Bureaucratic Intimacies

Stanford Studies in Middle Eastern and Islamic Societies and Cultures

Bureaucratic Intimacies

TRANSLATING HUMAN RIGHTS IN TURKEY

Elif M. Babül

Stanford University Press
Stanford, California

Stanford University Press
Stanford, California

Printed in the United States of America on acid-free, archival-quality paper

Library of Congress Cataloging-in-Publication Data

Names: Babül, Elif M., author.
Title: Bureaucratic intimacies : translating human rights in Turkey / Elif M. Babül.
Description: Stanford, California : Stanford University Press, 2017. | Series: Stanford studies in Middle Eastern and Islamic societies and cultures | Includes bibliographical references and index.
Identifiers: LCCN 2017020873 (print) | LCCN 2017022258 (ebook) | ISBN 9781503603394 (e-book) | ISBN 9781503601895 (cloth : alk. paper) | ISBN 9781503603172 (pbk : alk. paper)
Subjects: LCSH: Human rights--Turkey. | Human rights--Study and teaching--Turkey. | Turkey--Officials and employees--Training of. | European Union--Turkey.
Classification: LCC JC599.T9 (ebook) | LCC JC599.T9 B33 2017 (print) | DDC 323.09561--dc23
LC record available at https://lccn.loc.gov/2017020873

Cover design: Angela Moody
Cover image: Gökhan Deniz, "Hasat Mevsimi" (Harvest Time) Series, 2009.
Typeset by Bruce Lundquist in 10/14 Minion Pro

TABLE OF CONTENTS

ACRONYMS AND ABBREVIATIONS

AI	Amnesty International
AKP	Adalet ve Kalkınma Partisi (Justice and Development Party)
CE	Council of Europe
CIA	The Central Intelligence Agency
EIMET Program	Expanded International Military Education and Training Program
EU	The European Union
IMF	The International Monetary Fund
İHD	İnsan Hakları Derneği (Human Rights Association)
MAZLUMDER	İnsan Hakları ve Mazlumlar İçin Dayanışma Derneği (Association for Solidarity for Human Rights and the Oppressed)
NATO	The North Atlantic Treaty Organization
NGO	Non-Governmental Organization
PKK	Partiya Karkeren Kürdistan (Kurdistan Workers' Party)
STGM	Sivil Toplum Geliştirme Merkezi (Civil Society Development Center)
TİHV	Türkiye İnsan Hakları Vakfı (Human Rights Foundation of Turkey)
TTB	Türk Tabipleri Birliği (The Turkish Medical Association)
UN	The United Nations
UNICEF	United Nations Children's Emergency Fund
US	The United States

ACKNOWLEDGMENTS

This work owes so much to so many people in different times and places who helped me during the process of research and writing. I extend my thanks, first and foremost, to all of my informants and collaborators in Turkey, who allocated precious time and energy to answer all my questions, and who generously shared with me their everyday experiences. Many of them will unfortunately have to go unnamed, in line with the promise I made them to maintain their anonymity. Without the kind help and contributions of many government and civil society workers, translators, human rights activists, and project organizers whose stories I narrate in the following pages, this research would not have been possible.

During my field research, several individuals gave me their kindhearted help and support, including Sebla Arcan, Hakan Ataman, Gökçeçiçek Ayata, Metin Bakkalcı, Gökhan Deniz, Oktay Durukan, İdil Elveriş, Sevinç Eryılmaz, Gülden Gürsoy Ataman, Arezoo Jalalifar Ekinci, İhsan Kaçar, Seda Kalem, Zafer Kıraç, Şebnem Korur Fincancı, Nur Otaran, Özgür Sevgi, Emel Üresin, and Leman Yurtsever. Many conversations at the İstiklal cafes, Bosphorus teahouses, Asmalımescit taverns, and Boğaziçi University lawns with friends and fellow researchers of Turkey, Ceren Arseven, Sidar Bayram, Cem Bico, Başak Can, Ayça Çubukçu, Berna Ekal, Onur Günay, Zeynep Gürsel, Dilan Yıldırım, and Çağrı Yoltar, have made the research experience most stimulating and fun. At Boğaziçi, Nükhet Sirman and Nazan Üstündağ continued to be the most amazing mentors one can ever have.

At Stanford, I am most indebted to Liisa Malkki, Joel Beinin, James Ferguson, Miyako Inoue, and Sylvia Yanagisako for their invaluable advice, endless support, and thoughtful engagement with my work. I also greatly benefited at various stages from the indispensable guidance of Thomas Blom Hansen, Kathleen Coll, Matthew Kohrman, and Paulla Ebron in the Department of Anthropology; Woody Powell and Rob Reich at the Center on Philanthropy and Civil Society;

and Andrea Davies at Clayman Institute for Gender Research at Stanford. Across the Bay, Marco Jacquement and Cihan Tuğal have generously read excerpts and offered critical comments on different parts of my work.

My dear friends at Stanford, Nikhil Anand, Hannah Appel, Robert Samet, Rania Sweiss, Maura Finkelstein, Austin Zeiderman, Tania Ahmad, Ramah McKay, Zhanara Naruzbayeva, Kevin O'Neill, and Hillary Chart read and commented on several early drafts of my chapters. Lalaie Ameeriar, Fernando Armstrong-Fumero, Mun Young Cho, Oded Korczyn, Yoon Jung Lee, Serena Love, Tomas Matza, Angel Roque, Sima Shakhsari, and Thet Win have also been delightful to share both work and play spaces. I extend my gratitude also to the Stanford Turkish Posse, composed of Ayça Alemdaroğlu, Zeynep Alemdar, Fırat Bozçalı, Şamil Can, Yasemin İpek, Burcu Karahan, Sarp Kaya, Ekin Kocabaş and Burçak Keskin Kozat, with whom I shared camaraderie and many conversations on Turkish politics.

Feedback from audiences and participants at the Columbia University Human Rights Seminar, Haverford College Center for Peace and Global Citizenship, Five College Middle Eastern Studies Faculty Seminar, Harvard University Political Anthropology Workshop, Princeton University Institute for Advanced Study Policing and Ethnography Workshop, University of Massachusetts Amherst Meeting Ethnography Workshop, the College of Humanities and Social Sciences at Koç University, London School of Economics Programme on Contemporary Turkish Studies, Boğaziçi University Department of Sociology, Union College Department of Anthropology, and the Workshop on Emerging Regimes of Truth and Expertise in New Turkey has helped me immensely to think through many of my ideas and analyses. I particularly thank Ajantha Subramanian, Don Brenneis, Renita Thedvall, Didier Fassin, Daniel Goldstein, Esra Özyürek, Nükhet Sirman, Belgin Tekçe, Nazan Üstündağ, Meltem Ahıska, Ayfer Bartu Candan, Çağlar Keyder, Erdem Yörük, Başak Can, Hayal Akarsu, Fırat Bozçalı, Chris Dole, Hikmet Kocamaner, and Brian Silverstein for their thorough comments that enriched various parts of this book.

The nurturing and rigorous academic environment sustained by my students and colleagues at Mount Holyoke College has provided the utmost support and motivation for my scholarship. I thank my brilliant colleagues Debbora Battaglia, Lynn Morgan, Andy Lass, and Joshua Roth for their enthusiastic reception of my work. The smart and insightful comments of students in my Anthropology and Human Rights classes have been truly inspirational. Beyond Mount Holyoke College, conversations with friends and colleagues at the Five Colleges, including Hiba Bou Akar, Felicity Aulino, Nusrat Chowdry, Omar Dahi, Chris Dole, Pinky Hota, and Sahar Sadjadi, have helped clarify and tighten my arguments. My dear friend Sinem Akgül Açıkmeşe arrived at Harvard just in time to lend me her invaluable expertise on the EU-related parts of the book.

This research was made possible by the International Dissertation Research Fellowship of the Social Science Research Council, the Dissertation Fieldwork Grant of the Wenner Gren Foundation for Anthropological Research, the Mellon Dissertation Completion Fellowship awarded by the American Council of Learned Societies, the Graduate Research Opportunity Fellowship awarded by the Stanford University School of Humanities and Social Sciences, Diversity Dissertation Research Opportunity Award granted by the Stanford University Vice Provost for Graduate Education, PhD Research Fellowship awarded by Stanford University Center on Philanthropy and Civil Society, O'Bie Shultz Dissertation Completion Fellowship granted by Stanford University Freeman Spogli Institute for International Studies, and the Graduate Dissertation Fellowship awarded by Stanford University Clayman Institute for Gender Research. The American Council of Learned Societies Fellowship and several Mount Holyoke College Faculty Grants provided the much-needed support for final rounds of research and writing. The College of Humanities and Sciences at Koç University generously hosted me while I was finalizing my manuscript.

I owe special thanks to Rachel Jones, Kate Wahl, Micah Siegel, Emily Smith, Xenia Lisanevich, Sylvia Samet, Emily Jetmore, and the reviewers invited by Stanford University Press, whose evaluation made the book stronger. Gökhan Deniz—one of the most diligent human rights defenders I encountered in the field, who is also one of the most talented young artists in Turkey—generously allowed me to use his work on the cover of this book. The sprawling landscape he depicts in this warm yet melancholic painting reminds me of the numerous road trips I took together with many project teams (some including Gökhan himself) on the way to yet another training.

Finally, as always, I would like to thank my family for all the love, patience, support, and understanding they sent my way for all these years. My grandparents Nadide and Hakkı Işıksalan, my parents Aydan and Yılmaz Babül, and my darling sister Ebru remain proud supporters of what I do, despite all the longing it causes them by putting so many miles between us. My partner in crime and life, Robert Samet, has been the source of comfort, joy, affection, and enlightenment during the years we spent together in San Francisco, Amherst, Istanbul,

Schenectady, and South Hadley. In addition to giving me his big heart and unconditional support, he lent his brilliant mind to think through every single idea I put into this book. As I now wrap up this transformative experience, I look forward to many more adventures we will navigate together in the future.

With all its rewards and hardships, excitement and fatigue, not to mention all the laughter and frustration, joy and hard work that went into its writing, I dedicate this book to my delightful little Bou, who deserves to see the most beautiful days.

Bureaucratic Intimacies

INTRODUCTION
Standards and Their Tinkering

> *There are . . . few historical accounts of such imposition and transmission of ideas; and the historical process by which people, in both assessing and using the ideas presented to them, actually resist them, is scarcely considered.*
> **—Carolyn Kay Steedman**[1]

IN THE SUMMER OF 2013, Turkey became the subject of heightened attention due to the widespread urban riots that swept across the country. What started as a contained demonstration against the demolition of Gezi Park in Istanbul for commercial purposes quickly spread to other neighborhoods and cities. Hundreds of thousands poured into public places to express their grievances against the Justice and Development Party (Adalet ve Kalkınma Partisi, or AKP) government.[2] Following a series of clashes with the police, the protesters set up an Occupy-style encampment in Gezi Park, which lasted over a week. Similar camps were erected in public parks in Ankara and Izmir in solidarity. When a series of negotiations between the government and the activist coalition Taksim Solidarity yielded no results, the police retook the square, violently evicting the protesters. The demonstrations in the end succeeded in preserving the park.[3] The uprising did not go as far as ousting the government. Nevertheless, it made an important mark in the country's recent political history. What became known as "the Gezi spirit" brought to the fore a fresh repertoire of political action, incorporating new strategies for organizing and a new language of opposition.[4] Pulling together a diverse group of protesters that included environmentalists, secularists, workers, feminists, LGBTQ activists, anti-capitalist Muslims, professionals, students, football supporters, nationalist Turks, Kurds, Sunnis, and Alevis, it generated a new political experience and memory, especially among the country's youth.

In addition to sparking much-needed inspiration for progressive politics,[5] the Gezi revolts also elicited a spectacular display of state violence that until then

1

had prevailed in less visible places such as southeastern Kurdish provinces or maximum-security prisons. Circulation of the footage of police raids against peaceful demonstrators in social media was arguably the most important reason that the protests attained such a massive scale. During the demonstrations and in their aftermath, the scale of violence has also been the primary issue highlighted in domestic and international critiques towards the government's handling of the riots.[6] The European Union (EU)—Turkey's most conspicuous international interlocutor—immediately issued a resolution stating EU's "deep concern at the disproportionate and excessive use of force by the Turkish police" and stressing "the need for continued intensive training for the police force and the judiciary."

This critique alluded to a deep paradox, which serves as the departure point for this book. While the Gezi revolts were under way, the Turkish National Police was in fact running a project on the prevention of disproportionate use of force, which was being financed by the EU itself.[7] This €6 million project was conducted together with a German-Austrian consortium that included the German Foundation for International Legal Cooperation, the Federal Criminal Police Office, the Austrian Security Academy, and the Ludwig Boltzman Institute of Human Rights.[8] According to the latter's website, 452 officers were going through training on disproportionate use of force in May and June 2013, just as their colleagues were being ordered to crack down on the Gezi protests using tear gas, water cannons, and mass arrests.[9]

How to make sense of this situation? Does it suffice to say that the project is just another instance of the Turkish state paying lip service to meeting governmental standards required for EU membership? Or should it compel us to look more closely at the process with which these standards are implanted in Turkey's governmental realm?

Although attaining EU membership has been a national priority for Turkey since 1987, the relationship between the two parties has been deteriorating since 2005-2006. This downfall is visible in the deployment of anti-EU rhetoric both by president Erdoğan and the AKP government, as well as the Turkey-sceptic declarations of several EU officials. Notwithstanding this glaring rift, European standards of development, modernization, and good governance have been seeping into the lexicon of various state institutions since at least 2004. Particularly since the approval of Turkey's candidacy for EU membership in 1999, civil and military bureaucracies—including the police, the judiciary, the army, and healthcare services—have been employing lucrative tools of harmonization for "capacity building" to comply with membership criteria. Although Turkey seems to be drifting away from the prospect of EU membership, various harmonization instruments such as EU projects, twinning programs, and Technical Assistance and Information Exchange are widely used to organize meetings, workshops, training programs, and country visits for developing the administrative and judicial capacity of Turkey.

The conviction resulting in the research underlying this book was that projects aiming to build the Turkish state's capacity for good governance are far from unproductive, useless sites of whitewashing that help the Turkish state to continue business as usual. My curiosity about what actually takes place in the events and gatherings through which such projects are operationalized led me to a journey between 2007 and 2014 during which I conducted fieldwork alongside eleven different training programs—all with the stated goal to improve the government workers' ability to respect and implement human rights. The topics of trainings ranged from torture and maximum-security prisons to violence against women and children's rights. The target audience included judges and prosecutors, the police, prison guards, teachers, religious officials, and health care professionals.[10] In this ethnographic study of human rights training programs, I aim to scrutinize both the everyday governmental configurations of Turkey's EU accession and the effects of a particular framing of human rights engendered by the accession process.

In a nutshell, my findings reveal that the projects, trainings, and other tools of harmonization serve as key mediums of encounter between Turkish governmental agents and their various European interlocutors. It is by participating in such projects that the government workers both engage with and learn to manage the real-life effects of EU membership and the governmental standards that they entail. A close study of the training programs shows that human rights need to go through translation in order to be integrated into the governmental domain. Trainings accomplish this translation by disassociating human rights from their radical political connotations, and reframing them instead as relevant to and compatible with everyday practices of national governance. To this end, human rights are formulated as a requirement for expertise and professionalism to which all government workers should subscribe in order to better perform their jobs. This ethnography details how this reframing is administered and how it is received by the training audiences, who are socialized to be suspicious and reactionary towards the politics of human rights.

Overall, the ethnography of human rights training programs complicates the dominant conviction that EU accession is an all-progressive path for the advancement of human rights and democracy in Turkey. The good governance framework of EU renders human rights synonymous with governmental competence that is devoid of critical oppositional politics. This reframing ultimately carries the potential to delegitimize grassroots human rights movements in Turkey, which have historically been committed to speaking out against state violence in its various forms—such as discrimination against ethnic and religious minorities, economic exploitation, environmental decay, and gender disparity. With an aim to change the government workers' perception of human rights as "rights for terrorists," most training programs contribute to the transformation of human rights from a political tool to resist state violence into a resource that the state can employ to govern its subjects.

Nevertheless, it would be equally problematic to assume that human rights trainings completely neutralize the power and effect of human rights politics in Turkey. My research rather suggests that both the EU accession and human rights training programs emerge as dialogical processes, which involve negotiation, strategizing, and indeterminacy. The main analytical lens of this book invites the readers to view Turkey's EU accession as a pedagogical process, which revolves around the uneven yet dynamic relationship between the learner and the learned. Although pedagogical relations are primarily based upon (and reproduce) the clear demarcation between the educated and the non-educated, everyday educational situations are nevertheless saturated with dialectical encounters that generate contradiction and resistance (Bourdieu and Passeron [1977] 1990, Willis 1977). Seen from this perspective, everyday sites of EU harmonization emerge as fields of sociocultural production and encounter between multiple actors who have varying stakes in harmonization. Rather than clear-cut diplomatic positions whose outcomes are extensively discussed by policy analysts, these encounters instead produce diverse and unstable meanings, practices, performances, and feelings vis-à-vis human rights, national governance, the West, and Turkey's EU membership.

HARMONIZATION AS STANDARDIZATION

Human rights training programs are part of a larger "harmonization process" Turkey has to undergo for successfully completing its accession into the EU. An important means of the European integration, harmonization attempts to integrate the candidate countries' governments and their populations "not by overt coercion, but by instituting a host of 'harmonized' regulations, codes, and standards" (Dunn 2005, 175). Understanding Turkey's EU harmonization in terms of standardization highlights its processual characteristic. This is particularly important at a time when Turkey-EU relations are highly unstable. One of the most important points emphasized by the prolific literature on standardization is the need to pay attention to the long *dureé* rather than its end result. The multifarious networks, relations, practices, and rationalities that go into the making, implementation, and negotiation of standards often remain invisible, despite their influence in shaping the societies in which standards get operationalized. In a similar vein, although most commentators agree upon the near impossibility of Turkey's accession into the EU anytime soon, harmonization displays an ongoing dynamic process that generates encounters, prompts negotiations, assembles projects, and allocates resources in Turkey. It continues to influence the funding structures, work habits, and performances of productivity and accountability at government offices and beyond. These influences and the ways they infuse into the national governmental realm deserve attention regardless of whether Turkey attains EU membership in the end.

Another aspect of standardization that makes it a useful conceptual tool for understanding harmonization is the complexity it introduces into the power relations that mark transnational encounters such as those between Turkey and the EU. Standardization is heavily associated with acting at a distance on unfamiliar events, places, and people (Latour 1987) and with global neoliberal governance that attempts to create seamless, frictionless regulatory circuits for capital and power to function swiftly (Türem and Ballestero 2014). Standards seek to streamline procedures, regulate behaviors, and predict results primarily with an aim to render the standardized societies legible and intervenable (Collier and Ong 2005, 11). In addition to enabling intervention for humanitarian, developmental, and commercial purposes, standardization also involves evaluation of the people, products, practices, and techniques instituting technical, social, and moral hierarchies in standardized places (Coles 2002, 2008, Dunn 2005). Nevertheless, a detailed examination of the everyday sites of standardization also reveals the complications that take place during this seemingly straightforward process by exposing the amount of effort that is required for making, maintaining, and disseminating standards (Latour 2005, 227).

Despite pretence that standards have an inherent universal quality, social and technical engineering that go into them, as well as the political work that goes into persuading governments and publics in their efficacy, attest that they are in fact much less established than they seem. Focusing on the practices and processes of standardization opens up the spaces where standards are not just passively taken as matters of compliance but are also actively engaged with as issues of contestation, negotiation, and management. As Martha Lampland and Susan Leigh Star (2009) show in their influential work on standardization, instead of facilitating social processes, standards oftentimes end up frustrating people. Compensation and tinkering emerge as the primary modes of engagement with standards due to that reason—more so than simply conforming to them.

Finally, despite connotations of standardization as containing, streamlining, and reducing the things that are standardized, a closer look at its management shows that standardization in fact adds to the "vibrancy and multiplicity of its objects, potentially rendering them more complex and volatile" (Hetherington 2014, 57). In that respect, the ethnography of standardization refutes homogeneity as the final result. It also calls into question the immutability of what Bruno Latour calls "immutable mobiles" (1987, 227), referring to the devices through which standardizations are carried out.[11] As we shall see in the remainder of this book, principles of human rights and good governance that serve as the metrics of governmental harmonization in Turkey hardly remain constant throughout the standardization process. As they get translated into indices that would make them relevant for the everyday practices of various government workers, they get transmuted, at times deformed, resulting in situations close to what Julia Hornberger (2011) calls "forgery" or "fakery."

It might be tempting to read these mutations as deviations from the original intent and content of human rights. However, research on the local configurations of universal human rights discourse suggests that these in fact expand the transnational human rights register in a way to include multiple—even contradictory—meanings and practices (Allen 2013, Engelke 1999, Englund 2006, Goodale and Merry 2007, Merry 2006, Osanloo 2006, Slyomovics 2005, Tate 2007). In line with this argument, I also contend that the translations we come across in Turkey must be seen as constitutive of the European human rights repertoire. As much as they reflect the particular local conditions under which they are carried out, these translations also provide an important insight into the contours of the transnational regime that promotes them.

These contours become all the more visible in light of the readmission agreement signed between Turkey and the EU on March 18, 2016, according to which the EU agreed to instigate visa liberalization for Turkish nationals and promised to provide up to €6 billion in exchange for sending irregular migrants entering the EU from Turkish territory back to the country. Signed in the wake of the biggest refugee influx into the continent since the Second World War, the agreement particularly seeks to stop the Syrian refugees from entering Europe. Since the EU Asylum Procedures Directive allows readmissions only to a "safe third country," the agreement both assumes and declares that Turkey is a country that can guarantee effective access to protection for refugees and asylum seekers.[12] In light of widespread reports of labor exploitation, forced marriages, and child abuse, as well as the illegal detention and deportation of asylum seekers in Turkey, the agreement means an active disregard of the plight of 3.5 million Syrian refugees (and many others) on the part of the EU.[13] Signed in the midst of an alarming erosion of freedoms, as well as the return of violent securitization policies particularly in the Kurdish regions in the country, the agreement also demonstrates the ease with which the EU officials can overlook their interlocutors' abusive, authoritarian practices to pursue their own interests.[14]

At the local level, human rights translations for government workers reveal the sensitivities, moralities, and rationalities that shape the governmental field in Turkey. Examining the performances and conversations that accompany these translations shows how the actors work to navigate that uneven field, which is rendered even more volatile and unpredictable by transnational standardization. Human rights training programs add to the complexity of governance in Turkey despite their stated goal to regularize and systematize the governmental actors, procedures, and activities. Those added complexities in turn lead the government workers to develop new strategies to mitigate the contradictory demands of national governance and transnational standardization, which results in the transformation of the governmental field in Turkey in unexpected ways.

HARMONIZATION AS DEVELOPMENTALITY

Together with standardization, capacity building and auditing emerged as the primary means of international development in the late 1990s, with an emphasis on internal mechanisms of self-improvement (Strathern 2000). This new approach, which Jon Lie (2015) refers to as "developmentality," was marked by a shift in the donor-recipient relations wherein the donors withdrew from direct operational activities and the recipients became responsible for implementing the development programs. Embraced by key transnational agencies such as the World Bank, Oxfam, and the United Nations Development Programme, this new aid architecture stemmed from the conviction that recipient participation and ownership of development assistance were both more ethical and more effective. In this new configuration, the donors' roles became limited to providing technical assistance and know-how to build the recipients' management capacity for formulating and running their own national development policies. The donors also monitored the output of the programs by means of the recipients' self-auditing and reporting. This new aid relationship was also marked by an increase in "cultural sensitivity," an awareness motivating international donors and experts to take into consideration the customs, histories, and national sensitivities of target countries while planning, implementing, and auditing the development programs (Kyed 2009).

Looking at how harmonization is operationalized in various places including Turkey, it becomes clear that the new aid architecture heavily influences the EU's policies towards both candidate and neighboring countries. Several institutions in the EU engage in capacity building activities within Europe and beyond on topics ranging from education and gender parity to human rights and border control to ensure the countries' compliance with EU regulations or policy priorities.[15] Although it is definitely a catch phrase within the development sector, a clear definition of capacity building is hard to come by. As one commentator puts it, most development actors place capacity building "somewhere on a spectrum ranging from 'helping people to help themselves' at a personal, local or national level, to strengthening civil society organizations in order to foster democratization and building strong, effective and accountable institutions of government" (Eade 1997, 2). Often, capacity building is described as focused investment in a particular area, with the aim of enhancing skills, competence, and knowledge in the receiving agency or organization (McDonnell and Elmore 1987). Within the EU, capacity building is seen as a means of facilitating state compliance with international objectives by increasing the ability of local groups to address policy issues (Montoya 2008).

Although capacity building can target both the public sector and civil society, government institutions often emerge as the primary partners of development in the EU programs.[16] An important assumption underlying this approach is that the state's noncompliance with transnational standards stems from its limited political or economic capacity rather than its lack of commitment to a given policy issue. Capacity building programs aim to remedy this problem by instituting good governance to enhance the state's governmental power.[17] In order to promote good governance, most EU programs encourage state-civil society cooperation through project design. Actors in civil societies, the state, and international organizations are urged to form networks and work together for instituting an efficient, effective, and transparent governmental system in the country.

Like most development programs, EU's capacity building projects stem from and perpetuate the developmental understanding of the state "as a neutral vessel that is dedicated to improvement for people" (Li 2007, 134). The projects seek to rectify the flaws in this vessel by means of therapeutic measures such as human resource development, organizational strengthening, or institutional reform. It is believed that these measures would prevent unruly practices by consolidating the state apparatus as a rational legal bureaucracy. Improving bureaucratic performance is seen as the key for establishing democracy, human rights, and the rule of law in Europe and its periphery. This state-oriented approach to development overlaps with the self-perpetuating logic underlying both national and international bureaucracies, which sees intervention as necessary for improvement and interprets failure to improve as a call for further intervention (Lea 2008, Mosse 2005b).

Following the effects of this self-perpetuating logic becomes all the more pertinent for human rights, where debates about the best model for rights protection dominate the field. Whereas human rights ideology displays a heavily étatist (i.e., state-centric) structure (Arat 2008), critiques have long been pointing to the shortcomings of an international system that designates national governments as the main guarantors of human rights (Stacy 2009). Since the same state parties that are tasked with operating the international legal instruments also appear to be the primary human rights violators, the system often fails to deliver satisfactory results (Anders 2007). Although the European human rights system (with the European Court of Human Rights at its center) is cited as a unique model that functions effectively and as independent from its national constituents, EU's human rights agenda appears largely state-centric. Creation of a national human rights institution, standardization of administrative procedures, and fostering a pro-human rights organizational culture within administration are seen as important steps towards establishing human rights in countries. All of these measures foresee the state as the key protector of human rights rather than as the most notorious human rights violator. As such, they call for more government involvement rather than the withdrawal of the state from the human rights field. While this approach gets on board a good number of Turkish human rights organizations to cooperate with state institutions, others refuse to engage with the authorities, insisting on naming and shaming as a more ethical activist strategy.

The complex picture of human rights training programs in Turkey features multiple parties—national, international, governmental, and non-governmental—cooperating at different levels to improve the bureaucratic/governmental capacity in the country. Attending to the details of this partnership-based model challenges the assertions inherent to some dominant portrayals of development industry within the literature. The influential depiction of development suggests that it is an "anti-politics machine" (Ferguson 1994) that converts political problems into technical matters to be solved by a closed circle of experts. This conversion effectively shuts down political contestation by carrying the issue at hand to an inaccessible domain, guarded by professional qualifications required from anyone who wishes to join the debate (Illich et al [1977] 2000, Mitchell 2002). Contrary to this depiction, the ethnography of everyday sites of development partnership reveals that they are full of contestation and debate.

Human rights training programs for Turkish government workers are one example of those everyday sites where close encounters between various parties that are involved in harmonization produce opposition, tension, and resistance, among other things. They resemble "battlefields of knowledge" where disparate rationalities, social-political interests, emotions, values, and sensitivities meet and become articulated, manifesting friction, contradiction, and discontinuity (Lie 2015, 21). The particular makeup of human rights training programs reveals that the dividing lines within those battlefields go beyond the donor-recipient dualism. Composed of many different parties, including the EU, international non-governmental organizations (NGOs), Turkish human rights activists, foreign and domestic human rights experts, state institutions, and professional project managers, the harmonization industry in Turkey features multiple systems of knowledge and worldviews that coexist in varying degrees of tension. Observing how representatives of these parties interact at the everyday operational level introduces further complexity into the field, where differences based on the level of education, professional status, socio-economic background, ethnic belonging, and gender identity create an even more nuanced landscape within which particular actors are located.

A very important outcome of conceptualizing development as a field of contestation is that it draws attention to the group of actors who perform brokerage between the aforementioned competing systems, and whose service is essential for the minimal functioning of the development industry (Lewis and Mosse 2006). In my own analysis, I pay particular attention to the role of translators, who function as mediators between the human rights discourse and the official state language in the training programs. These mediators have an important role in managing the space of contestation and dissensus that shapes the everyday sites of harmonization.

Finally, paying attention to human rights training programs as sites where disagreement is both produced and managed enables us to further elaborate the kinds of politics that emerge out of the harmonization process in Turkey. As Tania Li (2007) points out, although development programs attempt to render various social problems technical and propose expert measures to overcome them, this rendering is not at all a secure accomplishment. Questioning the capacity of these expert schemes to absorb social, political, and technical critique reveals that expert discourses are often prone to be punctured by challenges they cannot contain. Therefore, aside from depoliticization and the closure of debate, "stimulation of critical communities and new practices" can emerge as "the unintended consequence of development projects" (151). It is true that the training programs strive to frame human rights violations as technical administrative problems that can be fixed by instituting a governmental system that is organized around principles of professionalism and expertise. Nevertheless, the participants constantly challenge this framing either by reasserting the political symbolism of human rights activism in Turkey or by drawing from competing technical rationalities. Instead of an absolute technicalization of the political, a particular kind of politics emerges from the training programs.[18] Contrary to what Li's account suggests, however, political communities, discourses, and practices that get generated as an outcome of human rights training programs often exhibit a staunch conservatism.

Even if training programs succeed in diverting the participants' attention from the historically established radical political connotations of human rights in Turkey, their reframing as part of transnational governmental standards still attributes human rights a foreign quality. This foreignness is perpetuated by their need to undergo translation in order to become relevant for the locality in which they intervene. As a result of their encounter with this powerful set of standards, most government workers resort to a particular repertoire of discourses and performances that coalesce around a reactionary nationalism. As I stated above already, it would be empirically wrong and totalizing to suggest that this political situation completely remains unchallenged. The dialectical spaces of harmonization pedagogy also contain the kernels of progressive human rights politics, no matter how contingent and tenuous they might be. Nevertheless, it is important to realize how the conservatism that comes into view in the human rights training programs reverberates in recent policies and regulations concerning security, immigration, and family. The surprising connections between liberal political projects such as human rights training and conservative governmental undertakings brings into view the uncalled-for affinities between harmonization and the much-debated emerging authoritarianism in Turkey.

Before proceeding with the detailed analysis of human rights training programs, one needs a historical and conceptual background to grasp both the politics of human rights and the meaning of EU accession in Turkey. An overview of methods will follow to discuss the larger implications of this research for ethnographic depictions of transnational phenomena. As many anthropologists argue, empirically grounded, ethnographic studies of global projects and processes are imperative to both demystify globalization as an elusive condition that is hard to pin down, and to account for the uneven local workings of the global.[19] Human rights training programs offer an example for locating the everyday sites where the global and the local interact, and they compel the researchers to reflect about their own place as they follow this interaction.

TURKEY AND THE EU: IN SEARCH OF RECOGNITION AND BELONGING

The roots of Turkey's bid for EU accession date back to 1987, when the country first applied for full membership to what was then called the European Communities. More than ten years following this application, Turkey officially gained candidate status in 1999. The accession negotiations were launched in 2005, another six years later. When the negotiations finally started, it was predicted that they would last for ten years minimum.[20] The Negotiating Framework stated that the negotiations were an "open ended process the outcome of which cannot be guaranteed beforehand." The document also noted that "in the case of a serious and persistent breach in Turkey of the principles of liberty, democracy, respect for human rights and fundamental freedoms and the rule of law on which the Union is founded, the Commission will . . . recommend the suspension of negotiations and propose the conditions for eventual resumption."[21]

Fast-forwarding to 2017, we see Turkey still continuing accession negotiations with the European Commission under thirty-five chapters, which cover a variety of national policy areas that require harmonization with the *acquis communautaire* (the total body of the EU law).[22] To this date, only sixteen out of thirty-five chapters have been opened for negotiations.[23] "Science and Research" is the only chapter that has been closed. Out of the remaining chapters, eight are frozen on the grounds that Turkey does not undertake its obligations stemming from the Additional Protocol to Ankara Agreement, mainly due to its refusal to open its ports to aircraft and ships of Cyprus (which Turkey does not recognize as a sovereign state although it joined the EU in 2004).[24] Following deliberations in December 2016, the EU decided not to open a new chapter in the forthcoming year because of the Turkish government's extensive crackdown on political opposition and independent media since the failed 2016 coup attempt.

Even if Turkey successfully completes negotiations under all thirty-five chapters, its membership is still not guaranteed. It has to pass the unanimous voting of all the member states in order finally to become a member of the EU. At that stage, securing the votes of countries such as Austria, Germany, and France, whose governments have expressed their hesitation about Turkey's full membership, might prove to be especially challenging.

A comparison of Turkey's accession process with other candidate countries reveals the extraordinary course of the former. Looking at the history of EU enlargement, we see candidate countries starting accession negotiations in one to five years after their initial application and negotiations lasting for three to eight years. For example, in the case of Greece, which applied for membership in 1975, the Commission decided to start negotiations the next year and Greece became a member in 1981 (in five years). In the case of Portugal, which joined the EU in 1986, the country applied for membership in 1977 and started the negotiations in 1978. Portugal is the country with the longest-lasting negotiations (eight years) among the current member states. In the latter phases of enlargement, Bulgaria and Romania became members in 2007 after negotiating with the Commission for seven years; both had applied for membership in 1995. In the last phase of EU enlargement, Croatia, which applied for membership in 2003 and started the negotiations in 2005 (at the same time as Turkey), signed its membership agreement in 2011 (Açıkmeşe 2014).

Although the official steps towards securing EU membership seem to indicate a purely technical administrative process, becoming part of Europe carries connotations that go beyond the mechanics of harmonization. Both for Turkey and the EU, Turkey's pending accession carries a symbolic meaning that exposes historical and current anxieties related to identity and belonging. For Turkey, accession to the EU denotes yet another enactment of its chronic "identity crisis" that forces the country to choose between the East and the West, Islam and secularism, and the Middle East and Europe (Deringil 2007, Keyder

1993, 2003). For many EU countries, Turkey's possible membership adds on to the current state of dismay stemming from the troubled integration of especially Muslim immigrant populations in Europe (Ewing 2008, Mandel 2008, Özyürek 2005, Uğur and Canefe 2004).

Turkey's identity crisis is closely tied on the one hand to a strong desire for recognition of its belonging to Europe and all that this symbolic geography stands for. On the other hand, the systematic failure of this recognition hurts national pride, leading to feelings of being spurned and rejected. It is the combination of the two—the desire to belong and the resentment of rejection—that pushes Turkey into a geopolitical identity crisis.

Although historically Turkey and the preceding Ottoman Empire never were officially colonized, the perception of Europe in Turkey displays a postcolonial undertone portraying "the West" as both possessor of an aspired-to development and perpetrator of a feared annexation (Ahıska 2003, Karaosmanoğlu 2000, Oran 2007). What is more, the promise of development, necessary to overcome this quasi-colonial relationship, depends on recognition by the West, which is itself conditional upon the successful imitation of and surpassing of the West by its own standards (Chatterjee 1986). The extraordinary course and length of Turkey's accession process leads to the belief that even if Turkey successfully completes the harmonization, this will never be rewarded with full membership.[25] The conviction that the EU holds a double standard for Turkey and that new rules are being made up as the game goes along results in Turkey's further pessimism about delivery of the recognition it so desperately needs. Under such circumstances, the performance of development becomes futile and frustrating.

The symbolic value of EU membership became more complex during the incumbent pro-Islamic, neoliberal AKP rule. When it first came to power in 2002, the party actively made use of its close alliance with the West and Western institutions—such as the US and the EU—to undermine the status quo of the Kemalist regime that institutionalized the French Jacobin model of secularism in Turkey.[26] It also effectively deployed the language of pluralism, democracy, human rights, and the rule of law to assert its legitimacy against the republican order that had ostracized fellow Islamists from the established political realm (Dağı 2004). The first two terms of the AKP rule witnessed a revival of Turkey's engagement with the EU, bringing a series of legal administrative reforms that were put in place in line with the accession negotiations (Müftüler-Bac 2005). Between 2002 and 2005, during what was considered "the golden age of Europeanization" (Öniş 2008), the government implemented eight reform packages that abolished the death penalty (2003), restructured the National Security Council (2003), revised the Anti-Terror Law (2004), shut down State Security Courts (2004), and instigated Article 90 of the Constitution that gave ratified supranational conventions priority over national law (2004). It also issued a new Penal Code (2004) that introduced serious measures for punishing torture and sentencing violence against women and children. Other reforms included allowing the use of Kurdish language in broadcasting and political campaigning, as well as giving citizens the right to learn Kurdish in schools. The United Nations' (UN) International Covenant of Civil and Political Rights and International Covenant on Economic Social and Cultural Rights were also ratified in the Parliament, three years after their initial signing (2003). All these reforms led to the inauguration of accession negotiations in 2005. It was during this period that then prime minister and now president Erdoğan famously declared that the government would change the name of Copenhagen Criteria[27] to Ankara Criteria and carry on with the political reforms even if the prospect of EU membership failed definitively.[28]

Ironically, however, the opening of accession negotiations in 2005 also marked the loss of momentum in Turkey-EU relations (Açıkmeşe 2010, Öniş 2008). One could say that the air had already turned sour in 2004, when Cyprus became a member of the EU. EU's decision to finalize Cyprus's accession despite its government's refusal to cooperate with the UN reunification plan (whereas the plan gained widespread support in the northern part of the island) stirred deep-seated nationalistic reactions within the Turkish state and society. The 2005 Negotiations Framework for Turkey, which included statements that did not appear in the previous enlargement cycles, strengthened the impression that the EU was implementing double standards. Clauses such as the open-endedness of accession negotiations and a possible permanent safeguard on full labor mobility even after Turkey becomes a full member led the EU to lose its credibility, even among its most vocal supporters in Turkey. This was followed by the suspension of eight chapters by the EU Commission in 2006 and the emergence of "a grand coalition" between the center-right parties of Germany, Austria, and France, who started voicing the option of "a privileged partnership" as an alternative to Turkey's membership (MacMillan 2010). At the domestic level, AKP's victory in the 2007 early elections resulted in the government's "exaggerated sense of its own power and a diminished sense of the importance of the EU anchor" (Öniş 2008, 43). Although the 2008 party closure case brought before the Constitutional Court against the AKP reinstated the government's view of the EU as necessary for its political survival and supremacy (Açıkmeşe 2010, 147), selective reforms in this era did not compare to the intense Europeanization of "the golden age."

Starting with the re-election of the AKP for the third time in 2011, Turkey-EU relations entered into a period of pronounced stalemate, which many commentators explain by a lack of domestic incentives and the government's growing authoritarian tendencies (Öniş 2013, Yılmaz 2016).[29] During this period, the Turkish public's support for EU membership also fell considerably. Whereas in 2004 74 percent of the Turkish public supported Turkey's EU membership, the ratio declined to 47.5 percent in 2013, and to 42.4 percent in 2015.[30] Although in 2012 the European Commission together with the Turkish government launched a new initiative called "the Positive Agenda,"[31] the government's current foreign policy is regarded as the recalculation of the country's national interests, which pushes Turkey further away from establishing itself as a liberal democracy through Westernization.[32] In 2015, Turkey and the EU agreed on a joint action plan on refugees and migration management. While the plan seemed to bring Turkey and the EU closer with a unified goal, critics (including the European Parliament) accused the European Commission of going silent on violations of fundamental rights in Turkey in return for the government's cooperation on refugees.[33] The July 2016 failed coup d'etat in Turkey further contorted Turkey-EU relations, when the government declared a nationwide state of emergency. The European Convention of Human Rights was put on hold and president Erdoğan signaled the possibility of reviving the death penalty to punish those responsible for the coup. Response from the EU came promptly, reminding Turkey that the unequivocal rejection of the death penalty is an essential element of the EU *acquis*.[34] To reinstate it would be tantamount to bringing the accession negotiations to a standstill.[35]

Turkey's membership has no smaller implications for the current crisis facing a unified Europe. The question of whether to include Turkey in the Union—a process regarded by many as "the most difficult enlargement ever" (Grigoriadis 2006)—has repercussions for the EU that go beyond its immediate institutional effects. This most difficult enlargement comes at a time when the EU—initially started as an economic community to recover from the adverse effects of World War II—faces some challenging questions regarding what the next step of European integration will be.[36] As the anxieties voiced in Turkey arising from a possible loss of national sovereignty upon joining the

EU (Canefe and Bora 2003), discussions regarding the European Constitution stir fears of losing national identity and sovereignty among the EU member states (Balibar 2004, 2009).[37] To overcome those anxieties and to solve the EU's chronic problem of legitimacy, EU politicians and officials seek to forge a distinctly European identity at the level of popular consciousness. The cultural politics of European integration appropriate various technologies of nation building such as statistical measurements, communications technologies, remapping, and rewriting history, as well as the invention of traditions, rituals, and symbols (Shore 2000). Oftentimes, the architects of this imagined European community emphasize its Greco-Roman and Christian roots, with the hope of uniting the diverse populations living in Europe.[38]

In addition to being hampered by political differences between member states regarding its desirability, the prospect of integration also appears particularly challenged due to the current fragmented state of populations living in Europe. Struggling to cope with the diversity resulting from internal and external migrations, both the states and peoples of Europe have had their cosmopolitan tolerance tested by encounters with constitutive outsiders. These domestic and foreign others, ranging from Mediterraneans to postsocialist Central and Eastern Europeans, and from Jewish populations to Muslim immigrants, increasingly make race and race relations relevant to everyday life in Europe (Balibar 1991, Bunzl 2005, Cabot 2014, Herzfeld 1987, 1997, Malcomson 1995, Pieterse 2002, Sirman 1997).[39] In the presence of soaring levels of racism and xenophobia, particularly in Western and Northern Europe, Turkey's membership becomes the synecdoche for how "the new Europe" will handle its relations with Islamic countries in general, and with its substantial Muslim minority in particular. These concerns are further escalated by the current crisis in Syria, where radicalized Muslim youth from various European countries have been running to join the ranks of the notorious Islamic State.[40] The recent Islamic State–led wave of attacks in Europe and the group's declaration of more to come have consolidated the prevalent perception that sees immigrant populations as a security threat. What is more, strong allegations of the Turkish government's underground support for Islamic State make Turkey's membership even more frightening and less desirable for many EU countries.

In search of a common identity, the EU emphasizes the metrics of rightfully belonging to Europe less in terms of the ability to integrate into a market-oriented economy and more on the basis of "values" and "principles" that are claimed to make Europe what it is. For example, Delegation of the European

Union to Turkey defines "accession" as "a carefully managed process, which helps the transformation of the countries involved, extending peace, stability, prosperity, democracy, human rights, and the rule of law across Europe," requiring the candidate country to "bring its institutions, management capacity and administrative and judicial systems up to EU standards."[41] A similar attitude prevails in the larger public realm, shaping the discourses of both governmental and non-governmental public figures in Turkey and Europe.[42] This is despite the fact that the majority of harmonization chapters pertain to the consolidation of Turkey as a functioning market economy. Harmonization of regulation regarding the free movement of goods, workers, and capital, the rights of establishment and freedom to provide services, public procurement, company law, intellectual property rights, competition policy, transport policy, fisheries, energy, taxation, economic and monetary policy, enterprise and industrial policy, and customs union is first and foremost geared to making Turkey's legal-administrative field commensurable and accessible to the European Common Market.[43]

Despite the weight of economic criteria in accession negotiations, it is the symbolically charged political criteria that are most emphasized both nationally and internationally. Human rights come forward in this particular context as a sign of Turkey's compliance with the political criteria. The well-documented involvement of many government workers in major human rights violations (such as torture, forced disappearances, forced migration, and extrajudicial killings) makes the government's human rights record one of the central tenets of Turkey's accession into the EU (Arat 2007, Arat and Smith 2014, Casier 2009, Hale 2003). This emphasis on political criteria is detectable in the Delegation's general language, where membership to the EU is defined not only as technical-managerial improvement but also as moral social progress. This value-based assessment of EU membership both adds to the vagueness surrounding the already indeterminate character of accession negotiations and raises the stakes of belonging to EU even higher for Turkey. Joining the EU does not just denote the structural adjustment of national governance to comply with the liberal capitalist order. It also requires the affirmation of Turkey's degree of civilization by confirming levels of stability, prosperity, democracy, adherence to human rights, and rule of law in the country.

In light of this sustained indeterminacy, much of the mainstream analyses concerning Turkey-EU relations focus on predicting the final outcome of Turkey's accession process. My ethnography diverges from this approach in that rather than trying to sidestep the aura of vagueness surrounding Turkey's EU membership, it delves more deeply into the effects of this vagueness. Instead of predicting the outcome of this process—whether or not Turkey is really going to become a member of the EU—I choose to pay attention to the harmonization itself, regardless of whatever its final result may be. I intend to find out what, in addition to a possible EU membership, the accession process produces.

The main portion of fieldwork for this study was conducted between 2007 and 2010, which corresponds to a period of more active engagement with the harmonization process in Turkey. However, even at its slowest pace, EU harmonization still displays a dynamic character that leads to many encounters, prompts numerous negotiations, and provides multiple resources, resulting in various outcomes. If nothing else, the Pre-Accession Assistance Turkey receives from the EU brings millions of Euros into the country each year. For instance, the European Commission's 2015 progress report for Turkey announced that funding in the amount of €4.45 billion was earmarked for Turkey for the period of 2014–2020. According to the 2016 progress report, the 2015 annual programme features a budget of €225 million, focusing primarily on rule of law and fundamental rights and on the building up of capacities in the field of migration and asylum. The Financing Agreements for the Sector Operational Programmes that entered into force in April and May 2016 feature a budget of €478 million in the areas of environment and climate action, education, employment and social policies, and competitiveness and innovation. Acknowledging the considerable pressure the Syrian refugee crisis imposes on Turkey, the EU also set aside €3 billion over the period of 2016–2017 to assist the country in setting up a facility to host over 3 million refugees residing in its borders.[44] This financial influx brings along new networks of spending, mechanisms of accountability, and ways of undertaking governmental work that alter the governmental sphere in Turkey in fundamental ways.

In addition to financial resources, harmonization also makes a considerable amount of human resources available by summoning experts from the member countries in order to assist institutional capacity building in Turkey. For instance, twinning projects match state institutions with their counterparts in EU member countries, where representatives from both sides take reciprocal field trips to exchange information, convey experience, and discuss best practices. In a similar vein, exchanges of information and personnel also take place within the realm of civil society as part of EU's agenda to support civil society development in Turkey. Focusing on the vivid socialization and exchange that happens around harmonization sheds light on Turkey's EU accession as an interactive process, "bringing into play different social actors who each express the European issue in their own way and according to their own potential" (Visier 2009, 4).[45] Some of the ideal sites to explore these "multiple uses of Europe" (7) are the EU projects, which indicate the primary format of the financial and human resources, made available by the EU, that are mobilized in Turkey.

The term "EU projects" is used in everyday life to depict a wide range of activities that are supported in varying degrees by the EU, which are undertaken by both the state institutions and civil society organizations. Each year the European Commission announces its spending priorities by issuing "Multi-Annual Indicative Planning Documents" for each candidate country. On the basis of those planning documents, the Commission then calls for proposals from both the state and civil society for projects that target the issues mentioned in the documents and in the annual progress reports prepared by the Commission for each candidate country. Proximity to EU circles also generates access to other agencies, such as the European Instrument for Democracy and Human Rights, which support projects geared toward the advancement of human rights and democracy in non-EU countries. Since designing and implementing projects has emerged as a new way of conjuring money and personnel to get things done, the form of thinking, planning and operating that is inherent to the project format becomes more and more internalized by both governmental and non-governmental circles. This new required fluency in project discourse has intense consequences for the administration of state apparatus, as well as for the organization of civil society in Turkey. With numerous funding resources becoming available, particularly in the realm of democracy, human rights, and the rule of law, the consequences of this new project mentality is perhaps most strongly felt in the area of human rights activism. It is to the history of this movement that I now turn.

HUMAN RIGHTS AND CIVIL SOCIETY DEVELOPMENT: FROM OPPOSITION TO PROJECT-MAKING

Although transnational standardization might cover a wide range of areas including economy, health, and security, standards pertaining to what are considered to be universal human rights are endowed with a particular moral and political force. An important indicator of development and political modernization, a nation state's human rights record has long been used to assess the legitimacy of governments, particularly in places labeled as "developing countries" or "transitional democracies" (Merry 2011). Despite forceful criticisms of this "new humanitarian order,"[46] the performance of human rights continues to serve as proof of a country's worthiness for international recognition, foreign aid, transnational investment and membership to institutions of global governance (Cizre 2001).

Much like anywhere else in the world, human rights in Turkey indicate a significant field of political action, policy-making, knowledge production, and world ordering. Although the idea of human rights gained some traction following the 1946 UN Declaration of Human Rights, the real emergence of human rights as the basis of a consistent political movement only happened after the infamous 1980 military coup in Turkey. On September 12, 1980, the leading generals of the Turkish Armed Forces, holding "immoderate, self-seeking and short-sighted politicians" responsible for the governmental crisis and the mounting political violence, disbanded the parliament, suspended the constitution, outlawed all political activity, and declared martial law until further notice throughout the country (Heper 1985, Paul 1981).

For the following three years, the country was governed by a nonelected Constituent Assembly composed of the National Security Council (the head of the military and the chief commanders of the army) and a civil Consultative Assembly (with 160 members appointed by the Council). The military regime directed a "sanitation campaign" against the entire society. Mass arrests, extended periods of detention, torture, ill treatment, executions, extrajudicial killings, expatriation, compulsory migration, and other forms of state violence were employed with the alleged aim "to remove the obstacles preventing the democratic system from working" (Paul 1981, 3). Between 1980 and 1984, there were roughly 180,000 arrests, 65,000 incarcerations, 42,000 sentences, and 27 executions (Mepham 1987). Altogether, the 1980 regime took 650,000 people under custody; put 1,683,000 people under surveillance; put 23,000 people on trial; expatriated 14,000 of its citizens; and forced another 30,000 to become political refugees (Türker 2005).

The language and politics of human rights were adopted during this period by a broad-based leftist political block as the only available means of political dissent and a channel to organize resistance against the ongoing persecution of their comrades. Although the coup initially outlawed both left- and right-leaning politics, close links between the military regime and institutions such as the United States Central Intelligence Agency (CIA) and the International Monetary Fund (IMF) positioned the regime and the post-coup governments more squarely against the leftist political ideology.[47] Turkey's longest-standing human rights organization, İnsan Hakları Derneği (Human Rights Association—İHD—established in 1987), was formed in this climate by the lawyers and mothers of political prisoners belonging to various leftist groups.[48]

As their Latin American counterparts, Turkey's early human rights defenders arrived at human rights consciousness upon their own victimization and under desperate circumstances, when they suddenly found themselves lacking every other means to demand justice.[49] In an environment where "politics" in every shape and form were rendered illegitimate and political association was widely criminalized, the rhetoric of human rights provided this group with a means to voice claims and demands—such as the abolishment of torture, ill treatment, and the death penalty—by taking them to an extra-political, moral realm, and by "invoking something bigger and more permanent" (Dembour 1996).[50] For the rest of its tumultuous path—especially during the late 1980s and throughout the 1990s—the İHD managed to sustain a fine line of opposition, effectively making use of the politics of the apolitical. The universalist, moral connotations of human rights allowed the İHD to forge transnational alliances to speak out against the Turkish state, and helped it navigate the precarious, prohibitionary national political field. Throughout its history, the İHD had to defend itself against accusations directed through various governmental channels, which alleged that its members had used human rights as a pretext for subversive political pursuits (such as socialist revolution or Kurdish separatism).

The transnational scope of human rights enabled human rights defenders to put pressure on the Turkish state by using extranational channels. As studies of what is called the "boomerang effect" show, the efficiency of this pressure is largely dependent upon the pressured country's investment in maintaining good standing in valued international groupings (Keck and Sikkink 1998). Similarly, it is fair to say that the success of the politics of human rights in Turkey was largely due to the fact that even before their official emergence as political criteria for EU membership, human rights have always carried implications for membership in the world society of nation states for Turkey (Kaplan 2001).[51] In fact, the reason the İHD could finally establish itself as a legal non-governmental entity after many unsuccessful attempts was the Turkish government's application to the European Communities later that same year.[52] Strategizing successfully around this official governmental sensibility, Turkish human rights defenders made an effective use of transnational advocacy networks to release shadow reports, mobilized their connections to generate international reaction against state violence, and held official institutions accountable in front of international judiciary mechanisms (Hicks 2001, Watts 2001).

Although political activism through international solidarity networks is primarily a leftist strategy, and mobilizing human rights discourse was originally employed by the left in Turkey, other social groups victimized by the official ideology—such as religious Muslims—also picked up human rights politics as a medium to express their opposition (White 2001).[53] One highly respected human rights organization in Turkey, İnsan Hakları ve Mazlumlar İçin Dayanışma Derneği (Association for Solidarity for Human Rights and the Oppressed, MAZLUMDER), was established in 1991, mainly around Islamic human rights sensibilities.[54] Widening the repertoire of the Turkish human rights movement, Islamic interpretations of rights added religious references such as the Ten Commandments and the Medina Charter into the history of the development of human rights (Mercan 1999).[55] Although it is actively involved in all human rights issues in Turkey, MAZLUMDER particularly assumed the flagship of the struggle against the headscarf ban in the country.

The subsequent establishment of other human rights organizations—such as the Human Rights Foundation of Turkey (1990), the Helsinki Citizens Assembly (1993), and Amnesty International (AI) Turkey (2002)—has led the agenda and profile of the Turkish human rights movement to branch out to a certain extent. Even so, the association of human rights with an antinational, antiestablishment political engagement has mostly remained. Within the İHD itself, the dominant political groups that influenced the position of the İHD have shifted over time, depending on the political conjuncture and the actual location of the particular İHD branch. Depending on the time and place, the Association has been dominated by liberal intellectuals, social democrats or groups from the socialist left and the Kurdish political movement (Türkmen 2006). In that sense, especially under the İHD roof, being a rights defender has never really emerged as a primary political identity. Human rights discourse and ideology have rather served as a loose associational basis that strategically pulled together an otherwise unstratified polity.

The ongoing consolidation of human rights activism as an exclusive political identity came with the end of the 1990s, as Turkey moved closer to economic and political integration with the liberal capitalist order and the country's candidacy for EU membership became official. As a result of the legal reforms in 2001 and 2004 that enhanced organizational freedom in the country, civil society activity increased remarkably.[56] The tragic experience of the 1999 Marmara

Earthquake, during which state institutions failed miserably to provide relief and civic initiatives rose to the occasion to compensate for this failure, had generated a plethora of groups who were ready to take advantage of this newfound organizational liberty. Due to EU's emphasis on civil society participation for establishing good governance, a wide range of resources to build a functioning, healthy civil society became available through Pre-Accession Assistance, especially after 2001. Perhaps one of the most emblematic gestures to encourage civil society development in Turkey was the launching of a project called the Civil Society Development Program in 2002. The Program, which transformed into the Civil Society Development Center (Sivil Toplum Geliştirme Merkezi, STGM) in 2005, was conceived as a means to forge a dynamic civil society in Turkey that would actively participate in the country's governance.

Since its establishment, STGM has been running trainings on institutional capacity building and project cycle management for local civil society organizations in order to help them institutionalize in a certain way, and to integrate them into the harmonization economy. During my interviews with the founders and personnel of STGM, I was told that the main point of departure for STGM was the initial lack of ability on the part of Turkish civil society organizations to make use of the Pre-Accession Assistance funds that were allocated to them. These organizations, in other words, did not know how to design projects, write project proposals, and implement their projects upon receiving funds. This lack of technical know-how had even resulted in the emergence of private companies that specialized in designing and writing projects for various organizations, and then charged them for their services. In order to forestall the emergence of project writing as a professional industry, STGM instead decided to help professionalize the civil society.

STGM trainings, in which I had the chance to participate while in the field, aimed to both help institutionalize civil society organizations and familiarize these organizations with the project format. The trainings encouraged civil society organizations to specify their identity by defining their "vision," "mission," "principles" and "goals," and to establish themselves by organizing their internal division of labor and responsibility. The next step was to teach these organizations how to translate their goals into concrete, feasible projects that could be expressed on a project sheet using specialized vocabulary such as "stakeholders" and "logical framework." In addition to helping civil society organizations gain fluency in an otherwise inaccessible, highly technical language, these trainings also led their participants to conceptualize civil intervention in a particular way. Instead of the naming-and-shaming strategy that the human rights movement has typically employed, this new style of activism asked the civil society to stop complaining and start acting.[57]

This new motto for civil society resonates with the neoliberal governmental rationality, which foresees a smaller government focused exclusively on security and on maintaining the conditions of a functioning market economy, while transferring welfare and social policy responsibilities to the private realm and to a civil society now defined as "the third sector" (Burchell 1996, Hindess 1996, Rose 1996).[58] In addition to "the promotion of an enterprise culture" (Burchell 1996, 29) at all levels of society, project-based activism also defines the "activists" acting upon the society's problems in a particular way. As opposed to the rights defenders that strategically used a universal human rights discourse for political means to address their own victimization, this new form of activism asks its executors to be professional activists who can conduct SWOT analyses, draw activity charts, and write concept notes to act upon the problems of their "fellow human beings" (Haskell 1985a, 1985b).

In addition to defining civil society as composed of professional activists, this project-based activism produces what anthropologist Marilyn Strathern, quoting Power, calls "rituals of verification" between the local actors and foreign donors of transnational standardization processes (2000, 3). Measures of accountability that are written into the project cycle regulate the organizations' access to resources that are necessary to carry out projects. To guarantee their continuing access, civil society organizations administering EU projects have to produce interim reports and evaluation documents in order to prove their compliance with the terms and conditions of project agreements. This burden of proof cannot be executed with equal ease for all kinds of projects. For instance, while it might be fairly easy to quantify the success of an environmental project aiming to restore the ecological balance of a lake, proving the success of human rights training programs may not be that simple. Even so, for projects with less quantifiable target areas such as changing the government workers' perception of human rights, the project teams are forced to come up with similar methods of accountability to prove their success, such as by reporting the number of people who participated in training programs. Because the short-term effects of attitudinal/behavioral transformation are extremely difficult to evaluate in quantifiable terms, these projects end up producing only the rituals of verification itself—including sign-up sheets, logs of meetings, and classroom schedules for the training programs.

The amount of paperwork that is required to produce these rituals of verification moves the members of civil society from the streets into the offices—a point critically acknowledged by the STGM representatives themselves. This withdrawal from the streets became all the more clear to me on December 2008, around the anniversary of the UN Declaration of Human Rights. Various institutions and organizations functioning in the human rights field had organized events including receptions, exhibitions, panels, and marches to commemorate this event. Among those, two particular events organized by the Istanbul Consulate General of the Netherlands and the İHD were the most telling. In honor of human rights week, the İHD's Istanbul offices had organized a march on İstiklal street—one of the busiest promenades in the downtown area that is historically associated with political organization and dissent. Although the İHD is one of the oldest and best-established of all the human rights associations, the number of people who showed up for the march was glaringly low. Less than twenty people accompanied by more than twenty police officers completed the march in under thirty minutes, weakly shouting classical slogans of the human rights movement such as: "Humans can only be human with their rights!" (*İnsan haklarıyla insandır!*) and "Don't be silent, or it will be your turn next time!" (*Susma sustukça sıra sana gelecek!*).

The next day, I participated in a reception organized by the Consulate General of the Netherlands, whose building happened to be located on the same street. The consulate, which is one of the leading foreign donors in the field of human rights in Turkey, had organized the reception to recognize some of the most distinguished "voices of human rights" in the country, selected from among the organizations that received funds from the consulate. As the awardees stepped up one by one to receive their prizes from the consul general, more than a hundred invited guests tasted wine and appetizers while energetically mingling among themselves. An old friend whom I ran into at the reception (who works for one of the leading foundations that support and administer civil society projects) took me around the room to introduce me to people, all the while repeating: "This is how small our sector is. Everybody knows each other."

Although they seemingly represent two entirely different worlds, the actors of the classical human rights movement and the new civil society are indeed much more intertwined than one would expect. Many of the activists I worked with in human rights training projects had been involved in left-leaning socialist movements or in the Kurdish political movement before they became frustrated by what they identified as the inefficiency and impracticality of those circles. One of my informants even told me that despite the suspicion and crim-inalization of associations such as the İHD, the work that organizations such as his were doing in fact required more strength. He said: "I could do it, too. I could go in front of Galatasaray [the famous midpoint of İstiklal street where most sit-ins and demonstrations take place] and yell 'Damn the state!' I also wish there were no prisons. But there are prisons. And as long as they exist, there will be people in them. You cannot make the prisoners' lives better by just yelling. That's our starting point. What we do is actually more difficult. We don't have the luxury to say 'Eww!' to the Minister of Interior. We have to shake that man's hand . . ."

On the other side, members of the İHD, who were critical of this new civil society that fed on the harmonization economy, called the people involved in those circles "tatlı su aktivistleri" (fresh water or pretend activists), meaning that the work they do does not involve any risk. However, İHD's position on taking advantage of this budding project economy was not that unified either. Because İHD had a loose structure, some of its offices in different cities tended more towards writing and administering projects that involved local-level gov-ernments such as municipalities. Some members differentiated between the governmental and non-governmental grants, refusing to work with donors such as the EU and the consulates while seeing no harm in cooperating with organizations such as the Council of Europe (CE)[59] and the International Reha-bilitation Council for Torture Victims.

Despite the seemingly clear-cut distinction between street-based grassroots associations such as the İHD and the project-based civil society that is fully in-tegrated into the harmonization economy, those two realms in fact appeared much more permeable on the ground. The people who belonged to those dif-ferent realms knew each other pretty well, and they interacted quite frequently. For instance, some staunch socialist organizations that refused to interact with the government coordinated with more mainstream civil society organizations that were willing to talk to the state. Similarly, some mainstream organizations insisted on being part of the meetings and conventions organized by classical human rights associations that still carried symbolic weight. Despite clear dif-ferentiations at the level of discourse,[60] the separations became a little messier at the level of practice.

Even though the structure of harmonization and its project economy orig-inates from a neoliberal agenda that aims to tame a political society by way of integrating it into the good governance framework, the actual practices of harmonization on the ground appear much less straightforward. In accordance with Steven Sampson's (1996) insightful observations on the transition industry in Albania, the harmonization process in Turkey is not experienced as a simple transfer of Western civil society models by way of their imposition. Rather, as Carolyn Steedman suggests in the opening quote to this introduction, the transmission of ideas and models is deeply entangled with the simultaneous refusal and thwarting of them (Steedman 1992, 76). Transition, as Sampson argues, has many agents—foreign and local—who accept the forms that come with the funding, and attempt to shape them according to their own interests (126).

Another paradox that runs through the civil society component of transnational developmental regimes is the fact that "many of the associations, which inspired the original faith in the power of civil society to act as a check on state power, arose in opposition to the imposition [of neo-liberal economic policies] by authoritarian regimes" (Jenkins 2001, 263). Just as in other aid-recipient countries, the very kernels of civil society that continue to symbolize the ethics of justice in Turkey emerged from a strong opposition to the establishment of market-oriented economic policies, such as the IMF-led structural adjustment programs. Whether this paradox and the complexity of the harmonization process really end up neutralizing the politics of human rights in Turkey still remains to be seen. But for now, it is fair to say that the human rights field in Turkey displays a dynamic and indeterminate character, involving multiple actors with varying stakes that respond to and make use of the current push for the depoliticization, normalization, professionalization, and bureaucratization of civil society in diverse ways.

ETHNOGRAPHY OF TRANSNATIONAL ENCOUNTERS: A NOTE ON METHODS

Although ethnographic sensibility urges us to attend to the particulars that define our fields of study, anthropologists long ago ceased to imagine those fields as disparate, bounded, homogenous entities (Gupta and Ferguson 1997). In addition to acknowledging the connectedness of specific localities they work in, anthropologists also turned their attention to transnational and global phenomena, seeking for a grounded understanding of global flows and assemblages.[61] The domains of state and bureaucracy emerge as particularly fitting sites to trace this global connectedness. Following the introduction of the concept of "good governance" by the World Bank in 1989 and the establishment of liberal democracy as the global norm in the post–Cold War era, institutions and mechanisms of governance mainly in places referred to as "the Third World" or "the Global South" have become the objects of intervention for reform (Jefferson and Jensen 2009).

This is particularly so for government workers, who are seen as the embodiments of the state. As primary operators of national bureaucracies, government workers performing various lines of administrative function are often designated as the quintessential targets of improvement through standardization. Programs and projects implemented for administrative reform and the transnational governmental standards that they aim to promote therefore constitute an important aspect of the everyday practices and experiences of government workers. Similarly to studies of global human rights regimes and the politics of humanitarian care,[62] ethnographic analysis of governmental standardization processes exposes the transnational as a powerful site for the making of the local (Malkki 1992, Merry 1992).

From an ethnographic point of view, what is interesting to trace is how the local governmental agents encounter these "traveling packages"[63] of transnational standardization and reform. The methodological question that follows is where we can locate these spaces of encounter so as to conduct prolonged ethnographic fieldwork. Through my own ethnographic study, I suggest that training programs offer an especially useful vantage point to observe how government workers encounter transnational norms and standards, which increasingly form an integral part of their local working conditions. I argue that the social spaces of training programs allow us to see how local governmental agents are not just subject to these norms and standards. Instead, they actively engage with them by way of questioning and negotiation. By analyzing how Turkish government workers speak back to the messages that are delivered in these training programs, we get to trace the established repertoires of governmental rationalities, social conventions, and moral convictions that inform the everyday practices of governing in Turkey. These rationalities, conventions, and moralities help us better understand who the government workers are, where they come from, and how they make sense of what they do in the context of the shifting terrain of governance instigated by accession into the EU.

As an ethnographic study of a transnational standardization process, which takes as its ocular the making of human rights as criteria for good governance in Turkey, this book examines a privileged elite site. Human rights training programs, where I conducted the main portion of my fieldwork, were exclusive sites with limited access, where members of the national and international governmental echelons met to transmit and acquire human rights rhetoric and sensibilities. This study, then, shares the perspective of some recent exciting ethnographies that focus on such exclusive sites of expertise as financial markets and investment banks.[64] Inspired by Laura Nader's (1988) famous call to anthropologists to "study up," these ethnographies share the conviction that the study of national and global elites is a necessary part of investigating how power works. By "making powerful actors culturally knowable" (Ho 2009a, 178), and by contributing to our understanding of how power becomes institutionalized and legitimized, "studying up" in fact expands the anthropological grasp and critique of power.

Extending the mode of basic anthropological research to the worlds of financial experts, bankers, and bureaucrats, of course, has significant consequences for fieldwork methods.[65] For one thing, studying the exclusive worlds of experts creates serious difficulties with regard to one's access to the field site. This limited access certainly has setbacks for the researcher. Nevertheless, the idea that not every field we wish to study might readily be available to us actually provides valuable insight into the terms and conditions of anthropological knowledge production. While anthropology is a discipline that did not shy away from coming to terms with its colonial past, the practice of ethnography to a large extent is still based on the assumption that the field of research remains within the anthropologist's reach. Although the actual entry to this field has always proved to be far from simple (one only needs to remember the frustrated accounts of the discipline's forefathers, such as E. E. Evans-Pritchard (1940 [1969]) and Claude Lévi-Strauss (1973)), the challenges associated with this entry have been largely attributed to the linguistic and cultural "otherness" that the ethnographers had to overcome by "going native."

The reflexive turn in anthropology has been largely successful in highlighting the power differentials defining the condition of this "otherness" between the ethnographers and their informants, who were essentially imagined as less advantageous. This reflexivity, nevertheless, was not in itself an equalizing act (Weston 1997, 172). Even though writing reflexively has led ethnographers to acknowledge the influence of their powerful position within the field for the particular presentation of their data, it did not necessarily lead to a radical alteration of "the field" itself (Gupta and Ferguson 1997). If anything, discussions about the relations of power within the field have helped consolidate the deep-seated assumption that it is the less powerful people that anthropologists find worth studying. As a useful corrective to this assumption, the study of the elite can actually prompt ethnographers to think further about the power dynamics that shape their fields and fieldwork. Providing a glimpse into the constitution of authority, studying up illuminates how people become seduced by and invest in maintaining asymmetrical relations of power and hierarchy. The arduous task of trying to gain access to exclusive sites of power can lead anthropologists to note the real merits of being at a place where one has no place to be.

My own place in the field was largely shaped by my own complex position of being an insider and an outsider at once. As a Turkish national who went back home to do field research, I experienced similar sentiments and concerns that are chronicled in the sophisticated testimonies of other native anthropologists.[66] As noted by many of those scholars, the seemingly straightforward position of being a native in fact obscures many different degrees of being an insider or an outsider, as determined by the conditions of gender, age, class, prestige, and expertise, as well as ethnic, racial, and political identity (Narayan 1993, Zinn 1979).

Being a native of Turkey did not necessarily put me in a more advantageous position to gain access to the exclusive governmental sites I sought to study. When I first arrived in the field and was still trying to figure out the logistics of how human rights training programs were administered, I tried approaching the state institutions directly by going to their education departments and asking to participate in their training programs. During one such meeting at the Ministry of Justice, the head of the education department told me that those trainings were "inter-family affairs," and since I was not family, I could not be granted access. Upon receiving this answer and anticipating similar answers from other state institutions, I tried looking for other ways into human rights training programs.

Eventually, entry to the field happened through the new civil society and by way of mobilizing the connections I never knew I had. Upon running into old acquaintances in places like the human rights reception at the Consulate General of the Netherlands, I realized that a considerable number of my old school friends were now working for the harmonization industry. Friends and colleagues with bachelor's and master's degrees in political science and sociology have become the main workforce for the harmonization process. My access to this group, with whom I shared a similar background, was much easier than going directly to government offices. As they were managing a tight project budget and trying to make ends meet, the civil society component of human rights training programs eagerly welcomed my offer to provide them with voluntary labor.

I finally gained access to my field through "collaboration and complicity" (Holmes and Marcus 2005, 248) and by working for the human rights training programs in an "embedded" fashion (Tate 2007). I worked for these programs in various capacities: as a field researcher, project assistant, project evaluator, workshop facilitator, and, in one instance, as a trainer. My duties ranged from making tea to preparing reports, taking notes, and photocopying; and from helping with translation and copy-editing to teaching a module inside the classroom.

Although I was born and raised in Turkey, and had an upper-middle-class, ethnically unmarked—therefore quite mainstream and unthreatening—background, I initially had to appease the deep suspicions of many of my informants, and had to work hard to earn their trust. Coming from a US institution and working on a sensitive subject such as human rights prompted repeated questions, asked in a teasing manner, as to whether I was working for the CIA or the Turkish Intelligence Agency. Both for government workers and the members of left-leaning civil society organizations, being a graduate student in the US also had strong class connotations. For the people who belonged to these groups and shared lower-middle-class or working-class backgrounds, studying in the US meant that I had rich parents who could pay for my school and living expenses, which immediately put a barrier between them and me. When I tried to correct this misunderstanding by saying that I was actually able to study at Stanford thanks to scholarships and grants, it further added to the suspicion that I might be working for foreign powers.

While my class status and educational background placed me above most of my government worker informants, my gender and age had exactly the opposite effect. In most cases, I met with the government workers while doing secretarial work for the training programs, which accentuated my informants' gendered perceptions of me. Although some of my friends who were my age worked in executive positions at those projects, my gender and work position always led me to be perceived as much younger than I actually was. After spending some time with the government workers at the training programs as the young female project assistant, I was able to explain to them what I was doing and what my research was about. At that point, rather than being perceived as a suspicious outsider, I was seen as a young student who needed help with her homework. Meeting under those circumstances and having the chance to establish rapport prior to explaining my real reason for being there made all the difference for gaining access. Higher-level government workers, such as judges, prosecutors, and medical doctors (both men and women), were especially happy to help me with things that I did not understand. Even though working for the state might have put them in a precarious position when expressing their views on sensitive issues such as human rights, my government worker informants rarely asked not to be recorded during the more than one hundred interviews I conducted.

The analysis in the following pages of this book is based on my extensive participant observation in human rights training programs, both during trainings and the planning process. Besides participant observation in the training programs, I conducted semistructured, in-depth interviews with various government workers, members of civil society, and human rights experts who participated in human rights training as both trainers and trainees. I also interviewed other actors involved in the training programs, such as translators, project assistants, and project organizers. I combine my ethnographic analysis with the analysis of legal/political documents that regulate Turkey's EU accession. The fraught relationship between some key regulations such as the Child Protection Law, the Law Regarding the Protection of Family, and Criminal Procedural Law and the discussions that take place during the seminars with regard to the everyday implementation of these regulations composes a major theme of my study. In addition to national regulations, I draw on some fundamental international documents, such as the annual progress reports on Turkey issued by the EU and the Multi-Annual Indicative Planning Documents for Pre-Accession Assistance of the EU. These documents establish the normative framework for Turkey's EU accession and the harmonization process that the country has to go through in order to become a member.

I also analyze the manuals, booklets and other materials that are used in training programs to understand the educational models and conceptual frameworks that ground human rights trainings. Just like national and international legal documents, these training materials establish the normative pedagogical framework that informs individual training practices. Throughout the book, I go back and forth between the normative frameworks and their operationalization in everyday life in order to illuminate how the distance between the two is employed strategically by different parties as a resource to cope with, manage, and take advantage of unstable governmental conditions and a constantly shifting political environment brought about by the EU harmonization process in Turkey.

ORGANIZATION OF THE BOOK

The book is structured around two parts that are organized to elaborate on the different effects of human rights training programs for government workers in Turkey. The first half of the book introduces the main historical and structural components of the bureaucratic field, and focuses on the transformations to this field that are propelled by Turkey's EU accession process. The historical configurations and transformations detailed in chapters one and two are meant to provide the context in which human rights training programs are situated. The second half brings the readers into the actual pedagogical settings of training programs in order to analyze their unforeseen, perhaps unintended, consequences. In chapters three, four, and five, I analyze the borders of state language and performances of statehood that these training programs both destabilize and help consolidate. The conclusion then discusses the findings of my research for understanding the latest developments in the fields of governance and human rights in Turkey.

Amidst the disquieting upsurge of authoritarian policies and populist politics in the country, I seek to comprehend how seemingly progressive and liberal projects such as bureaucratic reform and human rights trainings can coexist with (and sometimes even lead to) violent state practices and an illiberal form of governance. To that end, I conclude the book with an elaboration of the performance of bureaucratic intimacies during human rights training programs. Enabled by the particular structure and implementation of the trainings themselves, these performances end up generating a community of knowers of bureaucratic secrets instead of a community of believers in universal human rights values. The kind of understanding that emanates from such a community contributes to prolonging the environment of impunity and unaccountability that continues to shape the governmental realm in Turkey.

SETTING THE STAGE

The Bureaucratic Field in Turkey

THE COOL AND DIM INTERIOR of the Ankara courthouse stood in contrast to the bright, sunny day outside. It was early June 2008. I placed my purse on the moving band as the security guard asked whether I was a lawyer in training. I answered "No." The sign on the x-ray machine read "Judges, Prosecutors, and Attorneys Exempt." I told the guard who was examining my voice recorder that I was there to interview Judge Neriman[1] from the children's court and that I had an appointment. Stepping into the building, I found the courthouse surprisingly quiet. The signs on the grey walls directed me to the third floor. I looked for the elevator but ended up taking the stairs when I saw the posted warning: "Authorized Personnel Only." Climbing up the stairs, I found a small courtroom where the court was in session. I peeked in through the open door and moved silently to take a seat in the back. Judge Neriman saw me entering and gestured with her hand, pointing to the front seats that are usually reserved for the interns. I obeyed her and sat right by the bench.

The defendant was a boy in his late teens with stylish dark hair, fashionably ripped dark jeans, a white button-up shirt, and polished pointy shoes. He was standing in the front to the right, on the other side of the bench from where I was seated. I gathered from the hearing that he worked as an apprentice in a male hair salon and that he was accused of stealing a cell phone from his boss. His attorney, a soft-spoken young woman, explained that the defendant came from the provinces not long ago, without much money or acquaintances. When he stole the cell phone, his salary was past due. He had asked timidly to be paid a couple of times, but his boss delayed it, saying he had more urgent debts to close. The defendant then took the phone and sold it out of despair. Judge

Neriman interrupted the lawyer and finished the story herself. Looking over her spectacles and speaking directly to the boy, she said, "But then you confessed to your boss before he found out, after you got paid. And you apologized, right?" The defendant bowed his head to confirm. "I see that you still work at the same place," Judge Neriman continued, "and I'm sure that you've learned your lesson, and you will never repeat this mistake." The defendant complied again. Judge Neriman then turned to the court recorder directly seated under her, and she started dictating. She summarized the case and the attorney's defense, adding references to particular articles from the Child Protection Law. Next, she turned to the attorney and asked: "You will probably demand probation, right?" The attorney agreed eagerly. Judge Neriman finished dictating her verdict and she adjourned the court for lunch break.

Once the courtroom was emptied, Judge Neriman came to sit with me, and I interviewed her about the juvenile justice training program she participated in. She had a firm yet pleasant demeanor, which elicited both trust and respect. Her dark blue two-piece dress had black trim around the collar and the cuffs. With carefully coiffed short brown hair and light makeup, she looked elegant and serious. In her early fifties, Neriman has been on the bench for over twenty-five years. She was appointed to the children's court when children's courts were established in 2005. She has been involved in organizational meetings, trainings, and workshops since 2006.

When I asked her to comment on the latest training in which we both participated, she said that her experience was mostly positive. Although she particularly praised the multiday, camplike training setting that housed the participants, trainers, and organizers in a hotel outside the city for four days, she complained that the format added to her already-heavy workload. "Before they design such programs, they need to come and see our work environment," she said. "See, the colleagues substituting for me did not even issue the simplest verdicts. They all postponed cases. Now, instead of thirty files, I have forty that I need to get through this week. This demands quite a sacrifice from us."

Sacrifice and care were in fact recurrent themes in Judge Neriman's comments. "I hold trials at least three–four days a week," she said. "I need to review the files before the trial, I need to write down my verdicts. When am I supposed to do all these things? If I don't come to the courthouse on Saturday or Sunday, I cannot catch up. I also have health problems. I had to delay attending to my health because of all this." Judge Neriman talked about both her profession and her commitment to juvenile justice in terms of a selfless endeavor that she carried out despite limited resources and hardship. During the interview, she pointed to different parts of the courtroom, to wrapped doorknobs and felted chairs, which she had done personally to make sure that the furniture would not destroy the painted wall or the floor polish. She recounted that upon her initial appointment, she did not even have a designated courtroom. Through her own personal initiative, she transformed a file storage space into a small courtroom, decorating it with potted plants she had brought from her own house to make it less grim and more child-friendly. To further emphasize how she performed her job under inadequate circumstances, she narrated how she often lent her office to court social workers who needed to meet with children privately to prepare social investigation reports.

"I always convey to my personnel how much I appreciate them," Judge Neriman maintained. "I sometimes sit down and eat with them. We share. I don't know if you noticed, but none of them are badly behaved. They're not spoiled or impolite. They work relentlessly because I tell them how important their work is for what I do. Even if I'm the brain, I tell them that they're like my hands and arms." Her attitude towards her staff at times mirrored her approach towards children in the justice system, especially when she talked about her current bailiff—a young man raised in an orphanage who was hired through affirmative action: "The first day he arrived, I told Mehmet what he had to pay attention to, what I expected from him, how he should behave, and I had him watch me run a trial with an experienced bailiff . . . After the trial, I sat him down and told him that he was forbidden to wear heavy scents like *hacıyağı* [an oil-based heavy perfume that is made from attar of roses and is associated with hajis and/or worn by lower class, conservative people]—because I know that *onlar* (they—his kind) fancy it. I told him that he should not wear white socks. I told him all of this because I thought since he didn't grow up with parents, he might be lacking some things that are passed on through the family. He is a very attractive boy. He buys whatever he fancies. One day, I arrived at the courthouse and found him smelling very strongly of *hacıyağı*. He said, 'I wasn't thinking. My friends wore it, so I tried it as well.' I gave him the afternoon off so that he could go shower. I told him not to repeat it again."

Neriman emphasized the notion of leadership multiple times during our conversation. Her one criticism about the training program was that it did not highlight enough that judges are actually the head of the system. Although she enjoyed going through training with various government workers who work in different parts of the juvenile justice system, she nevertheless expected the trainers to be more explicit about who leads the system: "Now, physicians in particular have difficulty with this . . . They think that they studied for six years and when they start working they come under the authority of the governor, who only has a four-year education. But this is the law. That governor is there as an administrator, you are here as a staff member who is responsible for health care services. Management is different, health care, being a doctor is different. They have to accept this from the very beginning. Police, gendarme, social worker—they all need to accept that they are staff members within the judiciary. You need to see it from a distance. At the end of the day, it is the judge who issues the final verdict. The prosecutors only open cases; they make demands on the court. But the judges are not like that; they make decisions . . . Everyone has a set role and needs to know what his or her role is. Social worker, your job is to prepare this report. Doctors, likewise, prepare their reports. They don't interfere with how the judges will evaluate them. The judges may find the reports right or wrong, but they are the ones who will eventually decide . . . There has to be a chief. And the chiefs in this system are the judges. You must first and foremost accept their presence and authority. This might have been emphasized more in the training."

After the interview, Judge Neriman offered to take me to lunch. I gratefully accepted. "I can also show you around the courtroom on our way out," she suggested. We first stopped by her office. As she opened the door she warned me that a social worker was inside, interviewing a child. We said a quick hello to the young woman who was sitting with a notepad in her lap across from a boy in his early teens on two couches facing each other. Judge Neriman then took me to the court secretariat, where the staff was busily working. They all stopped to greet us. "Hello friends!" (*Merhaba arkadaşlar!*) Judge Neriman exclaimed. She then turned to me and repeated how the secretarial staff was essential for the functioning of the court. She introduced me as a university student preparing a thesis and she said that there are many students she helped out in the past. "If you need to see any case files, let me know," she said. "I can tell the secretariat to release them to you. Of course they erase any sensitive information—names, addresses. I allow many students like you to study my case files." I thanked her and the staff in advance. On our way to the cafeteria, Judge Neriman answered my question about how she decided to become a judge. "I actually always wanted to be a teacher," she said, "but life took its course, and I found myself here."

What I experienced firsthand in the courtroom that morning was enactments of deeply hierarchical relations that condition the worlds of government workers in Turkey. Those enactments were sometimes subtle, other times overt. One could read hierarchies through the spatial arrangements and enactments of deference and authority, as well as the organizational structure of government offices. Along with its hierarchical composition, another significant characteristic of the governmental realm in Turkey was its pedagogical makeup. A tutelary disposition defined the ways in which higher-ranking government workers related to those in the lower ranks and the ways in which most government workers related to citizens. Bureaucratic reform projects such as human rights training programs sought to undo those hierarchies and pedagogical relations in order to transform bureaucracy into a more egalitarian and collaborative field.

1 TRAINING BUREAUCRATS, PRACTICING FOR EUROPE

> *[Civil servants are] authoritative subjects with the authorization to subject others to authority.*
> —**Thomas Osborne**[1]

YASİN, a children's court judge participating in "the Juvenile Justice Training Programme" led by the Ministry of Justice and the United Nations Children's Emergency Fund (UNICEF), took the stage to explain what it meant to be a member of the judiciary in Turkey. His words clearly resonated with the general experience in the room, as the other participants listened to him with serious faces and nods of approval:

> As judges and prosecutors, we are not really encouraged to blend in with the people in places we are appointed to. We socialize exclusively with other bureaucrats and with the army personnel . . . A judge is also expected to display proper behavior on the street. We can't be seen eating something while walking on the street, for instance. We can't be seen doing [grocery] shopping at the neighborhood bazaar. We can't be seen riding a bicycle, carrying shopping bags. I know a judge who went through a disciplinary hearing because he was seen eating *simit* [a street food resembling bagels] on the street at Konak [district] in Izmir.

Yasin's account is perhaps the best depiction of embodying state power and authority in Turkey. The tutelary relationship between the state elites and the ordinary citizens has been a legacy of national governance in Turkey since the early Republican period (Frey 1965, Meeker 2002). The state elites, hailed as the civilizing agents of the newborn republic, were given the duty to raise the nation to the level of "modern civilization" (Ahmad 1993, Bozdoğan and Kasaba 1997, Finkel and Sirman 1990). This tutelary relationship finds its reflection in a sentiment that is traceable in the memoirs of many retired government workers, recalling both nostalgically and cynically their naïve ambition "to save the people."[2] The civilizing duty and the accompanying state-society relations have configured the state in Turkey as a social field that first and foremost produces hierarchies.[3] Bureaucratic authority and governmental legitimacy—two main products of this hierarchical field—depended on the distinction of government workers from *halk* (the common people). This distinction was based on the bureaucrats' ability to embody and channel the state—the traditional agent of modernization and development in Turkey—mainly due to their high level of education and proper institutional enculturation.[4]

This chapter explores the reconfiguration of this field and the recalibration of the terms of hierarchy and distinction that go into establishing bureaucratic authority and governmental legitimacy in Turkey—a process prompted by the country's pending accession to the EU. Turkey's EU accession hinges on a substantive reorganization of the governmental field according to European standards of good governance, which consider human rights a key component.[5] The accession framework renders human rights synonymous with governmental competence and more egalitarian, cooperative state-society relations. Hence, the human rights agenda of the EU aims directly at dissolving the strict hierarchy between the governor and the governed, viewing it as the main cause of human rights violations in Turkey.

As well as targeting the hierarchical relationship between the governor and the governed, human rights training programs also challenge the traditional role of government workers as educators of the people by portraying them as subjects who are themselves in need of education and reform. They feature the human rights experts of national and international non-governmental organizations as trainers qualified to educate the unqualified governmental actors. I argue that as government workers receive, resist, respond to, and accommodate these trainings, they strategically reposition their claims to governmental legitimacy in order to manage the challenges that are brought by transnational human rights standards. As their traditional hold on the markers of modernity are contested in EU-sponsored training sessions, Turkey's bureaucratic actors are compelled to recalibrate their proximity to *halk* and to base their claims to governmental legitimacy on being of the people rather than standing above them.

This inquiry is inspired by the prominent body of scholarship that grows out of the critical interrogations of the state as "an *a priori* conceptual or empirical object" (Sharma and Gupta 2006, 8). These interrogations have yielded a prolific literature on the everyday practices, symbolic representations, authoritative effects, and affective consequences associated with the normative institutional form of the state.[6] My work on bureaucratic distinction builds on this literature by examining the state also as a constellation of people situated within complex relations of class, gender, and transnational hierarchy. Bringing together Pierre Bourdieu's analysis of the state as "a meta-capital granting power" ([1977] 1999) and a source of "distinction" (1984) with Cornelius Castoriadis's (1987) depiction of "the social imaginary" as repertoires of meaning-making available in a given society, I seek to understand how Turkey's EU accession process affects the imaginaries of hierarchy and distinction that invest governmental subjects with the cultural and symbolic capital on which their authority is based.[7]

The encounters happening at human rights training programs in Turkey, and the ways in which governmental and non-governmental actors relate to each other during these encounters, are informed by the rivaling imaginaries of authority and elitism that come into circulation during Turkey's EU accession. These imaginaries provide bases for competing claims over status and distinction, and they situate government workers and their non-governmental counterparts in relation to one another. Human rights training programs reveal how those who govern acquire bureaucratic authority and governmental legitimacy through certain processes of interaction and practice that involve contestation, negotiation, and reconfiguration. These programs also demonstrate the conditional nature of bureaucratic authority and governmental legitimacy. Distinctions and hierarchies that produce bureaucratic authority and governmental legitimacy do not correspond to historically overarching, permanent structures of power and domination. These distinctions and hierarchies are instead products of highly contextual hegemonic practices, enabled and shaped by historical, socio-political and economic developments on both a national and international scale. Human rights training programs reveal how transnational encounters contribute to the making of the national state by situating the people who are its embodiments within the positions of distinction shaped by hierarchies of class, gender, and sociocultural privilege.

GOVERNMENTAL RESPATIALIZATION, BUREAUCRATIC DISTINCTION, AND LEGITIMACY

Human rights training programs are the products of a unique historical conjuncture that brings together Turkey's contested accession to the EU and the controversial role of human rights for the country's sense of sovereignty and its relationship to the West. It is in the intersection of these socio-historical, political phenomena that Turkish government workers make sense of themselves, and are made sense of by the non-governmental figures with whom they interact during these training programs. Bureaucratic imaginaries of hierarchy and distinction are built upon competing understandings of eliteness, and they are situated practices that take place in a highly transnational setting that expands the governmental realm beyond Turkey's borders. The expansion of governmental borders brought by transnational practices not only amounts to "the respatialization of various state functions" (Ferguson and Gupta 2002, Trouillot 2001, 133). It also respatializes the way in which bureaucratic authority gets established.

Today, the ongoing respatialization of governmental boundaries in Turkey is propelled mainly by the country's EU accession. The harmonization process that Turkey must undergo to meet EU standards requires the Europeanization of both the administrative techniques of government and the habits, attitudes, dispositions, and behavior that are often glossed as "Turkish political culture."[8] Especially for the kind of transformation that human rights training programs intend, this means the radical alteration of social conventions, historical registers, and webs of meaning that inform bureaucratic dispositions and the official governmental realm in Turkey. EU accession thus demands an expansion of the Turkish governmental sphere to include previously marginal fields such as human rights and civil society.

Human rights training programs epitomize the expansion of the governmental field to include human rights and civil society as essential components of a European model of good governance. These programs are intended to render both human rights and civil society non-threatening and acceptable for the government workers who have been socialized to perceive them as suspect. As such, they are also part of the EU agenda to encourage state-civil society dialogue despite the historical antagonism of the state towards a domain that posed a threat to its exclusive ordering authority (Gürbey 1997, Mardin 1990, Wedel 1997). Against this background, collaborations between state and civil society on human rights training programs ask actors from both domains to rehearse and challenge long-held convictions. These interactions are also where government workers encounter challenges to familiar models of distinction and eliteness that form the basis of their bureaucratic authority and governmental legitimacy.

The social imaginary that shapes the bureaucratic realm in Turkey is informed by a long-standing distinction between the governor and the governed, which the earlier literature refers to as the "bifurcated Turkey" (Lerner 1958), "the crucial chasm between the intelligentsia and the peasantry" (Frey 1965), or "the center-periphery dynamic" (Mardin 1973). This distinction is based on the cultural gap between the governing elite, who possess a bureaucratic *adab* (manners or etiquette), as well as formal education and the knowledge of the West, and the common people with mostly rural origins and conservative religious values (Heper 2000).[9] The governing elite's claim to governmental authority on political and economic issues is mainly secured by the unequal distribution of socio-economic resources between these two groups, which gives the center "the right of cultural superiority" (Mardin 1990, 44).

From the time of the Ottoman reforms to the early Republican period, education has formed the backbone of this cultural superiority. During successive periods of restructuring, both civil and military bureaucracies have been both an object and agent of political modernization through education. As civil bureaucracy prior to modernization was mainly organized around patronage, apprenticeship, and hereditary career lines, reformists saw education as the key to a modern civil service that was based on meritocracy. Although it allowed the entrance of some previously excluded social sectors into the governmental field, the reorganization of bureaucracy on the basis of educational merit did not necessarily translate into universal access. Access to education itself was mostly dependent on a cosmopolitan, urban family background. This started to change with the increased educational opportunities that accompanied modernization, as well as the transfer of the Turkish capital from Istanbul to Ankara. The result was the expansion of the social base of the civil service and the elite class, and the enlargement of the Anatolian element in it. This expansion, however, did not cease the hereditary and self-perpetuating character of the elite definitively (Chambers 1964).

Particularly since the end of the single-party regime in 1950, there has been a steady transformation of the composition of the governing elite from a closed circle of top-level families to a more open community of people with mixed backgrounds and diverse occupations (Arat 1991). In political life, this corresponded with the increased influence of local power brokers within the national parliament, notwithstanding the national urbanite elite (Frey 1965). With the spread of universal mass education, as well as the neoliberal socioeconomic transformations in the 1980s, the periphery started to gain further economic and political power, although this power was not distributed equally. The decrease in public funding for education was accompanied by deregulation and privatization of educational provision, which deepened the discrepancies between specific schools and their graduates' prospective careers (Acar and Ayata 2002).

Although they did not lead to a complete opening of the bureaucratic field, these transformations made government service more accessible. Particularly as a result of the steady decline in both the salaries and status of state employees, government service has appealed specifically to people with provincial and modest backgrounds. Combined with improved access through meritocracy, state employment has provided those groups with opportunity for upward mobility (Öncü 1991). University education in key institutions such as Ankara University Faculty of Political Sciences (Mülkiye) and Ankara University School of Law, certificate programs, and short-term appointments abroad, which give state employees *yurt dışı deneyimi* (overseas experience), have been critical to this upward mobility (Özer 2006).

Educated people from the provinces and the periphery who were drawn into bureaucratic institutions changed the nature of bureaucracy by challenging the traditional Kemalist-secularist state elite and their values (White 2002a). However, even though these structural changes caused the state to loosen its exclusive grip over society and transformed the bureaucratic profile from an exclusively Kemalist-secularist community to one of upwardly mobile rural origin with more conservative religious values, eliteness as a desired social status and an effective political institution remained intact (Navaro-Yashin 2002). Instead of a strictly ascribed status that was inherited from family, eliteness became an achieved social status accessible through education and merit. Although they did not fit in the prototype of the Kemalist-secularist state elite in the early years of the Republic, the new cadre of government workers continued to base their governmental legitimacy on their acquired bureaucratic distinction.

In addition to their distinction from the common people achieved via education, government workers also claimed governmental legitimacy due to their distinction from the *political* elites.[10] As opposed to the political elites who were expected to put their personal, socio-economic interests over those of the state, the bureaucratic elites perceived themselves as the guardians of Republican values and principles. The latter's claim to an unbiased standpoint allowed them to take on the duty of monitoring the political elite. The legitimacy of the bureaucratic elite, as opposed to that of the political elite, rested on the claim that being above society enabled the bureaucratic elite to see beyond the immediate interests of narrow political groups, thus making them fit to govern and shape the entire society.[11]

This history culminates in the popular personification of the Turkish state as a paternalistic figure, sometimes referred to as "the father state" (*devlet baba*) and other times as the "teacher" or "educator."[12] As many other nation states, the state in Turkey functions as a pedagogical tool as much as a governmental one (Kaplan 2006).[13] The state assumes the right and duty to educate its citizens, not only through institutions of national education, but also through sending enlightened government workers from the center to provinces all around the country. Government spaces such as courtrooms and factories, which house encounters between ordinary people and government workers, are imagined as educational environments where the latter guide the former about the proper ways of conduct.[14]

As the embodiment of state power and authority, government workers are expected to keep up appearances on and off duty in order to set an example for local communities. Anecdotes such as the one I opened this chapter with testify to the importance attributed to this aspect of bureaucratic authority. Yasin's statement is a perfect illustration of how closely bureaucratic authority is linked to the bureaucratic subject's distinction from the governed. This distinction requires government workers to disengage themselves from the community as much as possible, and prohibits them from undertaking the sorts of mundane activity that might put them in contact or on an equal footing with the people whom they govern. A similar story recounted by Neriman, another judge, and a woman, further elucidates how social distinction establishes bureaucratic authority:

> It is of course twice as hard for women judges. In one of the places I was appointed to, I lived at the top of this very steep street. It would be impossible to climb when it snowed during winter. I couldn't ask for help from anyone because it wouldn't have been proper. My neighbors wanted to help me too, but they didn't know what to do. I mean, I couldn't be [seen] holding on to anyone or anything . . . The idea is that you're someone who rules over the people. You can't be seen as weak, or caught doing something improper. As a woman judge, you have to be twice as careful. I was married and everything, but still . . . You have to set an example. The people should have respect for you.

Neriman's account illuminates the everyday conditions in which bureaucratic authority and governmental competence are constituted. The subjects endowed with this authority have to make sure that they appear competent and self-sufficient in all aspects of their daily lives. Any requests for help on their part run the risk of compromising their expected role as "rulers over the people." I was also told that "asking for help" could be regarded as a subtle way of asking for a bribe, which could in turn give rise to allegations of corruption. However, the most striking feature of Neriman's story is the additional hardship that comes with the gendered definitions of propriety in maintaining bureaucratic distinctions.

As the gendered embodiment of the Turkish state, Neriman had a duty to protect the state's honor. Modern state institutions in Turkey actively constitute gendered definitions of honor and they inscribe these definitions onto female bodies in various legal and governmental settings (Koğacıoğlu 2004, 2005). In line with these definitions, the condition of propriety Neriman was expected to uphold was strongly tied to guarding the boundaries of her female body.[15] She could not touch or hold on to anyone, even under the extreme conditions of walking up a steep, frozen slope. While her marital status designated her as a "taken woman" and protected her from indecent proposals or allegations of indecency, her honorable position was still conditional upon the regulation of her actual and metaphorical sexuality.

Yasin's and Neriman's accounts help to flesh out the social imaginaries of bureaucratic distinction that underlie governmental legitimacy and state authority in Turkey. Capacity-building projects that are designed to improve the compatibility of Turkish state institutions with EU's standards for good governance disrupt these imaginaries by introducing spaces where government workers, historically hailed as educators and the agents of development, are defined as themselves in need of education and development. Capacity-building projects bring together state and nonstate actors, historically framed as the governor and the governed, in a pedagogical setting that elicits novel dynamics. Within this setting, the knowledgeable one—the teacher—is not the state embodied by the bureaucrat. Rather, it is nonstate actors and civil society who, due to their international connections, are in possession of the desired knowledge and thus are better qualified to teach what it means to be "European."

THE PAROCHIAL BUREAUCRAT AND THE COSMOPOLITAN ACTIVIST

Human rights training programs, where government workers directly encounter challenges to their governmental legitimacy, are part of a historical process that started in the 1990s. Beginning with the rise of identity politics, especially the populist Islamist political project and Muslim popular movements, this period witnessed civil society gaining symbolic power and finding ways to challenge the state's authority (Özyürek 2006, Tuğal 2009, Turam 2007, White 2002b).[16] Although this process can hardly be defined "as one of progressive and favorable democratization," a discourse of civil society nevertheless became instrumental in claiming legitimate ownership of state power (Navaro-Yashin 1998). The current EU accession framework introduces a further twist to this process by summoning a particular kind of civil society that would interact in a particular way with the state institutions. As part of the agenda to establish good governance in Turkey, civil society is incited to take active part in governance by professionalizing and cooperating with the state to improve its governmental capacity. Meanwhile, to fulfill this demand for a professionalized, expert civil society, universities, interest groups, and professional organizations are invited to step up as civil society institutions.

Universities are among the most important institutions that are eligible to collaborate with state institutions on capacity-building projects. Both national and international institutions tend to prefer universities as proper civil society partners for the development of governmental capacity because of the widespread recognition of their academic authority. As loci of knowledge production, universities serve as important resources for the international agencies as they appeal to bureaucrats who demand that their trainers possess a certain level of proficiency and symbolic status. For universities and affiliated research centers, these projects are desirable because they provide an additional source of income and a new field of engagement outside the ivory tower.

The encounters between internationally connected academics and their less-connected bureaucratic counterparts in human rights trainings disrupt the elite positioning of the bureaucrats. Consider the account of Tahir, a university professor who is involved in capacity building projects for the Ministry of Justice:

> State institutions have a peculiar structure. There's *dantel* (needlepoint) all over the place, for instance . . . There's a TV set in the office of the minister of justice, and there's *dantel* on top of it. I mean this is a government office . . . Once, we were at the Ministry of Justice again, they invited us in, they asked what we'd like to drink. They said: "*Bizim kekik çayımız meşhurdur.*" (Our thyme tea is famous.) The ministry of justice's *kekik çayı* is famous, so they say. We had no idea. I had never had *kekik çayı* before. Thyme has a nice aroma to it, smells good, but I never thought of it as something that can be drunk like tea. We said: "All right, then, let's have *kekik çayı*." After some time, the teas arrived.

Light yellow colored water, served in glass teacups. Along with the teacups, in the saucers, there is *karanfil* (carnation flowers). Not with long stems, but cut short, and wrapped in tinfoil. So, they brought *karanfil,* along with *kekik çayı,* on the saucer. Now, whose decision is this, for example? Is it the tea maker's idea, serving *kekik çayı* along with *karanfil*? Does he wrap tinfoil around the carnation flowers in the kitchen? Is that the esthetic sensibility of the Minister? Whose sensibility is it? There's an intense *yerellik* (provincialism) that runs within the ministries, a very explicit *yerellik. Kekik çayı, lahmacun* [Turkish pita] go up and down in the ministry corridors.

Kekik çayı, dantel, lahmacun and other signifiers of provincialism depict the world of bureaucrats as quite distinct from that of the cosmopolitan academic elite. In the account of Tahir, a foreign-educated professor of law who frequents the international institutions of the elite academy, we see a sincere curiosity with respect to the provincial ways of national bureaucracy. In line with his multiculturalist sensibilities, Tahir was careful about not judging the parochialism he encountered in the Ministry of Justice while talking to me. Rather, he was eager to share his ethnographic observations and analysis of a particular social structure with a fellow academic. Even though his standpoint as an analyst of the Turkish bureaucratic realm positioned Tahir above the parochial bureaucrats, everyday situations in which Tahir interacted with them gave rise to instances where cosmopolitan nonstate actors were tested for their competence in national/local specificities:

At [government offices] of course, you realize that they're differentiating us from themselves. Now, we are a private university, they know it, we are internationally connected and stuff, I mean we're not an *Anadolu çocuğu* (Anatolian child) like them. We have to make an effort . . . to establish a common language there. They test us during the process, to see how much we fit in to their cultural environment. They say, for instance: "*Siz de alır mısınız Hocam? Size de bir dürüm söyleyelim mi?*" (Would you like one, professor? Shall we order a wrap for you too?) You cannot say "Ew!" in those instances. You have to put up with certain things even if you don't want to.

As the party who had to make an effort to establish a common language, Tahir felt that he needed to show tolerance toward things he might otherwise consider socially inappropriate, such as eating wraps during an official meeting. The "cultural environment" of the Turkish bureaucracy, from which Tahir clearly differentiated himself, wielded power due to the specific context of the encounter. Collaboration with the other party was an obligation both for the Ministry of Justice and the private university where Tahir teaches. The university needed to collaborate with the ministry to get project funding. It also added to the university's prestige to be involved in EU-related projects. By the same token, the ministry needed the university in order to fulfill its obligations arising from Turkey's National Programme.[17] Even so, the specific place of the meeting where Tahir and his team visited the ministry offices to plan the details of collaboration empowered state actors to approve or disapprove of the academic elite.

However, at other times, the capacity building projects and the appropriate forms of behavior required at the foreign places where these projects take place empowered the internationally connected party. The transnational nature of EU accession and the harmonization process compels Turkish government workers to travel to European countries and interact with people there according to the terms appropriate for those places. The cosmopolitan nature of this new governmental field, which extends from the ministry offices to workshops in Brussels, designates the internationally connected civil society and the cosmopolitan academic elite as the possessors of the skills necessary to operate within it. Capacity building projects, which are designed to push the Turkish bureaucracy to raise itself to European standards, privilege those familiar with European ways, thus complicating the power dynamics between the governmental and non-governmental figures.

In another account, Tahir recounted a field trip to Switzerland with a group of bureaucrats. His story clearly illuminates which group is cast as the expert within the cosmopolitan world in which the governmental forces are now expected to operate:

> It's not like we haven't come across judges who disappear during the field trips. All of a sudden they disappear. "Where have you been?" [They say] "We went sightseeing." There's almost a return to childhood . . . Most of the judges don't speak a foreign language, and although they have a very important status [in Turkey], in the [foreign] places they go to, this doesn't mean anything . . . It's a bit like taking schoolchildren to the museum.

Thus, the tables were turned. In an international setting, the powerful, competent Turkish government workers who tested the cosmopolitan academic elite at the ministry offices were suddenly infantilized. Their inability to express themselves or to understand and navigate without assistance in this foreign space was one of the major reasons for this infantilization. Stripped of their bureaucratic title, their high status in the national context, and their native tongue, they became powerless. The only act of protest they could display in these circumstances was to give Tahir a hard time (by disappearing). In turn, Tahir started to feel like a schoolteacher. Out of their element, Turkish government workers in foreign places experienced a discrepancy between the rules of conduct that they were accustomed to and those that regulated foreign places. This discrepancy often produced uncomfortable and even embarrassing situations:

> Once, while in Switzerland, at the institute where we hold the training, [the hosts] showed us around, classrooms, bathrooms, the kitchen and whatnot . . . And they said: "You're welcome to make tea, coffee here. Here are the mugs you can use, but please make sure you clean after yourselves because there's no one paid to do the cleaning here. If you don't want to be bothered by washing the dishes, you can use the paper cups and throw them away when you're done with them." Of course, none of *bizim zatlar* (our honorables) want to drink out of paper cups, but then [after using the mugs] they just fill them with water and leave them inside the sink. A couple of us in our team, we wash our own mugs and that's it. Of course, after a while, all the mugs got dirty, they got piled up in the sink. There were a couple of women judges. They started to clean up little by little. I said to them: "What are you doing? You don't have to clean this. Stop washing." They said: "Yes we know, but what else to do? We'd be ashamed in front of the Swiss."

Switching from a highly hierarchical order where they were served to one where they were expected to clean up after themselves signified the ultimate loss of status for the government workers. What is more, the codes of rank and gender that ordered the government workers' daily lives were not recognized in the training spaces in Switzerland. Failure of these codes and the expected forms of behavior that came out of them further alienated this group. In those foreign spaces, which operated according to different codes, Turkish government workers were configured not as the rule-makers but as the rule-breakers:

> Another funny event was about smoking cigarettes. As you know, smoking indoors is forbidden [in Switzerland]. You have to go outside to smoke. On a Sunday, there's nobody around. Taking advantage of it, *bizimkiler* (our folk) lit their cigarettes. But of course the built-in smoke sensors are so sensitive, the alarm went off with a huge uproar. *Bunlar* (those ones—the judges), of course, couldn't tell what was happening. You should've seen them. They didn't know what to do with the cigarettes in their hands. They were trying to put them out,

hide them, whatnot . . . The fire brigade arrived immediately, that way we got to witness how efficient Lausanne city services were.

Unfamiliarity with the place, with its ways, its regulations and registers, created distress among the Turkish government workers. As opposed to the cosmopolitan academic elite or the internationally connected members of the civil society, "provincial" bureaucrats lacked the skills and the attitude to feel at home in distant places:

> When you go abroad with groups like this, [getting] food becomes an issue. There's a widespread fear about eating pork. They get scared to death they may eat pork [by mistake]. For instance, even if they are served fish, they still don't want to eat it, out of fear that it might be cooked in pork fat. That's why they always look for places owned by [diaspora] Turks, such as *dönerci* (eateries that sell a distinct type of Turkish kebab, also known as a *shawarma,* or gyro).

Tahir's account of his adventures in Switzerland with Turkish judges and prosecutors clearly demarcates the distinction between "those who can feel certainty and self-assurance in a variety of places, even in distant ones, without feeling out of place" and those who feel "at a loss and out of place in unfamiliar spaces" (Yeğenoğlu 2005, 128). While the former have the ability to operate smoothly in various locations, the latter seek ways to deal with their anxieties "in a familiar and known manner" (ibid.)—like looking for *shawarma* eateries. This cosmopolitan distinction of "being comfortable in heterogeneous public spaces" and "moving comfortably in diversity" closely follows one's status as a frequent traveler (Calhoun 2002, 890–93). The "class structuring of social life," "systemic inequalities," "privileges of wealth," and "citizenship in certain states" grant certain people specific dispositions that allow "cosmopolitan appreciation of global diversity" (ibid.). These dispositions denote a specific way of relating to a place that "imprints particular habits" (like washing up after yourself), "modes of being in the world" (like being open-minded), and "forms of consciousness" (like transgressing established gender norms) (Yeğenoğlu 2005, 122).

Being a citizen of the world, therefore, bespeaks a position of privilege. Many Turkish government workers who came from lower-class backgrounds or the periphery (*Anadolu çocuğu*) and made their way to the center by entering government service lack the privilege of cultivating this disposition (through foreign language education, upper-class socialization, international media consumption, etc.). Their distinction as governmental figures in these circumstances causes them to experience not a gain but a loss of status. Looking from a cosmopolitanist perspective that builds upon the dichotomy between the "multicultural moderns" and the "monocultural traditionals" (ibid., 888), Turkish bureaucrats who do not speak a foreign language, know how to carry themselves in a cosmopolitan space, or comply with the aspired-to foreign standards (related to professionalism, gender roles, regulations concerning public spaces, etc.) appear as disconnected, parochial, and thus not worldly enough. As opposed to their traditional role as paternalistic educators of the provincial peoples in the national sphere, within these newly emerging transnational sites of interaction and governance (ranging from institutions abroad to five-star hotels in Turkey), the bureaucrats are the ones who appear provincial, infantile, ignorant, and in need of education. These new sites hence disrupt the old, established, elite position of the bureaucrats and urge them to recalibrate their claims to bureaucratic authority and governmental legitimacy.

While the Turkish government workers still enjoy a high degree of authority at the local/national level, their bureaucratic distinction starts to evaporate in increasingly transnational governmental domains. Government workers respond to this threat by challenging their cosmopolitan interlocutors, shifting the terms of power, and reframing the international connectedness of the cosmopolitan subjects in terms of a national disconnect. The privileged cosmopolitanism enjoyed by the academic elite and internationally connected members of civil society produces resentment in the form of nationalist backlash, especially when coupled with the perception that ongoing political reforms are being imposed from the outside. This "resentment toward cosmopolitan people—happily situated members of large, powerful nations, prosperous and mobile individuals able to serve on UN commissions, who participate in symposia, who plan the fates of other peoples while flying around the world and staying in splendid hotels"—fuels a fierce nationalism suspicious of all forms of social organizing at a nonstate level (Pinsly cited in Hannertz 2007, 75). A privileged cosmopolitanism thus yields a reactionary nationalism that justifies itself on the basis of class inequalities and geographical disparities at play in the cosmopolitan world.

GOVERNMENTAL LEGITIMACY AND KNOWLEDGE OF THE PEOPLE

Transnational circumstances currently in play in Turkey instigate a shift in the basis of governmental competence for government workers, who are now portrayed as in need of training about the correct ways of doing things. Challenged by the shifting grounds of establishing an elite status based on the knowledge of the Western ways, the government workers are forced to recalibrate the grounds of their bureaucratic distinction and to base their claims to governmental legitimacy on their familiarity with local contexts, practices, and facts of governance in Turkey. By condemning the content of capacity-building trainings as too theoretical, bureaucrats who work one-on-one with *halk* claim that they know better because of their everyday experience and their proximity to the concrete and the actual.

For instance, Hayri, a high-ranking police officer I came to know through the juvenile justice training program, explained to me why he thought these programs were useless for him:

> The professors start talking: "When I was in England," etc., etc., "there they don't even have an ID card." All right, fine . . . but it's not England or Sweden here. It's not. Forget about England. This is Turkey. You tell me what I can do here, in these conditions . . . There, they have a system, established centuries ago. They run everything without even a written constitution . . . Nobody comes and asks us what we need. [They say] "I already did the thinking for you. This is what you need to know. Off we go training!" Nobody asks [me]: "My friend, what are your problems? What are the difficulties you face during implementation?" The British Council, UNICEF, you name it . . . This is what they do to us all the time.

The form of thinking illustrated in Hayri's account disrupts the idea of connectedness at the international level, which is the central premise of human rights trainings. Hayri reframes international connectedness as the human rights training programs' lack of locally grounded knowledge. Because international standards are given priority over local needs, international connectedness becomes a disabling factor, rather than an enabling one. Being internationally connected becomes synonymous with being disconnected from the local/national reality and thus incapable of understanding and addressing the actual problems facing Turkey. Theory, in Hayri's critique, gets ahead of implementation.

As Hayri, Mehmet, a prosecutor who participated in a program on women's human rights, pointed to the elite position of the trainers as the reason for their disconnect from "the facts of life":

> Most of the presenters [at the training] were people from the upper strata of society. They haven't been much in contact with the lower strata. I am a prosecutor, but my father was a worker. My mother was a housewife. They were

both primary school graduates. I mean I know both sides. I have contact both with the upper and the lower levels . . . Of course, when you look at it in this way, things seem different. When you approach the issue from the luxurious neighborhoods of Istanbul, it looks different. When you look at it from the perspective of the poorer neighborhoods it looks different, now, doesn't it? . . . These are *hayatın gerçekleri* (the facts of life). These things haven't been touched upon during the seminar. In fact, those were the things that should've been talked about. But maybe the presenters don't know about the conditions of the village, the poor families, they're not familiar with these. Maybe they just know about the upper strata. Maybe that's all they can talk about. I am a villager, for instance, I'm from the Aegean region myself, but I am also familiar with the conditions in the Southeast . . . There's a saying that goes: "*Tok açın halinden anlamaz*." (A sated person cannot understand a hungry one.) Right?

In Mehmet's account, the facts of village life denoted the national reality, which needed to be understood and adapted to, rather than being transformed according to a universalist and elitist vision. This shows a stark contrast to the way in which the relationship of the bureaucratic machine to the Anatolian provinces was historically imagined. As I mentioned earlier, during the early years of the Republic, the official governmental attitude towards the Anatolian provinces (especially in terms of their tribal, feudal structure) was one of social engineering. In the "romantic vision of the Republican program," the village represented something backward that needed to be transformed through regulations imported from the national center, such as land reform and educational campaigns (Mardin 1990, 64–65). In line with this vision, what was expected from the bureaucratic elite was not a familiarity with the village as it existed and functioned. Rather, the government workers were expected to share the Republican vision, which was about the ideal conditions that had to be attained in the quest for progress.

In Mehmet's account, however, we see a devaluation of the ideal in favor of the actual conditions and situations, which corresponds to the everyday realities that the government workers cope with:

Most of the participants confront those problems on a daily basis. They come from places like Van, not from big cities . . . Here [in Istanbul], I can only spare so much time for each individual case . . . But in small places it's easy. Judges and prosecutors know the family structures well . . . Judges know very well what lies at the basis of domestic conflicts. It is hard to apply the international law for domestic situations . . . However, most of the speakers [at the training] were academics living in big cities. They never come across such events on a one-on-one basis. They only watch the game from *tribün* (the spectator box—from a distance). Nevertheless, things that happen on the [soccer] field look pretty different from *tribün* . . . Speakers from academia are not aware of these. They are unaware of the actual background of the events.

With the expansion of the governmental field brought by transnational circumstances and the advent of a new economy of governance, Turkish government workers like Yasin, Neriman, Hayri, and Mehmet feel the need to recalibrate their skills and abilities to continue claiming governmental legitimacy. In changing circumstances, where the cosmopolitan academic elite and the internationally connected members of the civil society appear more capable of channeling the standards of European civilization, government workers instead capitalize on their ability to channel Anatolian realities. This amounts to a recalibration of the terms of bureaucratic distinction. In order to maintain their accustomed superiority and governmental legitimacy, government workers have to transition from distinction based on universal claims in the local and national realm to one rooted in claims to local knowledge in a transnational realm.

A RELATIONAL PERSPECTIVE

Tracing the shifts in the imaginaries of bureaucratic authority and governmental distinction in Turkey allows us to attend to the state in its relationality, connectedness, and instability. Conceptualizing the state and bureaucracy as a dynamic field of distinction, I argue that the terms of distinction arising from positions of advantage and disadvantage brought by class, gender, race, ethnicity, geographical origin, level of education, and seniority also articulate with asymmetrical relations of power at the transnational level. Such a perspective moves away from examining the state as a dominant locus of power and instead analyzes it as a field permeated by conditions of dependency arising from global hierarchies (Coronil 1997).

Looking at the ways in which Turkish government workers recalibrate their governmental legitimacy and bureaucratic authority in the context of Turkey's EU accession, we see the negotiation of the terms of hierarchy that shape the governmental field in Turkey. This negotiation includes the recalibration of the sources of governmental distinction and legitimacy. As the reference of bureaucratic authority shifts from the standards of European civilization to Anatolian realities, the positioning of these two as binaries works to distance European standards from the realm of reality. Depicted as theoretical, abstract, ungrounded or decontextualized, transnational standards of good governance and human rights acquire the status of imposed fantasies.

By selectively employing themes from a set of imaginaries related to the state, governance, foreignness, locality, and elitism, both state and nonstate actors position themselves in relation to Turkey's EU accession and the institutional transformations it foresees. Following the ways in which these themes operate and define how bureaucrats make sense of the act of governing helps to map out what the state really corresponds to in Turkey. As opposed to the popular and scholarly depictions of Turkey's governmental apparatus as a "strong state," a close study of how the challenges to governmental legitimacy play out in human rights trainings reveals that the state in Turkey is a field of hegemonic power relations and a tool of upward mobility. It is populated by governmental actors situated differentially along lines of class, gender, and geographical origin, who have varying stakes in preserving the state as a field that produces hierarchy—something that many human rights defenders and civil society activists have been fighting against.

For the past three decades, human rights defenders in Turkey opposed an authoritarian mode of governance marked by strict hierarchies that have produced mass incarcerations, disappearances under custody, gender disparity, ethnic violence, forced resettlement, economic exploitation, and regional inequalities. In so doing, they made effective use of the transnational forces and institutions that obliged Turkey to keep up with universal standards if it did not want to jeopardize its membership in the interstate system. However, with Turkey's pending EU accession, human rights (along with other standards of good governance) are associated with cosmopolitan ways of being in the world and positions of privilege that go into achieving these. When paired with the specific class position and locality that often define the government workers' backgrounds, the cosmopolitan associations of human rights inhibit their force by stirring up further reaction against them. In an attempt to advance the idea of human rights by framing it in a cosmopolitan imaginary, many human rights projects end up pitting class hierarchies against bureaucratic ones. The result is a nationalist backlash that is justified by and framed as an opposition to socio-economic privilege, international asymmetries of power, and colonial impositions.

A study of the state and bureaucracy in a transnational context requires grasping the larger universe of historical and political relationships and their power dynamics for a fuller understanding of state actors. Failing to do so results in the production and widespread repetition of problematic categories such as "the rogue state" or "the failed state" in influential writings such as policy papers and strategy documents.[18] These categories are often used to condemn and target reactionary state mechanisms, which are portrayed as anomalies due to their noncompliance with international norms and standards, such as those related to human rights. What is rather necessary, I argue, is to disentangle and analyze the relationships and evaluations that underlie the designation of certain states as rogue or failed. Looking from there, Turkey's human rights record, which is a key point for Turkey's EU accession, becomes not an indication of the inefficiency of the state. Rather, it reveals a labor-intensive process of state making, underlining the entanglement of class, status, sociocultural privilege, gender, and nationalism in the assemblage that is currently the state in Turkey. In the next chapter, I focus on how bureaucratic reform programs that are brought by EU harmonization shape this state-making process by aiming to transform the bureaucratic field from one that thrives on hierarchy to one that produces service.

2 HUMAN RIGHTS, GOOD GOVERNANCE, AND PROFESSIONAL EXPERTISE

> *To the closed world of the police station, the gendarmerie unit, the*
> *village guard corps, and the armed forces, European promises of mar-*
> *kets and investments [remain] abstract, distant, and uninteresting.*
> **—Jonathan Sugden,**
> **the Turkey researcher for Human Rights Watch.**[1]

I WAS SITTING WITH YAKUP—the Ministry of Justice representative at the juvenile justice training—in the common area designated for coffee breaks. Inside
the adjacent conference rooms, two concurrent sessions were under way. Yakup
stopped by the training infrequently, so I wanted to take this opportunity to
talk to him alone. Taking a sip from his tea, he started telling me about the challenges of instituting a child-friendly approach in the public sector in Turkey:

We have such a hard time explaining this to our supervisors. They say, "[In
Turkey] we love our children. We take care of them, we raise them, we send
them to school. In the West, they throw children onto the streets . . ." It doesn't
matter if they throw children onto the streets. The state [there] has the duty to
serve those children . . . If you [as a state] are a signatory to the Convention on
the Rights of the Child, I now have the right [to service]. Someone once told
me a story: When he was in one of the European countries, he was traveling
somewhere by train. At one of the stations, when the train stopped, the in-
spectors lowered a platform for a child in a wheelchair to get on the train. He
said, "The inspector didn't act as if he was doing a favor for the child, nor did
the child act thankful to the inspector. The former was performing his job, not
doing a favor. And the latter did not feel obliged to him . . ." This is the complete
opposite of what we have [in Turkey] . . . [The politician] says, "If I provide this
to these people, they will vote for me in future elections." When [the citizens]
get something, they feel like they should give something in return. In reality,
this should not be a give-and-take relationship . . . Service needs to be a professional thing. Otherwise, the burden of receiving in fact weighs heavily. (*Hizmet
profesyönel bir şey olmalı. Yoksa almanın yükü ağırdır aslında.*)

A full understanding of human rights training programs in Turkey necessitates situating them within the larger framework of good governance. Good governance lies at the heart of the public administration reforms that are instigated by the EU harmonization process in the country. These reforms are central to the reorganization of the governmental field, which I began exploring in the previous chapter. By charting out the connections between good governance initiatives and human rights training programs, I aim to demonstrate in this chapter the process by which human rights are made part of the professional disposition that government workers are expected to acquire in order to become proper governmental agents. As the opening quote by Jonathan Sugden suggests, establishing the relevance of good governance imperatives—such as human rights—for the everyday lives of government workers calls for the invention of incentives other than the distant promises of EU membership. Professionalization as an incentive makes good governance more relatable for the government workers, and it helps to get them on board with administrative reforms. Contrary to ambiguous advantages of the European single market, attaining the qualifications of professionalism and expertise such as occupational prestige, social respect, self-esteem, and higher salary can provide very tangible benefits to a wide spectrum of government workers.

In addition to making them relevant to the government workers' everyday line of work, training programs sought to reframe human rights in terms of professionalization in order to overcome expected resistance on the part of the trainees. Socialized to perceive the politics of human rights as an anti-establishment, oppositional movement and as a form of treacherous political alliance that bypasses national loyalties, government workers were regarded as a particularly challenging audience to convince about the value of universal human rights principles. Project teams hoped to disassociate human rights from their controversial political connotations by incorporating them into other technical improvements that were deemed necessary to enhance the Turkish state's governmental capacity. By carrying human rights outside of the realm of politics, the programs aimed to preclude the eruption of possible contestations during the training.

Finally, as my anecdote featuring Yakup shows, inculcation of professionalism was itself considered a means of improving the governmental field in Turkey. Professionalism and expertise were widely promoted by administrative reform circles to transform the governmental field from a realm that thrives on the hierarchy dividing the government workers and citizens to one that produces service to benefit the latter.[2] Like maintaining the transparency and accountability of public offices, respect for human rights was considered a precept that would level the power relationship between society and state by enabling the former to control the latter. Before going into detail about how this framing played out in human rights training programs, I would like to further elaborate on the relationship between the liberal capitalist order, good governance, and the subsequent calls to professionalism in the public sector in general.

The idea of good governance rests on "the principles of openness, participation, accountability, effectiveness and coherence," which according to the EU underpin democracy and the rule of law in member states (Commission of the European Communities 2001). These underlying principles bear strong affinities with the logic of the liberal capitalist order and the market economy, and they are defined by the World Bank as essential for "sound economic policies," "the efficiency of the markets and government," and "economic development." Contrary to nepotism and arbitrariness, good governance brings "efficient and accountable management by the public sector, and a predictable and transparent policy framework" that are believed to benefit both ordinary citizens and corporations (World Bank 1992).

In addition to enabling the efficient and effective functioning of the governmental apparatus, the particular perspective of good governance also configures the rationality and principles of the private sector as viable tools to measure the level of democracy and rule of law in countries across the world. As Sally Engle Merry (2011) demonstrates in her work on global human rights indicators, the proliferation of these techniques of measurement signifies the expansion of the corporate form into the domains of state and civil society. In a similar vein, good governance initiatives adopt the models, practices, and metrics of the for-profit sector to reorganize the public sector (c.f. Graeber 2015). Markers of accountability and openness to scrutiny that come with the acquisition of "audit cultures" are employed to provide a stamp of democratic openness to governmental practices (Strathern 2000). Citizens are identified as stakeholders in public administration, patrons of public offices, and consumers of state services. In the meantime, economic efficiency and organizational effectiveness become hallmarks of the "quality of service" and they serve as indicators of democratic consolidation in various places.[3]

Reorganization of the governmental field as one of professionalism and expertise also implies the transformation of public administration from a patrimonial to a legal rational field. A dichotomy of the Weberian ideal types, patrimonial and legal rational forms of bureaucracy fall neatly within the terminology of good governance, which favors a depersonalized, routinized system (i.e., legal rational) over a personal, clientelistic one (i.e., patrimonial) (Weber 1978). The attribution of personal, possessive, clientelistic relations—as well as paternalistic/pastoral care and filial loyalty—to patrimonial order, and the association of depersonalized, technical, rationalized relations with legal rational order, often categorize non-Western and Western bureaucracies as stereotypical oppositions. As a result, non-Western bureaucracies are classified as anomalies that need reform to catch up with their Western counterparts.[4] Contrary to this binary model, real-life situations in fact feature an amalgam of different strategies and the coexistence of different characteristics attributed to both patrimonial and legal rational bureaucratic types (Alexander 2002, Best 2012, James 2012, Shore 2000). Oscillation between the two and a flexible use of different techniques are adopted to cope with and manage unstable conditions and a constantly shifting environment such as the one brought about by the EU harmonization process in Turkey. Although Weber's neat dichotomous categories fail to accurately capture the in-between, messy practices in real life, these ideal types both inform everyday common sense and "permeate international development thinking about 'good governance'" (Hetherington 2011, 147).

The harmonization process in Turkey is marked by the increasing ascendance of professionalism and expertise in public administration. Contrary to the argument that valuing expertise establishes an unavoidable hierarchy between experts and laymen and therefore runs counter to the ideals of democracy and egalitarianism (Illich et.al. [1977] 2000), institutionalization of governmental expertise and professionalization are seen as a key aspect of democratic consolidation in contemporary Turkey. It is believed that professional, expert government workers would make democracies safer by balancing the acts and decisions of interest-driven professional politicians, if expertise itself is made democratic—i.e., accessible, pluralistic, and transparent (c.f. Schudson 2006).

Similar to what Hwang and Powell (2009) describe with regard to the rationalization of the nonprofit sector in the US, the reorganization of the governmental field in Turkey includes hailing state officials as actors with clear professional identities whose formalized activities can be measured for purposes of efficiency.[5] Training programs for government workers on a number of issues including human rights are among the primary means of installing this new system of values based on professionalism. Through socialization processes (including capacity-building activities and certificate programs), security forces, members of the judiciary, health care providers, and many other govern-ment workers become experts by acquiring specific repertoires and by learning to act as such in their specific occupational fields (Brenneis 1994, Carr 2010).

In the particular context of Turkey, subsuming human rights within good governance also indicates an important change in the official discourse about human rights violations in the country—a shift from denial to a conditional acceptance of state-inflicted human rights violations. With the advent of legal reforms in tandem with the harmonization process, state policy for address-ing human rights abuses became predicated upon the assertion that these were not systematic but individual cases.[6] Promotion of expertise and professional-ism as a remedy for human rights abuses is part of the government's claim that those violations are inflicted by rogue figures, and institutional standardization would prevent these abuses. This reasoning is starkly different from the claims of human rights defenders in Turkey, who accuse the state of promoting an in-stitutional culture that normalizes state violence.

The good governance framework that upholds institutional standardization carves out a specific field of professionalism that is supposed to be devoid of emotions and empathy, and is required to exclude political beliefs and ideol-ogy. Both personal morality and politics are regarded to have adverse effects on government service that is supposed to be depersonalized, standardized, and accountable. Contrary to the normative framework of good governance, my ethnography of human rights trainings reveals that the practice of these admin-istrative reforms can hardly exclude emotional and political realms. As I dem-onstrate in the remainder of this chapter, the trainers in human rights training programs regularly evoked personal empathy and individual conscience to per-suade state officials of the importance of human rights for their professional formation. More importantly, my research shows that it is in fact impossible to communicate an effective pro-human rights message in the absence of a strong political orientation.

REPLACING PATERNALISTIC CARE WITH PROFESSIONAL SERVICE

In almost all of the human rights trainings I attended as a participant, overcom-ing the paternalistic framework in how government workers related to citizens was a major concern for the training team. This paternalistic framework shaped the relations between the government workers and citizens over a wide spec-trum of the bureaucratic field where the judges, prosecutors, police officers, doctors, and many others felt entitled to and responsible for making decisions on behalf of the citizens according to what they thought would serve them best. This mind-set led the physicians to force-feed the prisoners on hunger strike, the police officers to keep street children under custody over time to keep them out of trouble, and the judges to refuse processing divorce cases because they believed it would put women in a more precarious situation even if they were victims of domestic violence.

With the conviction that relating to citizens on the basis of paternalistic care was actually the main cause of human rights violations, the trainers of human rights training programs asked the government workers to instead relate to citizens on the basis of "bureaucratic indifference" (Herzfeld 1992). They instructed the trainees to act like experts and professionals in their field, which meant strictly applying the law despite their contradictory personal feelings and beliefs.

The particular way the government workers related to citizens was heavily determined by the way in which they related to their professions. The majority of the government workers I worked with thought of their jobs in terms of "public service," which they understood to be starkly different from the way that service was configured in the market economy. For them, public administration indicated something beyond "professional" work defined by "the time value of money" (Riles 2010, 805). Many government workers instead associated their jobs with altruism, devotion, self-sacrifice, and as something that they did to serve a higher purpose. For instance, judges and prosecutors often contrasted themselves to attorneys, who, they claimed, were doing their jobs for money.

As opposed to the idea of bureaucratic service that is grounded in the social production of depersonalized "indifference," this idea of service to the nation or the country was deeply engrained in practices of "masculinist protection" (Young 2003) and care. Unlike the good governance framework, which advocates disinterested professionalism as the necessary basis to serve citizens, government workers such as Judge Neriman associated the meaning of being a government worker with personal endeavor, empathy, and self-sacrifice that were necessary to care for citizens and serve their country. Contrary to its positive connotations for the government workers who experienced and performed their duties as a calling, the good governance framework associated this form of care with arbitrariness, inconsistency, and irrationality.

Human rights training seminars, thus, often instructed trainees to act professionally by keeping their personal conviction and feelings at bay. For instance, during the program on "the role of the police in preventing domestic violence against women," the trainer Chief Inspector Sertan emphasized the importance of "being professional" for the role of the police in preventing domestic violence: "Professionalism. Objectivity. Not being affected by anything ... Isn't this what we've always been taught in the first place? ... We want to be experts in this topic ... (*Biz bu konuda uzman olmak istiyoruz.*)"

By teaching government workers how to act professionally, the trainings invited them to relate to their professions in terms other than selflessness and dedication to the public good. The trainers told trainees that their responsibility was limited to their job description. "To do your own part" and to refrain from transgressing the boundaries of one's own profession was one of the most significant messages conveyed in these trainings. Sertan, for instance, often reiterated that one of the most important purposes of the training was to ensure that police officers "would not do things that aren't their business" (*üzerine vazife olmayan işleri yapmamak*).

Similarly, Dr. Simden, the trainer of health care professionals on the prevention of torture, emphasized that physicians should not take the duties of judges and prosecutors upon themselves. She advised the trainees to concentrate on "medical findings" such as scars, burns, and lesions, as well as anamnesis,[7] while treating "*alıkonulmuş hastalar*" (detained patients), rather than evaluating whether or not the detainees deserved harsh treatment. It is clear that this discourse of professional demarcation produces different messages within different professions with regard to human rights—as it does in the case of the physicians and the police. I will further detail the comparison between these messages later in this chapter. Before getting into that, though, let me concentrate on the outcome of this call to professionalism that ran across all occupational groups.

FIXING THE SYSTEM THROUGH
PERSONAL COMMUNICATION AND RELATIONALITY

The obligation to find creative solutions to manage the lack of resources and financial difficulties in fact constituted the everyday reality of many government workers in Turkey. Under those circumstances, most government workers found the human rights trainings' emphasis on professionalism and expertise, and a strict adherence to the letter of law, unfeasible and unrealistic. They often got frustrated about the discrepancy between their actual working conditions and the aspired-to governmental standards, which the human rights training programs kept referencing.

For instance, during the police training to prevent domestic violence, the participants were shown an instructional video about how a domestic abuse victim who comes to the police center to file a complaint should be treated.[8] In the film, police officers played by professional actors took the plaintiff into a designated interviewing room, assigned a woman police officer to take her testimony, and distracted her young son with toys while her testimony was taken. The prosecutor was notified of the situation immediately. Meanwhile, because the plaintiff was assessed as "high risk," someone from the social services agency was also notified. She was then taken to the hospital for medical examination. After being brought back to the police center, she was promptly transferred to the women's shelter.

Before showing the film, Sertan emphasized that it reflected the institutional ideals and aspired to best practices. Even so, participants continued to crack jokes and make comments about the discrepancy between what they saw on the screen and what happened in real life. One police officer jokingly asked whether the personnel in the film paid for the toys out of their own pockets. Another participant expressed his amazement that there was a woman officer available at the police center. Similar comments were made regarding the ease with which the low-rank officers called the prosecutor without the fear of being told off. And finally, the participants all applauded when someone from the social services agency actually answered the phone.

In these instances, the glaring discrepancy between actual working conditions and what was presented as universal standards ran the risk of leading the practitioners to question the relevance of such standards for the localities in which they worked. Fatma, a woman police officer in the training, summarized her feelings: "My concern with this training is that I'll go to my district and tell my colleagues that they can call the social services agency if they decide that the plaintiff is at high risk. They are going to call and nobody will show up. I understand that we have raised our standards and raised the bar [for public service]. But we're jumping over a bar and there's nothing to catch us on the other side."

Feelings of despair such as these were the last thing that the trainings aimed to evoke. To appease their frustration, training teams encouraged their audiences to better communicate and cooperate with other parties within the bureaucratic system to overcome their unfavorable working conditions. Unable to generate change at a structural level due to their limited scope, training programs instead focused on building human relationships. These relations were

believed to be central to creating a networklike bureaucratic structure organized around the division of labor among government workers who work together to produce the required government service.

This message was made particularly explicit in the juvenile justice training
program, which brought together government workers from different institutions. Following a test training with isolated professionals, the program held
two one-week sessions in which the police, gendarmerie, judges and prosecutors, physicians, social workers, psychologists, and lawyers, who worked in the
security forces, the judiciary, institute of forensic medicine, and probation centers, were brought together for a joint training. The purpose of the program was
to make these professionals recognize themselves as part of the "juvenile justice
system" that was recently established to fulfill Turkey's obligations as a signatory to the UN Convention on the Rights of the Child.

Right from the start, Dr. Onur Çelikkan, the project's training coordinator, announced that they aimed to implant a "feeling of belonging" (*aidiyet
duygusu*) and raise "team spirit" (*ekip ruhu*) among the participants. In his
opening remarks, he declared that the training's goal was to raise awareness
among participants of how they "complete each other with [their specialized]
knowledge of psychology, law, security, public order, and medicine" and how
they "all need each other." Similarly, Selma, the project advisor, asserted that
the training was "not so much about transfer of knowledge but about the development of an attitude and behavior" among the participants in order to
establish a habit of "working together in coordination." For that purpose, the
training was designed in a camp format: the participants were housed in a
resort hotel outside of the city and the daytime training sessions were complemented with extracurricular evening activities to build interpersonal relationships among participants. In addition to participating in sessions, which
involved preparing group projects and presentations, the trainees were also
divided into two teams and were given the responsibility of preparing an evening program that included skits, games, music, and dancing. According to
Dr. Çelikkan, these extracurricular activities were every bit as important as
the formal training sessions because the main purpose of the program was
community building.

Throughout the training, all of the trainers endorsed "inter-institutional dialogue" (*kurumlar arası diyalog*) as the primary solution for the problems that
juvenile justice professionals were facing while performing their jobs. This di-
agnosis was starkly different from the way in which the practitioners under-

stood their problems. From the perspective of the trainees, the difficulties they faced were mainly due to harsh working conditions, inadequate resources, and material shortcomings. Whenever they raised such issues, however, trainers and project advisors at once reframed these structural failures in terms of co-operation and communication problems. Consider this lengthy discussion be-tween Gizem, a psychologist working for the police, and Kemal, a judge and the trainer for the session on the Child Protection Law:

> *Gizem*: We encountered difficulties in the field of preventive services. We wrote to the social services agency. We said, "Look, we have a child here convicted of such-and-such crimes. This child is at high risk: let's do something about it together." After one month, we received a reply saying: "It was not deemed necessary to examine this case because the child was deemed not at risk." One week later, the child came back, this time convicted of another crime.
>
> *Kemal*: We do experience conflict with social services [agencies]. We found an unattended child at the Ankara bus terminal. The entire responsibil-ity was left to the police . . . How is this child supposed to be transferred to social services? The law says that the police pick up and deliver the kid to social services. The social services [agency] says: "How do I know whether this child has fleas or not? Bring him/her back in three days." This is against the law . . . The police and the prosecutor are only respon-sible for reporting and delivering the child. The social services [agency] is responsible for protecting and accommodating the child.
>
> *Gizem*: Of course, the social services [agency] isn't open on the weekends. The police, on the other hand, work 24/7.
>
> *Kemal*: Well, it has to be from now on . . . What we need to look at is the law. Who is responsible [for the child] according to the law? All the stones should be in their proper place and everybody should perform their duty. (*Taşlar yerine oturmalı, herkes de görevini yapmalı.*)
>
> *Gizem*: Things don't always happen as they should on paper. In the province (*taşrada*) I took another child to the social services [agency] on Friday afternoon with a court order. They refused to take her in because she didn't have the doctor's report testifying that she didn't have any contagious dis-ease. I went to the medical center; there was no one working. Maybe you can find someone in Ankara or Istanbul, but in the provinces you can't find anyone. It was a sexual abuse case and the girl had to spend the weekend at the police center.

Kemal: These things happen for two reasons. First of all, people don't know their responsibilities and duties. Also, none of us are working on a voluntary basis—we are not civil society organizations.

Here, although Kemal was himself a judge and a practitioner working within the justice system, he kept couching Gizem's complaints about inadequate resources and frustrating working conditions as problems arising from a lack of knowledge and professionalism. Even though a considerable portion of Gizem's difficulties was related to understaffed clinics and overpopulated, underfunded shelters, Kemal kept steering the discussion back to the code of law.

In these instances, the glaring discrepancy between actual working conditions and the aspired-to universal standards ran the risk of leading the practitioners to question the relevance of such standards for the localities in which they worked. Some of the participants who were first-response practitioners and therefore worked closest to the field—such as police officers and social workers—reacted especially strongly to what was expected of them. For instance, Hasibe, a social worker working for the children's court in the eastern city of Antep, shared her concerns with me regarding the relevance of the "child centered" approach to her working conditions:

If this had been Finland, and if I'd grown up in Finland, for instance, in their system there, everything would've been different. Why? [Because] they have so many resources there (*Adamın bir sürü imkanı var*). They have group therapy, they have camps. If you have an interest in woodwork they have carpentry workshops, roofing, masonry, whatever you like. You don't feel yourself hanging in a vacuum there. The system holds you there. It doesn't let you fall into pessimism. (*Orada insan kendini boşlukta hissetmiyor ki. Sistem seni tutuyor çünkü. Karamsarlığa düşmene izin vermiyor.*) If I were there, I'd know that what I do would produce results. I'd have so many resources. I'd be supported. It's nothing like that here. You know, in the class someone asked whether there are similar problems in socio-economically developed countries. I think that's the right question. So much depends on that. What can I do here, anyhow? (*Ben burada ne yapabilirim ki?*) Trainings like this are fine and everything. I'm not saying that they shouldn't happen, but we're discussing an ideal here. We could dream further if they let us, but there's also the reality. What I'm against is losing sight of that reality. (*Bıraksalar daha da uçarız yani, ama bir de gerçekler var. Ben onların gözden kaçırılmasına karşıyım.*)

Government workers like Hasibe who felt the urgency of practice were left with feelings of inadequacy and frustration, which the trainings aimed to eliminate. In the words of Selma, the juvenile justice training program's project advisor, the message the training wanted to get across was: "There might be difficulties arising from [working] conditions, but you have the authorization to resolve these" (*siz bunu cözme yetkisine sahipsiniz*). By restoring the capability and responsibility of government workers, training projects aimed to divert the participants from using obscure concepts such as "the system" as a pretext for not changing their habits of governance. Shortcomings in "the system," a phrase that was indeed repeated widely by participants across various training programs, worked to mystify the functioning of the state at many levels. It also helped the participants to evade responsibility for their actions. To prevent the use of this mystification as a convenient way to avoid accountability, the trainers and project teams emphasized that the participants themselves were the system. "The system," Kemal asserted during one of his sections, "is you and me. Things happen if we do them."

Since the government workers had neither the power nor the authority to change the material conditions of their work, they were instead urged to cultivate a collaborative governmental sensibility in order to build a "child-friendly," "child-centered" system. Since a deep structural transformation was beyond the reach of the participants, this sensibility instead called upon the management skills of government workers to save the day. Solutions such as these not only encouraged highly personalized, creative ways to approach problems, but they also ran counter to the original mission of public administration reforms to consolidate an impersonal, systematic, legal rational bureaucracy. Let me clarify this point by recounting one extra-curricular activity organized during the juvenile justice training.

Aiming to illustrate what a child-centered approach to juvenile justice should look like, one evening the project team organized a special screening of the Turkish feature film *Dondurmam Gaymak* (Ice Cream I Scream) for the training participants. Very well received both nationally and internationally, this 2006 release by director Yüksel Aksu tells the story of a group of misbehaved children in a small village in Muğla who abduct the local ice cream vendor's trolley with the hope of securing free, limitless ice cream on a hot summer day. As the story unfolds, we see how this small incident is blown out of proportion by the vendor, who mistakes this theft for a conspiracy planned by big ice cream brands in order to destroy his small business. The film ends at the local police station, where the fatherly police chief—who personally knows all of the village residents—persuades the vendor not to file a complaint. The police chief decides to close the case on the condition that the trolley be returned to its owner, thinking that the children must have already learned their lesson since they had to spend the night at the hospital as a result of their excessive ice cream consumption.

During the conversation that followed the screening, the project team urged the participants to think about how the police chief in the film had successfully managed the situation in a child-friendly way. Selma, for instance, argued that his intimate familiarity with the village had allowed the police chief to understand the incident and its parameters correctly, enabling him to restore justice while saving the children from a lifetime of stigmatization as criminals. This call for management and personal initiative stirred a lively discussion among the participants. Especially the judges and prosecutors claimed that their commitment to neutrality prohibited them from making personal connections with other government workers to bypass the system. One of the police officers, Superintendent Fırat, said: "This is our official duty, we are all working in hierarchical professions. It pains me to see that empathy and personal initiative are promoted as the way to solve problems. The system should be built in a way that leaves no room for personal initiative."

Fırat had a point. As part of the larger public administration reform, the juvenile justice program in fact promoted the systematization of the governmental field. This reorganization was regarded as necessary to prevent human rights abuses that allegedly arose from the individualized responses of government workers. Because of this, resorting to personal discretion was inconsistent with the larger framework of the training. Nonetheless, most human rights trainings in effect culminated in this call for discretion and personal ethics. Similar to juvenile justice training, project teams often found themselves back at where they started, advocating that the government workers perform their jobs in an empathetic and conscientious way. Oya, the coordinator of the training for health care professionals on the prevention of domestic violence, expressed her frustration and despair in the following words:

We come across impossible stories. For instance, there was a midwife from Kars [in eastern Anatolia]. She's working alone. She's already under so much pressure. If she ever reported [domestic abuse] she wouldn't survive . . . The rationale behind the law [obliging health care professionals to report cases of abuse and ill treatment to the office of the prosecutor][9] is to get the prosecution to pursue these cases. But then you come across horrible prosecutors . . . There was this one prosecutor, for instance, investigating a child abuse case. The child, in her testimony, had told him everything. But the prosecutor played deaf. He didn't hear it. He gave the child back to the abuser, thinking that children make up things anyway. Even we, who are the pioneers [of these trainings], feel despair under these circumstances. All we can say in the end is "It's up to your conscience." Funny, isn't it? There are all these laws and regulations but in the end, what we end up with is conscience.

Reverting to empathy and conscience, the projects allowed personal relations and individualistic approaches to come in through the back door. In the end, the constitution of a legal rational bureaucratic realm ironically had to subsume the encouragement of governmental sentiments and sensibilities.[10]

To be sure, the attitude and mind-set of government workers were an undeniable part of the system that produced violation, abuse, and ill treatment. Prosecutors overlooked abuses, thinking that children made up things. Physicians ignored signs of torture and ill treatment, thinking that the criminals probably deserved them. Police officers shared confidential information about women's shelters with abusive husbands because they believed that protecting family unity was more important than preventing domestic violence. Social workers at social services agencies refused to admit at-risk children to shelters, thinking that they would corrupt the "innocent" children residing there. During the juvenile justice training, I witnessed one of the children's court judges claim that most allegations of rape were baseless since sexual intercourse was impossible without the woman's consent. Patriarchal values, sexism, and the paternalistic mind-set of the government workers were just as much to blame for human rights violations as poor working conditions. Nevertheless, in an environment where economic distress, institutional shortcomings, and a lack of material resources were immediate, pressing issues, glossing over these problems to focus on what was thought to be within the power of state officials did not necessarily help to persuade the trainees of the salience and feasibility of human rights.

POLITICS OF EXPERTISE:
CONTESTING JUDICIAL PROCEDURE WITH MEDICAL ETHICS

As I mentioned earlier, the emphasis on governmental competence, expertise, and professionalism in human rights training programs was also geared to reframe highly politicized human rights issues in technical, professional—and therefore apolitical—terms to preclude their contestation by training audiences. In line with the elimination of individualistic approaches towards governance (which ended up coming in through the back door), it was thought that a technical reframing of human rights would establish them as professional imperatives that government workers would have to follow regardless of their personal beliefs and political or ideological convictions.

However, a call for professionalism and expertise did not have the same effect on all government workers. Depending on their specific realm of expertise, different occupational groups operated with different priorities. Judges, prosecutors, police, and health care professionals had different approaches towards issues such as internal physical bodily examinations, hunger strikes, and handcuffing children. Contrary to the expectations of the project teams, which deliberately emphasized expertise to establish human rights as uncontested phenomena, occupational differences ended up making trainings highly contested pedagogical spaces.[11]

For instance, during the juvenile justice training, Superintendent Fırat challenged Judge Kemal, one of the program's trainers, regarding the law against using handcuffs on children. He argued that handcuffing was an issue related to security, and thus should be left to the expertise of the police rather than to the judiciary:

> When a law is issued on a topic that falls under the expertise of the security forces, they should be consulted. This is how things are done abroad as well . . . You should let us determine [what is appropriate] here. In the Netherlands, in the US, this issue falls entirely within the field of policing . . . This is a topic that should be left to the experience and expertise of the police. Can you imagine issuing a law that details the specific angle from which the police are supposed to hit with their baton?

Another issue that stirred fierce disagreement between different professionals was the "internal physical bodily examination" (*iç beden muayenesi*) (Exum and Yenisey 2009) or gynecological examination (*genital muayene*), which refers to the medical examination of the genital organs or the anus for forensic purposes. Article 76 of the Turkish Criminal Procedure Code No: 5271 allows "the judge or . . . the public prosecutor [to] decide to conduct an internal physical bodily examination on the victim . . ." (81). This examination plays a key role in the prosecution of sexual assault and abuse cases, since it makes it possible to trace and document the physical signs of sexual violence, which can then be used as evidence in the proceeding. The physicality of those signs endows them with an aura of incontestability and this makes judges and prosecutors turn to internal physical bodily examination as the primary means to collect evidence for cases involving sexual violence. Despite its judicial efficacy, however, this examination can be highly traumatic for the victims, causing their further victimization within the medical and judicial systems. Especially for minor victims, the process may inflict additional trauma both due to the difficult nature of the examination, and due to the controversial situations that may arise while obtaining the victim's consent.[12]

While internal physical bodily examinations constituted a key forensic tool for the judicial process, health care professionals saw them as a delicate medical procedure that required the patient's informed consent. Especially for (although not limited to) cases of sexual abuse against children, obtaining the victim's consent for an internal physical bodily examination proved to be extremely challenging. Already scared and traumatized victims usually did not want to go through this difficult procedure. For children between the ages of fifteen and eighteen, Turkish Penal Code No: 5237 Article 104 considers sexual intercourse that did not happen as a result of force, threat, or deception punishable only on the grounds of complaint. In cases where the complaint originates from the legal guardians, the child may not want to go through the examination. Situations such as these, in which the victim's consent was not readily available, led the judicial and medical experts to find themselves at odds with each other about the status and conditions of an internal physical bodily examination.

The issue of gynecological examination and its forensic uses came up regularly in multiple human rights trainings that focused on juvenile justice, domestic violence, and torture. When the issue came up during one of the juvenile justice meetings, Judge Kemal, who is otherwise known for his progressive interpretation of the Child Protection Law, argued that upon the judge's decision, the physician should conduct a gynecological examination no matter what. Responding to the complaints of a doctor who worked in the Institute of Forensic Medicine,[13] he said: "[Physicians are] to conduct the examination by force, by tying up [the victim] if necessary. Otherwise, of what use is the judge's decision? (*Zorla alacak. Gerekirse bağlayarak alacak, yoksa niye karar veriyor hakim?*)"

In another training for judges and prosecutors on the effective investigation and documentation of torture and other cruel, inhuman, and degrading treatment or punishment, the participants argued with Dr. Nedim, the trainer of the session on medical ethics, who himself was a physician specializing in forensic medicine:

> *Participant 1*: [Concerning] the issue of informed consent . . . in the case of a fifteen-year-old victim . . . [a genital examination] is the most effective [way to collect] evidence in rape [cases]. Let's say she didn't consent to examination. Is it possible to document torture based solely on psychological findings? Is there a precedent [of such a case] that went through [was ratified at] Yargıtay (the Higher Court—Court of Appeals)?
>
> *Nedim*: Informed consent may pose difficulties. If the victim is unconscious, consent can be obtained from his or her legal representative. [If not] we consider it against medical ethics and we don't conduct [a genital examination].
>
> *Participant 1*: How come? It is conducted upon the court's decision . . .
>
> *Nedim*: No way . . .
>
> (The participants start rumbling)
>
> *Participant 2*: Criminal Procedure Code Article 76 says that if it is the only way [to obtain] physical findings, then the examination is carried out upon the court's decision.
>
> *Participant 3*: Never mind Article 76. If there is consent, you can carry out the examination anyway. Let's say you are [the doctor] on duty, and you receive a court order. What do you do?
>
> *Nedim*: I won't do it.
>
> *Participant 3*: This goes all the way to breach of duty, neglecting duty . . . You could stand trial for concealing evidence, for preventing the manifestation of justice!

The main issue of contestation in this exchange was whether forensic medicine belonged to the juridical or the medical field. If forensic medicine was primarily part of the juridical process, then it should have been subject to the laws governing the juridical field. On the contrary, if it primarily belonged to the medical field, then it should have been bound by the ethical rules governing the field of medicine. Due to the priorities of their specific fields of expertise, judges and prosecutors thought that an internal physical bodily examination should be carried out according to the guidelines of the judicial process. The main motive of this group was to obtain the least-contestable evidence that would help them evaluate the legitimacy of alleged victimhood. Their primary professional concern was to make sure that the court decision was not appealed in Yargıtay. Nedim, on the other hand, was coming from a very different set of priorities, shaped by his specific profession. He considered himself more of a physician than a member of the judiciary, and he considered genital examination to be a medical intervention rather than a judicial procedure. While the judges and prosecutors based their arguments on the regulations governing the judicial process (Criminal Procedure Code), Nedim extensively cited Hippocratic principles and argued that in the event that these two sets of rules contradicted each other, it was the latter that should be given priority since it represented a universal consensus based upon a "2,500-year-old heritage."

The message that genital examination fell under the precepts of the medical field was given all the more strongly in the training directed towards the health care professionals, which was part of the same program that trained judges and prosecutors. The trainer of the session, Dr. Simden, gave an unequivocal answer to the question asked by a participant on whether genital examination was a matter of "judge's order or physician's judgment" (*hakim emri mi, hekim takdiri mi?*): "There is nothing superior to your word [on this]. (*Sizin sözünüzün üzerine söz yok.*) As physicians, you are the ones who come into direct contact with the patient. The minute you say [the examination] would harm the physical and psychological integrity [of the patient] she or he cannot be examined."

In addition to the necessity of informed consent for conducting genital examination, an equally salient matter of contestation was whether psychiatric findings constituted legitimate evidence for cases of torture and rape. Campaigns for the recognition of clinical psychological certificates to establish the authenticity of the allegations of torture and ill treatment have been one of the most fundamental causes for the human rights struggles both in Turkey and elsewhere (Fassin and Rechtman 2009).[14] The Turkish Medical Association (Türk Tabipleri Birliği—TTB) and the Human Rights Foundation of Turkey (Türkiye İnsan Hakları Vakfı—TİHV) have extensively contributed to these struggles, both nationally and internationally. Both of these institutions actively took part in the preparation of alternative medical reports for torture cases to contest the reports coming out of the Institute of Forensic Medicine, and spearheaded international initiatives such as the Istanbul Protocol.[15] These organizations were also the initiators of the training program on effective investigation and documentation of torture, targeting the professionals working in the medical and juridical fields.

Since the early 1980s, both THİV and TTB have been successfully employing medical expertise as part of their human rights advocacy to define torture
and other violations as "above and beyond politics" (Dembour 1996). Continuing to use the powerful universalistic underpinnings of medicine and the
medical profession, both THİV and TTB remain at the forefront of campaigns
against torture, ill treatment, and forced disappearances in Turkey (Can 2015).
Contrary to the widespread criticism of the discourse of medicalization as disabling and depoliticizing (Ticktin 2006, Zola [1977] 2000), THİV and TTB continue to use the medicalization of torture and ill treatment strategically in order
to create political effects.

Even though both the trainings for the judiciary and for health care professionals were part of the same program co-organized by TTB and the Ministry of Justice, the messages conveyed in those trainings were starkly different.
Health care professionals left the training with a strong conviction that forensic medicine was part of the medical field, that physicians had the final word
on whether to conduct gynecological examinations or not, and that psychiatric
findings were as authoritative as physical findings to prove allegations of torture and rape. But judges and prosecutors who went through similar training
were left with no clear messages regarding any of these issues. As opposed to the
trainers of juridical experts, the trainers of health care professionals successfully
drew key human rights issues (such as the compulsory medical examination of
the arrested persons before and after detention) within the medical field to in-
terpret them in a progressive way in line with the politics of human rights. They
regularly referenced the specificities of the medical profession and effectively
mobilized the "internationalist occupational solidarities" it allowed for (Malkki
2007a). In this way, they were able to argue convincingly that the subjects with
whom the participants came into contact as part of the judicial processes should
first and foremost be regarded (and treated) as patients. In a setting where being
a medical subject guaranteed better treatment than being a juridical subject, reminding the physicians of the requirements of their expertise did produce pro-
human rights results. A comparable message underlining the requirements of
juridical expertise, however, failed to produce a similar outcome.

Nevertheless, it would be a mistake to think that it was only the nature and
essence of the medical field that allowed for a progressive, pro-human rights
interpretation of these key forensic and judicial processes. For instance, in another training on the prevention of domestic violence, targeting the same group
but organized by the Ministry of Health and United Nations Population Fund,

genital examination was mentioned only in relation to court orders. The physicians were told that, in the absence of court orders, they were prohibited from conducting a genital examination. Similar to the training on the prevention of torture, this program also employed a strategic medicalization of human rights issues by defining domestic violence and child abuse as "public health concerns" (*halk sağlığı sorunu*) in order to bring them under the purview of heath care professionals. However, as opposed to the training conducted by the TTB, the Ministry of Health program mainly focused on the obligations of health care professionals within the judicial system (such as the obligation to report domestic violence) to ensure its smooth functioning.

The uniqueness of the effect of TTB-led trainings had everything to do with the ideological orientation and political involvement of both the trainers and the organization. Medicine as a professional field certainly did contain a specific repertoire including the Hippocratic oath and a universalistic claim to surpass national borders and policies, which in turn allowed for its strategic use for human rights-related ends (Redfield 2005). Nevertheless, the availability of this strategy did not automatically lead to its use by all medical experts in an equal fashion. What Dr. Simden and her team practiced was "an overtly motivated form of [the use of medicine geared to] finding facts in the name of values" (Redfield 2006, 1).

All of the physicians who served as trainers in the training for health care professionals were human rights defenders who had been involved in campaigns against torture and had long-term experience in the preparation of alternative reports. Dr. Simden herself was a very well-known figure within the TTB who had been extremely vocal on many issues, including the prison death fasts in 2001, the controversial Institute of Forensic Medicine report related to a high-profile child abuse case involving the Islamist columnist Hüseyin Üzmez in 2008, and the ongoing efforts to retrieve forensic evidence for the investigation of forced disappearances and extrajudicial killings.

It took a specific political project and ideological conviction to ensure the political efficacy of the apolitical rhetoric of medical expertise. The trainers' involvement in the politics of human rights enabled those who served in the training for health care professionals to convince the participants of the urgency and feasibility of effective documentation and investigation of torture and ill treatment. The same political involvement, however, disqualified them from participating in the training for judges and prosecutors. Almost all of the trainers who ran the health care professionals' training—including Dr. Simden—were vetoed by the Ministry of Justice, with the reason that they were too involved in the politics of human rights. It was more the absence of those trainers rather than the disparity between the medical and juridical fields of expertise that caused the two sets of trainings to look starkly different from one another. In the absence of politics and ideology to guide the direction of performative neutrality, referencing expertise and professionalism to disseminate human rights values did not work.[16] It did not even help to maintain an uncontested training environment that conveyed a coherent message.

POLITICS OF PROFESSIONALISM AND EXPERTISE

The emphasis on professionalism and expertise in the governmental reform in Turkey should be understood as the reframing of public administration in line with ideals of good governance that emphasize the rationalization of the bureaucratic field. Personal morality, emotions, and politics are regarded to have adverse effects on government service, which is supposed to be depersonalized, standardized, and accountable.[17] Emanating from the same framework, human rights training programs were also geared to accomplish a similar reframing. By reframing human rights as a matter of good governance, the programs sought to make them relevant to and acceptable or desirable for the government workers.

Human rights training programs advocated for institutional standardization as a way to curb a personalized approach to government in order to institute a systematic framework operated by indifferent service providers. However, a detailed analysis of the practices of those training programs reveals that the messages that were conveyed during the trainings often contradicted this notion of standardized public service. Since state employees were bound to operate within highly nonstandardized working conditions, the standardization of treatment could only be achieved via promotion of personal initiative in order to manage unfavorable, real-life working conditions.

High-level administrators and decision makers who may have had the power to change these working conditions usually remained out of reach for many training programs. Under those circumstances, the training programs ended up resorting to "non-instrumental," value-driven motivations (Kiser and Baer 2005). These motivations referenced a highly personal morality based on conscience and empathy in order to hail government workers as agents who were capable of changing the bureaucratic field. As a result, the personal and the emotional, which are relegated outside of the good governance framework, came in through the back door to manage the discrepancy between the universal standards and the everyday conditions that defined the governmental realm.[18] Perhaps the most discernable outcome of this unintended consequence is the simultaneous definition, once again, of the rights-seeking citizen as the passive victim who is both reliant on the conscience and empathy of, and at the mercy of, the professional service provider (Babül 2015).

Reframing human rights as a technical matter of expertise and professional service provision aimed to detach human rights from political values and ideologies in order to prevent their contestation by government workers. The particular pedagogical approach of human rights training programs aimed to forge a standardized governmental treatment of torture victims, abused children, and victims of domestic violence regardless of whether individual police officers, judges, prosecutors, physicians, and social workers personally believed in the legitimacy of the use of violence against suspects and/or detainees, or whether they resorted to violence against their own partners and/or children at home. However, analyzing the expert dialogues that took place during human rights training seminars, we see that the technical reframing of human rights issues did not necessarily preclude their contestation by training participants. The realm of the technical did not emerge as a domain of quiet reason but one of fiercer controversies (Coles 2008, Latour 1987). Alternative ways of coding, highlighting, and representing professional issues—such as handcuffing children and conducting internal physical bodily examinations—while enacting different forms of expertise, indeed configured these issues as highly contested phenomena.

As I pointed out above, the successful resolution of these expert contestations with a pro–human rights outcome only happened in the presence of a clear political agenda—one thing that human rights training programs generically tried to get around. The majority of the programs that actively sought to exclude the politics of human rights from their pedagogical framework failed to communicate a convincing pro–human rights message to their audiences, leaving participants with feelings of frustration and inadequacy due to their compulsory resort to individual conscience. Alternatively, the programs that employed training teams that were equipped with the repertoire of both professional expertise and human rights politics were much more likely to succeed in conveying progressive and convincing pro–human rights messages.

As the history of the human rights movement in Turkey illustrates, the politics of the apolitical can be a strong tool to forge an effective opposition against authoritarian regimes. Professionalism and expertise can indeed be the perfect tools for the politics of the apolitical due to their universalistic, technical connotations, their character of calculability, and their association with transparency and accountability (Mitchell 2002). In a similar vein, standardization of the governmental field in Turkey can be used strategically in order to forge a pro-human rights organizational culture in that field. This, however, can only be achieved as part of a political project, not as a project of administrative reform that buys into the rhetoric of professionalism and expertise as it tries to keep the politics of human rights at bay.

Image 1. Non-hierarchical classroom arrangement at a human rights training. Organizing teams attempted to counteract the hierarchical structure of the training programs by arranging the classroom space in less hierarchical ways. Classroom arrangements such as this were adopted to emphasize the desired egalitarian relationship between the trainers and the trainees. They were also seen as a good way to deemphasize the professional hierarchies between the trainees. Source: The author.

Image 2. Small group work during a human rights training. Another way of counteracting professional hierarchies between the trainees was to have them work together on small group projects or case studies. Organizing teams often assigned specific trainees to particular groups. Here, the trainees are working together in mixed groups that are composed of representatives from the judicial, legal, medical, social work, and security fields. Source: The author.

Image 3. Simultaneous conference translation. This type of translation came closest to what Nilay described as the ideal translation situation. Although in these events the translators were indeed made invisible by way of their removed location, translation still maintained a tangible presence in the conference in the form of headphones and occasional technical difficulties. Source: https://www.flickr.com/photos/peacecorps/4861220362/. Public domain.

Image 4. Consecutive translation during a human rights training. As opposed to the simultaneous conference translation, these types of translation events put the translator onto the stage with the presenter. This increased visibility emphasized the role of the translator as a mediator and it marked the foreign source of the message that was being translated. Source: The author.

Image 5. Private simultaneous translation during a human rights training. A third type of translation took place on the sidelines of the training programs. Pictured is the instructor addressing his class with the translator and two listeners sitting off to the side. Here, although translation was only meant to be audible to the people sitting next to the translator, the event in fact drew everyone's attention in the classroom. The participants conducted themselves with the knowledge that what they said would be translated to the foreign observer. Source: The author.

Image 6. Mustafa Kemal Atatürk, the founder of Modern Turkey. The cultlike figure of Atatürk gave rise to some of the most tense translation situations. Because of the sensitivity surrounding Atatürk's symbolism, human rights issues pertaining to the Atatürk era were exclusively dealt with using the "domesticating method" while translating into Turkish. Source: Segafredo18 own work. CC BY-SA 3.0.

Image 7. YBS and PKK fighters holding up a painting of Abdullah Öcalan. Öcalan is marked as the ultimate enemy of the Turkish Republic. As opposed to his glorifying depiction in this image, he is often portrayed in the national media as a criminal, posing in front of the Turkish flag with his hands shackled. Similar to official sensitivities concerning Atatürk, sensitivity about Öcalan also gave rise to tense translation situations. Source: https://www.flickr.com/photos/kurdishstruggle/21446138934. CC BY 2.0.

Image 8. Opening ceremony of a human rights training program. Formal ceremonies marking the beginning or the end of the training programs provided the representatives of government offices, donor organizations, and the EU with an official platform to perform on behalf of their institutions. Source: The author.

Image 9. Participants playing musical chairs at a human rights training. Most training programs adopted games and ice breakers to reduce the degree of formality in the classroom, and to establish collegiality between the participants. Organizing teams considered these as crucial for establishing an open and sincere training environment. Source: The author.

Image 10. The mock trial at the juvenile justice training. Participants in this mock trial assumed each other's institutional roles while portraying how an ordinary trial at a children's court proceeds. Although it was meant to to be an exercise about professional cooperation and best practices, the event quickly turned into a parody of the judicial system in Turkey. Source: The author.

PEDAGOGIES OF ACCESSION
Translation, Management, and Performance

ON AN IMPOSSIBLY HOT AFTERNOON in August 2007, I tiptoed into the meeting room of a think tank in Ankara, where a training program on the juvenile justice system was in the making. I had approached the think tank just a couple of days ago to volunteer for the project they were running together with the Ministry of Justice and UNICEF, and to ask for permission to conduct fieldwork at the same time. After checking my credentials, Hilmi, the head of the project team, had eagerly welcomed me, adding that they needed all the help they could get. Afraid to interrupt the meeting that was already on its way, I perched on one of the chairs around the long table positioned in the middle of the room and tried to catch up with what was going on.

The meeting room was large, with shelves full of books covering the walls and a table that could seat about twenty people. Of the seven present in the room, I had only met Hilmi and his assistant, Sinan. An obviously foreign blond woman in her early forties was standing up in front of a white board with a marker in her hand, explaining the different roles a trainer could assume in various pedagogical settings. She was wearing a loose cotton shirt and loose pants that didn't match, along with sandals and pendant earrings—an appearance that contrasted with those listening to her around the table. Everybody else was dressed more formally, in suits and button-up shirts. Standing up in front of the board, she listed "facilitator," "instructor," "coach," "trainer," and asked the others around the table for suggestions to add to the list. She was speaking in English with a Germanic accent, making big gestures and facial expressions and trying to make eye contact with the members of her audience, half of whom did not understand English very well. Sinan, who was one of the

English speakers in the room, struggled to keep up with Karin, the training advisor commissioned by UNICEF, and to translate her for the others. Hilmi, a
professor of sociology working at the Police Academy, could speak English as
well. He kept interrupting Sinan, commenting impatiently on the translation or
the thing being translated.

The mood in the air was tense. There was lots of huffing and puffing, eye
rolling, and nervous pen-tapping on the audience's part as the voice and gestures of Karin got louder and louder to compensate for the obvious impatience
growing in the room. She went on to explain how different training techniques
shaped the experience of learning differently. She wrote on the board: "Lecture," "Power Point," "Discussion," "Reading," "Small Group Work," "Role Play,"
and asked her audience to guess what percentage of knowledge these different
techniques transferred. Belma and Sami, both of whom were employed by the
Turkish National Police's Department of Education and were working on this
project as part of the national team, nervously took turns to answer the question when Karin called on them. They asked Sinan to repeat the question once
more in Turkish to make sure they got it right, and answered in question format: "*Yüzde on mu?*" which they repeated after Sinan in English as he translated their answer: "Ten percent?" "Yes, ten percent."

Belma was a police officer with a degree in psychological counseling. In
her late thirties, she was a chief inspector, a rank higher than her current shy
demeanor suggested. She was responsible for both preparing and teaching the
child development and psychology section of the juvenile justice workbook,
and Karin wanted to make sure that she understood the principles of interactive training before she moved on to writing. Belma had already started
writing her module. Since she already had a full-time job, she wanted to get
the project work, which she did for a little bit of extra money, done as quickly
as possible. When Karin told her that she needed to make changes to her text
she did not seem happy, but did not refuse either. She jotted down some notes
and mumbled that she would include some games and Q&A sections to make
the training more interactive. Karin asked Sami to note down that Belma was
going to change the text. Sami looked tense. Both his age and his rank were
even higher than Belma's. Nevertheless, with his communication skills sev-
ered by his lack of proficiency in English, he looked hesitant and disjointed.
He obeyed Karin's directives, while at the same time agreeing with Hilmi, who
kept complaining about what Karin said or did in Turkish, and then spoke
back to her in English.

Karin did not understand Turkish, and asked Hilmi not to interrupt as she called Belma to stand up and assume the role of the trainer, to try out the interactive training techniques they had been discussing so far. Belma was not eager to do so. Nevertheless, she stood up and started to deliver her part. Sinan started translating for Karin. Karin began to take notes on her manuscript as she watched Belma explain different stages of child development. Belma saw Karin taking notes, and sighed in an anxious manner. She said in Turkish: "Oh no! She is taking notes again. She is going to criticize the text all over!" Hilmi burst out once more in Turkish in a stressed-out tone: "She is treating us as if we are Ethiopians! We've got it! All right! Belma, don't you crouch like that! Stand up straight! Speak up! Be confident!"

Hilmi was not discrete about his dislike of Karin. He thought that she was clueless about Turkey and that working with her was a waste of time. Originally from Holland, Karin was married to a Bangladeshi and she lived there. Whenever the project team wanted to comment on their annoyance with her ways, they claimed that she confused Turkey with Bangladesh, a country they considered much more backward than Turkey. This, obviously, offended them. Karin realized that she was losing control of the room. It was already past five o'clock. Everybody was tired. They needed to get going.

As some people excused themselves to leave the room, the rest of the UNICEF team appeared at the door. Anika, the coordinator of the project for UNICEF, was also from Holland. She arrived with Ceyla, her assistant, and Selma, a freelance lawyer and a legal consultant for UNICEF in Turkey. With the arrival of the UNICEF team, the language of interaction turned to English. Sinan struggled to make himself heard by Belma, Sami, and Selma, who did not speak English either. With a desire to be useful, I stepped in and suggested translating for Belma and Sami. I realized, only after it was too late, that my suggestion was not at all welcome, and was found a bit irritating. Having unintentionally made myself visible, I ended up contributing to the friction between the UNICEF team and the national project team led by Hilmi. After the meeting, Anika came up to me, introduced herself, and asked who I was in a polite but suspicious manner. Upon hearing that I would be working with them, she followed up with Hilmi about it, expressing her objection to making any changes to the team at this point. Already agitated, Hilmi said that as the head of the national team, he had the right to decide with whom he would be working. As he packed up his notes to leave, he told Anika they could talk about the issue later, clearly signifying that it was the end of both the discussion and the meeting.

The complicated sociality and dynamics of the juvenile justice training program that I found myself thrown into that afternoon was by no means an anomaly. During the following two years that I spent in the field, I discovered that most project teams contained an amalgam of constituents composed of actors who were differentiated along complex markers of belonging. These actors were simultaneously unified and differentiated on the basis of their nationality, level of education, linguistic ability, political allegiance, professional affiliation, class status, level of distinction, and social aspirations. They formed and broke alliances with each other frequently, as they sought to advance their perceived interests and cope with the volatile conditions they worked in.

3 HUMAN RIGHTS EDUCATION AND ADULT LEARNING

IN 1997, D. Michael Hinkley, the supervisor for the US Naval Justice School's Expanded International Military Education and Training (EIMET) program,[1] writes how in the early 1990s the program crafted a brand-new training method to provide "military human rights training to emerging democracies":

> After much thoughtful analysis, the school decided that *participative learning*—emphasizing role playing, problem solving, and small group discussions—would be the most effective way to teach the specific blocks of instruction to the *anticipated adult audience* . . . This was an experimental approach that, to the best of the school's knowledge, had not been tested before in any such foreign training programs . . . It was apparent that US efforts to provide human rights training under the auspices of security assistance in the past had been, in many respects, less than effective in their final results . . . Given these data, the Naval Justice School decided it was time to shift paradigms from traditional military training methods (e.g., lectures, rote repetition, one-way communication of information) and break new ground (Hinkley 1997, 300—emphasis mine).

Hinkley reports that one of the strengths of the EIMET program's teaching methodology, which found its first application during the 1992 seminars held in Sri Lanka and Papua New Guinea, is that it appeases the host country's "concern for 'independence' and 'sovereignty'" (301). Participative learning helps to bypass reluctance among trainees that might be caused by "a strong sense of student patriotism and national pride [preventing them from listening] to 'outsiders' or 'foreigners' (or, worse yet, neocolonialists) trying to tell them what's right or wrong" (298):

> By avoiding ramming "the American way" down the students' throats, by breaking away from traditional military training, and by letting the students themselves logically work through nonoffensive [sic] hypothetical problem scenarios and apply generally accepted principles of basic human rights, we have crafted a proactive and preventive strategy both for human rights education and for the fight to prevent human rights abuses. In accordance with this strategy, the students see more than human rights principles. They see, in a practical setting, how respect for human rights is: common sense, relatively cost free, internationally expected of civilized nations, and conducive to public support for the government in a democratic society. *This realization comes from the students themselves as they struggle with the discussion problems, and not from the "outsiders" (instructors)* (307—emphasis mine).

Fast forward a decade to 2007 in Turkey—a context that seemingly has nothing to do with either the US foreign assistance or the EIMET program—and we see that the predicted success of the Naval Justice School's human rights training model has held true. Interactive adult education and participative learning methodologies indeed constituted the dominant pedagogical framework of the human rights training programs for government workers that I worked with in Turkey. Aiming to train government workers to respect human rights as they perform their duties, these programs employed techniques that went beyond the classical one-way model of education in order to maximize the trainings' effectiveness. As Hinkley's foreign assistance cases, human rights training programs in Turkey also generated discomfort and reluctance among their audiences due to the perception that they were "imposed from outside." Interactive adult education and participative learning methodologies were employed to overcome this resistance, to encourage government workers to own the trainings, and to persuade them to embrace the human rights standards.

This chapter explores the pedagogical models that underlie human rights training programs for government workers in Turkey. The influence of the participative adult education framework on these programs testifies to the proliferation of the educational methods that were also employed by the US military/ aid complex. As I show in the remainder of this chapter, techniques of education that are currently used in Turkey are promoted by some of the major players in the transnational human rights field such as CE, AI, and UNICEF.

The actual historical connections between these institutions' pedagogical trajectory and military/developmental aid programs such as EIMET are beyond the scope of this chapter, and they remain to be further explored. What is important to note for the purposes of my research are the effects of these educational models on the practice of human rights education in Turkey.

Regardless of whether it really emerged from the US Naval Justice School, the adult education framework has had an undeniable effect on the pedagogical approach that determines the tone and scope of transnational standardization efforts in the field of human rights. Pedagogical tools in the form of training manuals or instructors' guides that are introduced in various localities such as Turkey are often produced at the in-between spaces of transnational governance, which include grassroots organizations, international agencies, and supranational bodies. The seeping of these pedagogies into the porous areas of national governance underline the fact that it is not only the financial structures and state bureaucracies that become stratified as a result of transnational developmental programs. What emerge as equally salient fields of standardization are the ethical regimes of governance that feature a particular moral economy, in which a new hierarchy of values takes shape and certain ethical configurations gain credence (Ticktin 2006).

Participative adult education methods that are employed to ensure the effectiveness of human rights training programs in Turkey provide a glimpse into the techniques that go into the establishment of transnational ethical regimes and standardization processes. Participative adult education methods and interactive learning techniques condition the environment in which the normative harmonization frameworks—such as Accession Partnership and the National Programme—are enacted to produce effects on the ground. These models of education and the pedagogical settings that they forge have a considerable impact on how the harmonization process is experienced in Turkey. It is this impact that leads us to the unintended consequences of Turkey's accession to the EU.

Focusing on the adult education models through an analysis of the manuals used in human rights trainings, interviews conducted with advisors and trainers, and episodes from the actual training seminars, I argue that these educational techniques produce two important results. First, by hailing the trainees as professionals and defining the training as part of their professional development, adult education models help to reframe human rights as part of the professional expertise that government workers must acquire to improve their capacity. Second, by working to create non-hierarchical, power-free training environments out of concern for their audiences' sensitivities, these educational models reframe the encounters between government workers and human rights experts as devoid of confrontation and accountability. Both of these results contribute to the incorporation of human rights into the governmental realm in Turkey by actively reframing this highly politicized field as one of governmental capacity-building and expertise.

A close examination of the models of education used in human rights trainings in Turkey exposes their affinity with models that are used for similar trainings in places such as Sri Lanka, Papua New Guinea, and the Philippines, undertaken by institutions such as the US Naval Justice School and the John Jay College of Criminal Justice. Throughout the chapter, I often address these affinities to point out the larger framework of these models of education and the type of learning that they promote. This larger framework is about projects and processes of standardization, foreign assistance, and international development that constitute the field of transnational governance. I use the affinities between human rights training programs in Turkey and elsewhere to delineate the notion of human rights that these transnational pedagogical schemes help to produce.

NAMING THE TRAINING

Human rights training programs employed the adult education approach primarily to prevent a negative reaction from their target audiences. Not unlike Hinkley's "key players and power brokers" of society, government workers in Turkey were extremely offended by the idea of being educated (*eğitilmek*), especially by an outsider. Traditionally hailed as the bureaucratic elites and the embodiments of state power, Turkish government workers considered themselves highly educated figures who were entrusted with the duty of educating the rest of the society. Additionally, the subject of human rights training antagonized Turkish government workers, mainly due to the historical context of human rights activism and the political connotations of human rights in Turkey. With this antagonistic environment in mind, training programs for the most part focused on rendering the training acceptable for their audiences.

The naming of training, and the word choice in the project title, were important components of the training's acceptability. This resembles the accounts of Marc DuBois of John Jay College of Criminal Justice, who writes about his experience of training the police. In order to make the trainings acceptable for these audiences, DuBois (1997) advises: "not (to) focus expressly on human rights but upon human dignity, professionalism, or other 'disguised' subjects," and to "find an expanded vocabulary." In a similar vein, project teams of human rights training programs in Turkey sought to bypass the terms "education" and "human rights" when naming these programs—so much so that due to negative connotations of human rights within the official imaginary, the term "human rights" rarely appeared in program titles. Instead, the issue was reframed and rearticulated in terms of the detailed focus and administrative impact of the human rights problem that the project was aiming to address. This sensibility often led to unusually long and winding names such as: "Juvenile Justice Training Programme towards Good Governance, Protection and Justice for Children in Turkey," "Training on the Role of the Police in Preventing Domestic Violence Against Women and the Application of Related Procedures," "Training of Trainers for Health Practitioners in Combating Domestic Violence Against Women" and "Training Programme on the Istanbul Protocol (The Manual on Effective Investigation and Documentation of Torture and Other Cruel and Inhuman, Degrading Treatment or Punishment): Enhancing the Knowledge Level of Non-Forensic Expert Physicians, Judges and Prosecutors."

Along with anxiety about the expected reaction of participants against human rights, training teams were also concerned about the reception of the word "*eğitim*" (education). Almost all of the training programs began with a disclaimer made by the training team assuring the trainees that the program they were about to undergo was not education per se. For instance, Meral, the program manager of AI Turkey's Rights Education Office, spent a good amount of time at the beginning of each session explaining to the training audience why they did not like to use the word "*eğitim*" to define their program:

> [We] don't like the word "*eğitim*." You cannot further educate people who are already educated. How should we translate the word "training" [into Turkish]? *Antreman* (workout/exercise), perhaps? We're not seeking to directly teach something to people. This is mostly a process through which people [mutually] learn from each other. (Human Rights Workshop for Teachers)

* * *

> [We have to call it] "*eğitim*" for lack of a better word in Turkish. In fact, we're not interested in educating anybody [here]. You're all educated people already. It's not like we can educate you or anything. It's just that there is a problem at hand, and we want to get together with you and talk about the possible solutions. Because [the solution] can only be [reached] together with you. There can't be any other way. (Human Rights Workshop for Detention House Teachers)

* * *

We call it "*eğitim*" because there isn't a better word. We didn't come here to educate anybody. *Estağfurullah* (not at all)! Who are we to educate you? There is a problem going on, and we will evaluate it, discuss it with you. (Human Rights Workshop for Religious Personnel)

As these examples clearly illustrate, the acceptability of trainings was established by strategically renaming them so that the words "human rights" and "education" did not appear up front. Although the name of the AI office that ran these trainings was "*İnsan Hakları Eğitim Ofisi*" (Human Rights Education Office), the training team felt obliged to deny by all means possible that they were conducting education. As such, these programs did not make human rights training acceptable for government workers by convincing them to change their minds about human rights or education. They were not set up to confront or challenge the established convictions of government workers. Instead, they were run with the intent to appease and accommodate their audiences. This was because the specific type of learner who stood at the center of the adult education framework was assumed to learn best if his or her thoughts, beliefs, and ideas were accommodated—not confronted. According to this framework, adult learners and their convictions could not be changed by confronting them. Change could only happen by working around those convictions.

SETTING THE RULES OF LEARNING

The pedagogical approach underlying the majority of human rights training programs that I attended was based on the theories and methodologies of adult learning, such as interactive adult education, participative adult learning, and cooperative learning. This approach described adults as a special group of learners with specific qualities that should be taken into consideration when developing a training program. For example, "Adult Education Guidebook for the Project for Combating Domestic Violence Against Women" defined adults as different from younger learners due to the diversity of their motivations, interests, values, attitudes, physical and emotional skills, and educational background. The guidebook listed six basic principles that condition the learning experience for adults:

- *The need to know:* Adult learners want to know why they have to learn something before they actually learn it.
- *The learner's ego:* Adults want to decide for themselves, and they want to bear the responsibility for their decisions. They do not accept the imposition

of other people's will, and react to it. This might cause a problem in adult education. Because "to be educated," "to be raised," or other such concepts remind them of their childhood.

- *The role of experience*: Adults come to the educational setting with numerous experiences they have had throughout their lives . . . To dismiss or overlook their experiences has the effect of dismissing their personality, which sets a barrier to reaching the goal of adult education.

- *Readiness to learn*: Adults want to learn about issues that will ease their lives and solve their problems.

- *The goal of learning*: As opposed to the topic-based learning approach of children and youth, which is not based on their needs (at least in school), adults' will to learn is oriented towards solving problems and overcoming obstacles that they come across in their daily lives. They tend to learn about issues that will help them solve the problems they encounter in real life. They tend to learn all kinds of knowledge, behavior, values, and skills that they can apply in real life more effectively and permanently.

- *Motivation*: For adults . . . the most important things are the internal incentives and pressures (work satisfaction, self-confidence, quality of life, etc.) . . . Motivation to learn is mostly affected by internal factors. ("Adult Education Guidebook for Combating Domestic Violence Against Women Project")

The target audience of the human rights training programs were defined according to this framework as "adult professionals," who both due to their adulthood and their professional status had a set of sensitivities and soft spots that needed to be appeased in order to ensure a successful (i.e., less-resistant) training. One way of satisfying the adult learners' need to be in control was to make them responsible for their own learning. With this concern in mind, the workbook for the juvenile justice training program started with a personal exercise for the trainees' self-assessment of their training needs. A similar exercise was repeated for every section of the workbook, inviting the participants to comment on their current level of knowledge and skill related to each section (such as communication with children, different stages of child development, main texts of international law on children's rights, and the recent changes in national law). A clear statement preceded each exercise, reminding the participants that the form they were about to complete was not a test, and that it was only intended for them to follow their own development throughout the training. This self-evaluation technique was thought to validate the training by incorporating the trainees into their own needs assessment. In the long run, it was hoped that this self-assessment would raise awareness among trainees that they actually needed the training. Self-evaluation was also believed to help persuade the trainees that the training had actually worked, and that it was not a waste of time, by providing them with the immediate means to see that their knowledge and skills had improved.

Another way to put the adult learners in charge of their own learning was to encourage them to come up with their own classroom rules. This was achieved by enacting the "group contract" method, which asked the trainees to collectively make a list of acceptable and unacceptable behaviors that would be upheld during the training. The trainees were then held accountable for their compliance with the set of rules that they themselves had made. The "Manual on Interactive Adult Training for Institutional Trainers of Juvenile Justice Professionals" described this classroom activity under the title "Your Rules, Your Penalties":

> Your first class. You encounter nonstop ringing of cell phones. Participants arrive ten minutes late, or they leave after five minutes without saying a word and never come back. What can you do? You have to set some ground rules together with the participants at the beginning of the training.

Ground rules, produced in class during the training, were intended to maximize compliance with those rules by making them appear not imposed from the outside but collectively created in a democratic way (Lea 2008).[2] Together with self-evaluation, self-created rules aimed to enhance the self-disciplining aspect of the training program by both sharing and legitimizing the pedagogic authority behind the pedagogic action. The participants were hailed not as tutelary subjects but as self-governing liberal learners (Hunter 1996). They were expected to better internalize the form and content of the training because specific techniques of participative learning would prevent the trainees from perceiving the training as an imposition. This educational model instead sought to internally motivate the trainees by encouraging them to be their own masters and evaluators (cf. Cruikshank 1996).

The participant-centered approach of the training framework was also maintained by informing them up front about the learning objectives of the training. This was done by way of exercises such as name games, introduction pairs, and "the tree of expectations and contributions." Also used as icebreakers at the beginning of training sessions, name games and introduction pairs were carried out by dividing the participants into groups of two and then asking them to introduce each other to the rest of the group after talking among themselves for five minutes. This exercise was then followed by a game called "the tree of expectations and contributions," in which trainees were given small pieces of paper to write down what they expected to gain from the training and what they would be contributing to it. These pieces of paper were then attached to a picture of a tree, which remained on the wall in the classroom for the rest of the training. During the training, the trainees were invited to revisit their expectations and contributions. These games and exercises enabled the trainers and trainees to get to know each other. Additionally, they urged the trainees to contribute to determining the training objectives. As a result, the trainees were encouraged to co-own the training, which was believed to enhance the adults' investment in learning.

The internally motivated and invested adult learners were expected to actively participate in training by way of sharing, discussing, acting, and playing during the training sessions. Adults, the juvenile justice training manual maintained, "remember 10 percent of what they read, 20 percent of what they hear, 30 percent of what they see, 50 percent of what they hear and see, 70 percent of what they hear, see and discuss, and 90 percent of what they hear, see, discuss and do." According to the adult education model employed by the human rights training programs, participation and active learning enhanced the effectiveness of training because it kept the participants' attention alive. Additionally, this method was seen as coherent with what adult learners were assumed to expect from training—applied, practical knowledge that they could use while performing their everyday professional duties.

ON THE USEFULNESS OF HUMAN RIGHTS

The postulate about the learning preferences of adults considered the adulthood of the trainees to be synonymous with their professional identity. This point was especially relevant for the human rights training of government workers, in which their professional identity was the main reason why this group was designated as the target audience in the first place. The participants were trained about human rights with the expectation that they would use the knowledge and insight they gained during the training while performing their everyday professional duties. In a similar vein, Hinkley advises taking the professional identity of trainees seriously when designing human rights trainings that have a professional, practical orientation. This, he argues, is essential to "minimize the natural reluctance" of the trainees:

> It is not enough to lecture adults; *they must see how what you are telling them will benefit them* or how they can use your information to their advantage . . . *following "the law" in protecting against human rights abuses is not only easy (and, of course, right), but also makes good common sense*: why, as a military leader of troops, would you waste time, money, and effort destroying civilian structures, pursuing or harassing noncombatants, and allowing your troops to plunder villages, when all these activities use up valuable time, squander supplies or ammunition, cause hate and entrenchment in the civilian populace, heap international scorn on your activities, and lead to a breakdown in unit discipline as your soldiers become more interested in lining their pockets with loot than in your mission accomplishment? When phrased in such terms, heads begin to nod in agreement: *to the military commander, this makes sense, and helps him* (Hinkley 1997, 303—emphasis mine).

What Hinkley calls "appeal to self-interest" or "the greed factor" is a means of rationalization that was widely employed in the human rights training of the law enforcement agents in Turkey as well. During a training organized by the General Directorate of Security, in which police officers were taught about the disproportionate use of force, Chief Inspector Sertan—the session's trainer—explained why it made sense from a professional point of view not to interfere with the medical examination of detainees before and after their detention, which was required by law:

> *Sertan*: *Arkadaşlar* (friends), I think obtaining a [medical] report is actually in our interest. I mean we should definitely get reports [for the detainees] before and after detention . . . Because there is nobody who gets arrested according to his or her own will anyway. Have you come across anyone who gets into a police car willingly, without resisting?
> *Trainees*: No!
> *Sertan*: Do I have the legal right to use force during the arrest?
> *Trainees*: Yes, of course!
> *Sertan*: Of course! The real problem arises not at that point [arrest] but afterwards [in detention]. Because we don't get [medical] reports [after the arrest, before the detention], the bruises that happen during the arrest appear in the latter reports [causing the bruises to look like they

happened while in detention]. That's why we shouldn't intervene in the doctors' business. On the contrary, we should encourage them to report whatever they see . . .

Ordinance No: 25832 Regarding Apprehension, Detention and Interrogation allows the use of force by security forces during apprehension because it considers the use of force at that stage necessary. However, the use of force during detention—once the suspect is captured—is regarded as unnecessary and therefore illegal. Medical examination of the detainees before and after their detention is instituted as a control mechanism through which the illegal use of force can be traced and documented. Many police officers resist this regulation and try to interfere with the medical examination process. They refuse to leave the room while the examination is carried out, intimidate the detainee or the doctor or try to find ways to skip the process altogether. Sertan's approach to the disproportionate use of force by security forces, which results in severe human rights violations such as torture and police brutality, was informed by this normative framework. The point of departure for Sertan's rationale not to interfere with a medical examination derived from a professional standpoint. His argument for the need to obtain medical reports for detainees was not based on the belief that police brutality was wrong. Rather, it was based on the claim that medical documentation actually benefited the police by allowing them to perform their duty for which the use of force was necessary. According to this instrumentalist reasoning, medical documentation did not impede the use of force by the police. On the contrary, it enabled the use of force by documenting that it was used legally.

The main factor enabling this line of reasoning to be displayed in a human rights training program was Sertan's intentional conflation of human rights and the rule of law. The law bounded the security personnel while performing their duty. As such, the law was the connection that made human rights relevant to the security personnel's professional identity. In line with the adult education framework that advocated orienting the training to the professional identities of the trainees, the code of law that regulated the trainees' professional duties became the medium of human rights training. In that sense, Sertan's statement was in line with Hinkley's message above: It was good to abide by the law because it made sense from a professional perspective. Abiding by the law made the use of force hassle free, which was useful to the police while performing their duty. It was thought that this utilitarian rationality would motivate the participants to act according to law because it would help them realize that abiding by the law "actually worked." Despite its usefulness, however, Sertan's call to allow for medical examination did not lead to the condemnation of police brutality during the training. Instead, it led to a utilitarian affirmation of the law, which apparently allowed for the use of violence under certain circumstances. As the above quote demonstrates, under those conditions, the training ironically turned into the mastery of the circumstances that allowed for the legal use of violence by the police.

ETHICAL SUBJECTS OR PROFESSIONAL ADULTS?

In order to better analyze the professional adult education framework, I would like to juxtapose it against another pedagogical approach I came across in the field. This approach, led by the internationally renowned philosopher Ioanna Kuçuradi,[3] conceptualized human rights in terms of ethics and human rights training as "ethics education." As opposed to the adult education framework, which hailed its participants as professional subjects that should act according to law, ethics education hailed the participants as ethical subjects and asked them to internalize universal human rights ideals. During the tenure of my research, I was able to observe only one training that was led by Professor Kuçuradi and her team, which was organized according to the ethics education perspective. The training was directed towards the local human rights commission of an Istanbul district, composed of members representing different local state institutions such as the Directorate of Security, the Directorate of Health, and the Directorate of Education. The reason for the rareness of the ethics perspective in human rights training for government workers was due to its anomaly when compared to the dominant adult education approach. When I asked her about it, Sinem, the project advisor for the police training, explained why they distanced themselves from an ethics education framework:

> While on the education commission of the Human Rights Directorate, we spent three months with Ioanna *Hoca* (Professor Kuçuradi) discussing how human rights education should be conducted. Ioanna *Hoca* argued that the philosophical aspect [of human rights] should be taught . . . But what really needs to happen is that . . . Adults learn a subject only to the extent that they can associate it with what they do and where they stand.

Contrary to this, Ayfer, a student of Ioanna Kuçuradi and a social worker by training whom I encountered as one of the trainees in the juvenile justice training program, argued that the pragmatic/legal standpoint of professional adult training had considerable setbacks:

> These types of programs [with a professional emphasis] are also run in Sweden, for instance . . . But over there, the notion [of human rights] is already covered in primary education . . . People are brought up with it. [Here] if you [suddenly] tell government workers, who until now were encouraged to say "Down with human rights!": "Here you go! These are human rights. You have to pay attention to them. Take a look at the Beijing rules," of course it wouldn't have any effect. Human rights training programs are usually prepared as law-centered. They should instead be based on ethics. The idea of human . . . What is the idea of human at the heart of human rights? Otherwise it becomes an entirely technical issue.

The difference between the ethics of humanity and the technique of law, and the kinds of learner they were geared towards, became all the more clear during my interview with Ioanna Kuçuradi. While explaining her teaching philosophy, Professor Kuçuradi underlined the difference between installing an obligation among trainees to abide by the law and implanting a desire within them "to do the right thing":

> They [the law enforcement agents] should not do it [violate human rights] *because they* [themselves] *are human. You can teach them the rules, but in the end it's they who will decide when to apply which rule* . . . Looking at my own students, I have personally witnessed that this [ethics] method actually works. I tell them: "You could torture me right here, right now. It would only take you two minutes, and nobody would know. *But you shouldn't want to do it, yourselves. You! Because you're human, you shouldn't want to do it!*" They come and tell me [afterwards], "*Hocam* (Professor), I actually did it [torture] before, but it was wrong. I shouldn't have!" (Emphasis mine.)

As the above quotes demonstrate, Kuçuradi and her pedagogical approach understood human rights to be a fundamental ethical issue that needed to be integrated into the process of subject formation. That was why, according to Ayfer, technical approaches to human rights law could produce the intended results in Sweden but not in Turkey. This was because in contrast to Turkey, human rights were already part of the people's ethical formation in Sweden. Under the Swedish circumstances, a technical reference to law did not remain superficial. However, in the absence of such an ethical formation in Turkey, what primarily needed to be generated were ethical human beings.

The difference between the adult professional training and ethics education was that while the former aimed to minimize human error by instituting a standard system to cordon off individual initiative, the latter approach invested in the individual's moral-ethical capacity to be human. Ethics education imagined its audience as composed of individual human beings who naturally shared an ethical human condition, which instead of being suppressed should rather be encouraged to generate self-realization. This belief in the individual human capacity showed stark contrast with the way in which professional adult education approached individuality. The primary goal of professional training was to mold the trainees into proxies so that they would act in a standardized manner in their workplace, despite their individual/personal differences—just like cogs in a wheel. For example, when explaining the goal of the police training, this was how Sertan had addressed his audience:

> What we are aiming for in administrative operations is *to establish a system, a move away from individual behavior to establish an institutional approach . . .* The goal of the training is *to systematize things . . . an impartial, standard, non-individualistic approach.* (Emphasis mine.)

Contrary to a move away from the individual towards the more systematic, ethics education aimed to maximize the human potential of individuals. Rather than appealing to the learners' professional identities, ethics education hailed the participants through their human subjectivity. According to this view, human rights education was about instilling the consciousness of being a human being and sharing a human dignity (Kuçuradi 2008). With its roots in Kantian humanistic ethics, ethics education relied upon the universal faculty of reason that was assumed to be inherent in every individual, and which needed to be brought into consciousness by means of education. Once this faculty was restored, individuals would then be capable of evaluating in an ethical manner the specific conditions under which they would be conducting themselves. Even if legal loopholes might exist, government workers trained as ethical human beings would not take advantage of those loopholes and violate human rights.

Bearing similarities to the Christian spiritual discipline and pastoral guidance with its call for confessional catharsis (Hunter 1996), human rights training as ethics education treated its subjects on the basis of a moral-private self-governance model, instead of a professional-public one. Professor Kuçuradi's account of her student's coming to her after the class to confess his previous involvement in torture is a perfect example of the catharsis that the training ultimately aimed for. However, as opposed to the confessional moments recounted by Professor Kuçuradi, during the training I participated in, government workers in the audience continuously challenged Professor Kuçuradi and other trainers by giving examples from their everyday experiences that did not fit into the universalistic model from which the idea of ethics was derived. For example, one of the participants who was working as a doctor at the local community clinic objected to the assertion that the notion of human rights was necessarily tied to universal ethical principles of behavior:

> I am a doctor. I work at the local clinic. I work for sixteen hours per day and the money I earn is not enough to support my household. We aren't treated according to human rights either. We may be government workers, but it's not right to expect doctors or police officers who have been working for thirty-six hours to treat citizens right. It's not right to assign one teacher to a class of eighty students. Am I making myself clear? Government workers should be treated right, too. Under the current circumstances, I cannot be a good doctor. The police can't be good police either; neither can a teacher be a good teacher.

Other participants voiced similar protests, highlighting the specific conditions of their professional environment and the particular everyday situations within which they operate. They argued that these particularities made it impossible to behave in ways claimed to be universally valid. One of the most cited justifications for the government workers' failure to adhere to human rights principles was the ban on political activity.[4] Most participants argued that the political nature of human rights and the particular power relations and legal regulations they had to consider due to their professional status prevented them from critically engaging with the political circumstances that formed the basis of human rights violations in the country. In those situations, the trainers tried to avert these challenges by repeating that human rights should be thought of in ethical terms and that the political conditions, although important in other ways, should not be allowed to interfere with the actual focus of the training (cf. Fassin 2012). Despite its divergence from the ethics education approach in many essential aspects, this was also the attitude of the professional adult education approach. Trainings that addressed their audiences as adult professionals also worked to keep the particular socio-political circumstances that conditioned the human rights situation in Turkey at bay.

A SECURE TRAINING ENVIRONMENT: CORDONING OFF POLITICS

Inherent in both Ioanna Kuçuradi's and Ayfer's criticisms of professional adult education was a disapproval of what they viewed to be a disengagement of human rights from ethics. Both contended that without the ethical basis, the technical/professional approach to human rights training would be superficial. Advocates of professional adult education, on the other hand, specifically promoted a technical approach to human rights in order to detach it not from ethics but from politics. They saw political schisms and ideological differences as major obstacles that could impair the internal motivation of adult professional learners. Similarly, Edy Kaufman, who writes about the human rights education program for law enforcement agents run by the Centre for Human Rights of the UN, specifically advocates "job oriented instruction," especially in countries where human rights are perceived to be a "subversive issue." According to him it is necessary to make human rights "a constituent part of [law enforcement agents'] being as professionals" in order to avoid the "development of partisan attitudes" against human rights (Kaufman 1997, 283–86).

In the same way, both DuBois (1997) and Hinkley (1997) define the optimum setting for the human rights training of law enforcement agents as a "non-threatening," "secure" environment, where both the trainers and the organization of training (the materials, training activities, etc.) display a "non-judgmental," "not accusatory" standing. Hinkley suggests the use of "hypothetical," i.e., nonthreatening scenarios for case studies, such as "a shipwreck on a deserted island," which would not bear any suggestion of the actual socio-political condition of the country in which the training is being held. Along the same lines, AI, for instance, used a board game in its training programs in Turkey that featured a spaceship crew trying to survive after making a forced landing on a deserted planet. As the crew moved along the path on the board leading to the space station on the planet—their only chance of survival—the players (a small group composed of four-to-five trainees) were challenged with a question at each step, forcing them to make decisions about balancing individual rights with group needs in dire circumstances.

Hinkley reports that the use of hypothetical case studies in the EIMET program is an important component of its "future-oriented" approach, which means that it is "essentially preventive, not corrective in nature: it is geared towards progress and development, rather than focusing on any sins of the past" (1997, 303). This preventive approach is seen as the condition of creating an ideal educational atmosphere, envisioned as a setting in which the participants would feel safe enough to actively participate in the training. Coming from a similar angle, Kaufman also maintains that "proactive learning and experiential techniques such as role-playing, facilitating discussions, and so on" are important "to make [human rights education] *not only an informative but also a formative experience*" (1997, 298—emphasis mine). The definition of ideal education as active and participative designates the ideal educational setting as one that encourages the voluntary contribution of the trainees. Such a setting automatically excludes the political—evoking accountability, confrontation, and facing the past—from the process of learning, based on the belief that the political would alienate and shut down the trainees, and inhibit them from partaking in training.

ENCOURAGING PARTICIPATION, OOZING AWARENESS

Preventing the alienation of trainees and encouraging their participation were central concerns for human rights training in Turkey too. Training programs accepted that participative, active learning was the ideal condition for adult professionals, and they aimed to create safe spaces to encourage the participation of the trainees. Training was not seen solely as a transfer of information. It was instead imagined as a process of re-formation, not just by way of enhancing the knowledge of trainees but also by transforming their skills and attitudes. In order to achieve this transformation, active participation and interaction of the trainees were viewed as necessary components of the training process. In the document "A 12-Point Guide for Good Practice in the Training and Education for Human Rights of Government Officials" published by AI, this issue was addressed in the following way:

> For any training and educational program to be consistent with human rights principles, it has to provide knowledge and information about human rights and it also has to develop attitudes and behavior respectful of those rights. To achieve a meaningful effect, the educational program needs to be sustained over a period of time, involve direct and constant interaction between the trainers and the trainee, and include practical, hands-on learning.

The point of a successful human rights training was not to expose the trainees to a stream of information about human rights. Instead, a successful training was supposed to initiate a substantive transformation among the trainees and make them respect human rights while performing their duties. The manual for the juvenile justice training stated that the change in knowledge did not necessarily lead to a change in attitude: "Attitudes cannot be learned. Neither can they be trained. Trainers cannot change attitudes, but they can create opportunities to have an effect on them." Hence, merely providing information was not enough to alter established forms of thinking and behavior. Nesrin, the advisor for the project for preventing violence against women, stated that this pedagogical approach was quite similar to that of women's empowerment projects. Comparing the professional training of the police to women's informal training, Nesrin stated that both pedagogical approaches refused a unilateral transfer of knowledge. Rather, in both women's empowerment and police training on women's rights, the pedagogical trajectory started with building awareness, then went on to consciousness raising, and then gave way to agency.

A major problem for the training programs that aimed to transform the skills and attitudes of their participants was the difficulty of measuring their success. As opposed to the relatively easy task of measuring a change in the trainees' level of knowledge, changes in the skills and attitudes of the trainees were rather difficult to assess. As a result, the ultimate goal of the training projects, which was to create an attitudinal change in government officials in order to prevent human rights violations, was often regarded as a distant ideal that was hard to achieve. Instead of this distant ideal, many of the trainers felt that the most they could hope for was "to ooze snow melt into the ears of the trainees."

The expression *kulağına kar suyu kaçırmak*—strange as it may sound in English—was used extensively by the trainers to explain the kind of impact they hoped to have on government workers. Most of the trainers I interviewed also likened their job to the well-known story of the man who dedicated his life to saving starfish. The story, which was recounted at one stage or another at the majority of the trainings in which I participated, was about a man on a vast beach who spent all his time picking up the dying starfish that had washed up onto the shore, one by one, and throwing them back into the sea so that they could live. Even though there were probably millions of other starfish dying as he rescued only a handful of them, the man did not give up on his mission, thinking that saving even one starfish was better than saving none. The idea behind both the "snow melt" expression and the starfish story was that no matter how insignificant and ineffective the thing one does might seem, one still had to keep doing it because even the smallest difference had an effect.

From this perspective, the ultimate aspiration of a successful human rights training emerged as creating a suitable—i.e., safe—environment for purposes of active learning and participation, with the hope that it might effect the smallest change. Training, thus, became all about the learning environment and how best to create it. The juvenile justice training manual, for instance, described this training environment as one that is built in cooperation with the participants in a democratic fashion, allowing the participants to feel that "this is our education." Such an environment required non-hierarchical, egalitarian relationships both between the trainers and the trainees, and among the trainees themselves. This, in turn, obliged the training environment to be cleared of all relations of power and of even the most basic structures of hierarchy—including the one between the learner and the learned—that defined the educational field.

DOING AWAY WITH HIERARCHIES

One of the primary objectives of the interactive, participative human rights training for government officials was to strip the participants of their markers of hierarchy, which might have prevented their participation in training activities. Every human rights seminar, almost exclusively, started with encouraging the participants to relax, be informal, and have fun:

> *Trainer*: *Arkadaşlar* (friends), please make yourselves comfortable. Dress comfortably. I repeat this at the beginning of each training program we have. The participants say [that they dress formally] due to their respect for us. Thank you very much! But, really . . . you can be comfortable and dress comfortably. (Training for religious personnel on women's human rights)

* * *

> *Trainer*: Now let's put our identities aside. Let's take off our jackets, too. Let's get rid of the formalities as much as we can. (Juvenile justice training for judges and prosecutors)

* * *

> *Ministry of Justice Representative*: Now, *arkadaşlar* (friends), this is not one of those training programs that we're used to. So, forget about those [old] training programs. This is not formal. Look, I am [dressed] informally too. (Training on women's human rights for prison teachers)

* * *

> *Trainer*: Earlier, the idea of in-service training was to gather [the officers] from the periphery to Ankara. And someone would come and talk for hours. Boring, suffocating . . . Now we're trying to make things fun. We go on tours and stuff. (Training on women's human rights for the police)

Another way to downplay hierarchies was to arrange the classroom space in less hierarchical ways, such as by arranging the chairs so that the participants would sit in a circle, half circle, or in v-form (Image 1), rather than in the classical classroom format. The latter was deemed undesirable because it usually resulted in a seating arrangement in which the front seats were occupied by the high-ranking officials, while the back ones were left to those with lower ranks. Another form of spatial arrangement was to divide the participants into smaller groups that would rotate during training in order to make all of the participants get up and move (Image 2). This method was also popular because it enabled all of the participants to work with one another across professional hierarchies.

As for minimizing the hierarchy between the trainers and the trainees, training programs carefully employed forms of address other than "the trainer" and "the trainee." This is how the training manual for the juvenile justice training addressed the issue:

> The subject we often discuss with regard to adult education . . . is whether to name ourselves as "trainers," or whether terms such as "teacher" or "instructor" are appropriate for trainers. The same discussion goes for the words "trainees" or "students."

The terms "*eğitmen*" (trainer) and "*kolaylaştırıcı*" (facilitator) were widely used within the human rights training programs. The term "*hoca*" (professor) was usually reserved for trainers from academia. The term "*öğretmen*" (teacher) was never used. As for referring to the trainees, the term that the project teams used almost exclusively was "*katılımcı*" (participant). The term "*öğrenci*" (student) was never used. Although the goal was to render the relationship between the trainers and trainees as less authoritative, expertise on the subject of the training was still an imperative to be considered a good trainer. The trainers were required to be less authoritative in their relationship with the trainees. However, they were still expected to be authorities and experts on the subjects they addressed during training. During the training session for Combating Violence Against Women Project, Cemil, the interactive adult education trainer, explained the importance of expertise for a successful adult educator in the following words:

> You have to establish credibility by displaying your experience: "I have been working on this issue for this amount of time. I am competent." What have I done, for instance? I [came here and said that I] am a clinical psychologist . . .

I have been working on this since this [amount of] time . . . Otherwise, "Hi, I'm here. I came to talk about these issues." Fine, pal . . . But who are you? What kind of training do you have?

In the light of the egalitarian aspirations of the adult education framework, master–pupil relationships between the trainers and trainees were considered highly inappropriate. Nevertheless, as the above quote demonstrates, the mastery of the trainers over the subject of training still emerged as an essential requirement for the success of training. Paradoxically, however, the credibility of "mastery over the subject" inevitably defined an unequal relationship between the trainers and trainees. Even though the trainees were imagined as "experienced," "already educated" and not just the receivers but also the participants/contributors of training, the structural difference between calling and being called to education (and different degrees of receiving/responding to this call) situated the actors of training differentially. Relations of power and hierarchy in the educational environment of human rights training did not disappear or become stratified that easily.

In their work on the reproduction of relations of power, Pierre Bourdieu and Jean-Claude Passeron ([1977] 1990) argue that education is perhaps the primary means of maintaining ascribed positions of privilege and domination within society. Inherent to their argument is the axiom that no matter how legitimate and natural it may seem to its participants, "pedagogic work," "pedagogic communication," and "pedagogic action" always presume "pedagogic authority." According to Bourdieu and Passeron, it is by definition impossible for a pedagogic action to destabilize the power relations that it is built upon. It is not viable for a pedagogic action or communication to break free from its constitutive power relationship—the inequality between the object and the subject of pedagogy, and the discrepancies between the subjugator and the subjugated of the systems of value, which education helps its audiences to internalize.

It is due to this paradox that even though the human rights training programs for government workers in Turkey sought to democratize the learning environment, they were nevertheless required to take into consideration the perceptions of authority and hierarchy among their audiences in order to establish the legitimacy of training. It is exactly for this reason that all of the training programs I worked with included at least one representative from the government institution for which the participants were working. Some training programs even included a session that was run by the government representative. Rather than eliminating the hierarchical structure of the classroom, these situations further consolidated the pedagogic authority of the trainings by borrowing from bureaucratic hierarchies. Despite the belief that abolishing classroom hierarchies would lead to a more effective training, the presence of an institutional representative—situated above the trainees in the bureaucratic hierarchy—set the tone of the training environment hierarchically.

The validation of trainings by a bureaucratic authority was necessary to prove to the audience that the program was officially approved by the state, as human rights trainings may have at first seemed suspicious. The previous quote from the Ministry of Justice representative, encouraging participants to dress informally by referring to his own attire, is the perfect illustration of what institutional authority was capable of and why it remained necessary for the training's validation. In another training program, organized by AI, the representative of the Ministry of Education clearly articulated that his presence was proof of the training's legitimacy. This was yet another instance demonstrating how pedagogical environments, especially the ones containing participants stratified by bureaucratic hierarchies, could not be conceived of as free of power relations:

> Democracy and human rights are both rising concepts in the global world, and they are concepts that our government is sensitive about. They also form a basis for the development of our country and macro programs oriented towards this development. The reason we are here today is that *we want you to realize that we are supportive of this work.* (Emphasis mine.)

POWER OF EDUCATION

In their attempt to generate a democratic learning environment, models of adult education employed by human rights training programs bear close affinities to methods of critical pedagogy. Critical pedagogy aims to transform the practice of education to generate self-empowerment among learners, and to trigger eventually the revolutionary transformation of society (Darder, Baltodano and Torres 2003, Leistyna, Lavandez and Nelson 2004). Following the legacies of Paulo Freire, Jurgen Habermas, Antonio Gramsci, and Raymond Williams, studies of critical pedagogy focus on alternative methods and forms of education, empowerment, and "the pedagogy of the oppressed." Due to its empowerment framework, critical pedagogy also has direct influence on studies of "transformative adult education." With its strong emancipatory emphasis, it is believed that transformative adult education can enable active citizenship and radical community development (Mayo 2009). The direct link between critical pedagogy and adult education is the reason why the latter is embraced by human rights movements all around the world. Civic education and rights education is considered one of the primary means through which oppressed people can be made aware of their rights. The proponents of civic education and rights education argue that these trainings can enable the oppressed to fight back against their oppressors by means of acquiring and mobilizing the human rights rhetoric.[5]

Scholars of adult learning, following Habermas, emphasize the importance of "encouraging an environment that recreates the ideal speech situation" for an education aimed at empowering the oppressed (Cowie 1997). They believe that the ideal speech situation would enable communicative knowledge as well as improve interpersonal relations by creating an environment in which understanding others is rendered possible. Citizen school projects in places like Porto Alegre are based on such educational environments. Although civic education, rights education, and citizen school projects are designed to educate and empower the powerless, it is argued that through challenging and transforming "the official knowledge" these initiatives also have the indirect effect of "educating the state" (Gandin and Apple 2004). Yet in projects that directly aim to train state actors, such as human rights trainings in Turkey, the affinities between the pedagogic models that are used to educate the oppressed and the ones that are employed to train the power brokers of society appear more than just "indirect."

Such an affinity is traceable when, for instance, Nesrin references her experience in women's education as an influence over the pedagogical model she helped develop for the training of police. This strange affinity leads to a situation in which educational models and pedagogical techniques that are used to empower women are also appropriated while training the law enforcement agents who are part of the structural violence those women experience on a daily basis. Educational practices addressing those in positions of power entail relations of domination and authority, which are quite different from those that emerge during the education of the powerless or the socially marginalized. What is more, the goal of education directed towards government workers is quite the opposite of the aim of women's education. While women's education seeks to equip women with knowledge to empower them, human rights trainings for government workers seek to persuade those powerful public figures (who are usually in cahoots with rights violators) to contain their power.

When thought of in this way, it becomes even more puzzling to see the use of similar pedagogical techniques for purposes of both empowerment and disempowerment.

The use of interactive, participative adult education techniques in human rights training programs for government workers stemmed mainly out of a need to convince their trainees of the acceptability of the training programs. Acceptability of the training, as I have illustrated above, was dependent on the successful portrayal of the training environment as egalitarian, non-hierarchical, and nonthreatening. The aim was to level the unequal relations of power among trainees that arose from their bureaucratic stratification, as well as to eradicate the hierarchical relationship between the trainers and trainees. This leveling within the training environment was ultimately employed to compensate for another set of hierarchies at play—namely, the transnational hierarchies generated by the asymmetrical relations of power between the EU and Turkey, which enabled this specific pedagogical activity to take place in this specific geography in the first place. Turkey-EU relations, rife with colonial connotations and transnational tensions of power and domination, provoked a highly reactionary response in the audience for human rights training, especially among members of the Turkish bureaucracy. Delineation of a democratic training atmosphere was employed as a way to contain the expected reactions of the audiences of human rights training programs towards the unequal relations of power that shape Turkey's EU accession process.

Following Bourdieu and Passeron ([1977] 1990), I have argued that the acceptability of the training activity was conditional upon the acceptance of the legitimacy of the pedagogic authority from which the pedagogic action derives. Making human rights training programs appear to derive from the sovereign authority of the Turkish state (rather than being imposed by the EU) or placing responsibility for the training's success on each individual trainee (rather than on the trainers) aimed to establish the trainings as legitimate. This proves once more that the universal ethical connotations of human rights and references to a universal human condition are not sufficient to constitute a legitimate pedagogic authority in human rights training programs for government workers in Turkey. These programs instead need the state authority's affirmation to establish themselves as legitimate. As a result, training environments that supposedly sought to eliminate hierarchical relations in fact became sites for the display of bureaucratic power and state authority—a factor that project teams had to take into account.

Tracing the establishment of pedagogic authority enables an understanding of the kind of learning and learner that is produced by means of these training programs. As I demonstrated throughout this chapter, the kind of learning generated by the professional adult education framework is one that oscillates between a technical capacity building that aims to standardize the participants' bureaucratic operations and a general exposure to a universalistic sensibility that aims to seep into the trainees' psyche to affect their professional behavior. To this effect, human rights as the subject of training was delineated, on the one hand, as a technical, professional issue, and on the other hand, as a universalistic ethical framework that excluded the messiness of particular socio-political conditions in Turkey. As a result, these trainings aimed to produce bureaucratic subjects who were both conditioned to be cogs in a wheel and motivated to have consciousness that would lead them towards a common humanity. The most important thing, however, is that by refraining from upsetting the nationalistic/bureaucratic sensitivities of its participants, this kind of training was careful to leave the egos of its learners intact.[6] As such, it defined the engagement of the governmental realm with human rights as devoid of confrontation and accountability, which would have necessitated governmental agents to face past and current state atrocities, as well as their own complicity in them. Rather, human rights became the subject of imaginary scenarios that made their way into board games, or they became the tools that enabled the legitimation of certain types of violence. The following two chapters are intended to exhibit what happens when these models of learning actually hit the ground during human rights training programs.

4 TRANSLATION AND THE LIMITS OF STATE LANGUAGE

Traduttore, traditore (the translator is a traitor).
—Italian Proverb

I FOLLOWED SELİN TO HER KITCHEN, where she put some water into the kettle to make us coffee. When I had asked her if she would talk to me about her experience as a translator for human rights training programs, she had kindly invited me to her house. She was busy making a glossary of the key terms related to agricultural machinery in preparation for a meeting at the Ministry of Agriculture the next day. I told Selin that I had no idea how prevalent translation work was in the public sector before I started this research. Selin agreed. The public sector in Turkey was a lucrative market for translators. In fact it was so lucrative that some foreign translators were looking to cash in:

> They said, you know, with Turkey's accession into the EU, the accredited translators in Europe, let's say they translate from Spanish to English, they will come to Turkey to study Turkish for like four-five years to learn the language and then get the jobs . . . You know, because they're already accredited . . . And I laughed so hard when I heard this. I thought, sure let them come and after they learn Turkish, let's see how they spend another ten years deciphering the Turkish state officials' way of speaking.

Translation is a theme and a metaphor through which many scholars have investigated the relations between the local and the global, the configuration of the universal, and the establishment of transnational standards in a variety of fields, including human rights, law, science, social movements, and histories of modernity.[1] Translation in those studies brings to attention the processual characteristic of transnational standardization and the labor that is required to establish what are considered to be universal standards as relevant to local specificities. Studies of standardization that appropriate translation as an analytical medium conceptualize universalism as composed of "complex global encounters" that indicate continuous processes of negotiation over the terms, stakes, and meanings involved in the making of universals. What these studies make apparent is that despite their widespread association with homogeneity and commensurability, standardization processes in fact produce and highlight diversity and ambiguity.

In addition to being a useful metaphor for understanding the standardization process that is put into motion by Turkey's EU accession, "translation" also refers to a set of actual practices that took place during human rights training programs. Due to the format and funding of EU projects, project teams often included foreign experts or project advisors who did not speak Turkish. This made translation an indispensable part of the training process and introduced translators as central actors for training programs, mediating between the Turkish-speaking audience and the non-Turkish-speaking project manager, project advisor, or observer. This chapter is primarily focused on those events and practices of translation and the work of translators that constituted an indispensable part of what human rights training programs produced.

Examining the simultaneous and consecutive translation practices that formed an essential part of human rights trainings, I argue that translation, on the one hand, emerges as an articulation of the foreignness of the universal human rights discourse during these training programs. This foreignness is one of the major reasons for the perception within Turkey's governmental circles that human rights is unacceptable and unsettling. On the other hand, translation also provides the tools necessary for the management of foreignness, with the hope of making human rights acceptable to Turkish government workers. Tracing how the politics of acceptable and unacceptable come into being through the practices of rephrasing, editing, silencing, speaking out, replying, and performing that take place during translation, I argue that translation processes in human rights training programs produce two important results: First, by actively editing the utterances of foreign experts to fit them into the official state language, translation mostly reinforces the boundaries designating the speakable and the unspeakable within the Turkish official domain. Second, by enabling access to "the foreign" in less threatening ways for Turkish government workers, translation processes lead to a reconfiguration of the transnational into a domestic governmental technology. This modified figure is then taken up by some government workers and used strategically to position themselves within the bureaucratic mazes that they navigate. I focus on this positioning in more detail in the following chapter.

Following translation practices in human rights training programs also reveals the contours of a particular discursive domain that hosts the interactions within the Turkish governmental field. What Selin refers to as "the Turkish officials' way of speaking" indicates a set of morals, values, and sensibilities that shape the norms and forms of communication to and among the government workers. I call this "state language." Translators like Selin have to take these norms and forms seriously as they translate the universal human rights rhetoric for the local governmental agents in Turkey. Tracing how translators orient themselves as they translate in the training programs provides a valuable insight into how global power relations shape local conditions from a linguistic point of view. Particularly, it shows how and to what extent postcolonial linguistic power asymmetries condition the translation of putative universals that shape relations of domination in different settings. Looking from here, the relationship between Turkey and the EU resembles the kind of encounters Mary Louise Pratt (1991) delineates in her account of colonial "contact zones." I will develop this argument more, again, in the following chapter.

HUMAN RIGHTS AS THE ENEMY OF THE STATE

The current EU-related transnational standardization process in Turkey is best understood as a field of encounters and negotiations that takes the form of contentious translations aiming to establish the relevance of "universal human rights" for the practices and processes of governance in the country. However, a quick glance at Turkey's political history reveals that EU accession is not the initial generator of such a translation process. As I mentioned in the introduction to this book, the emergence of "universal human rights" as a language to express political discontent was an immediate outcome of the 1980 military coup in Turkey. A time of mass political persecutions, prohibitions, and widespread incriminations, the coup and the following military regime left no space for the mobilization of politically marginalized, mostly left-leaning groups—thereby forcing them to recourse to the transnationally accredited rhetoric of human rights. This has led to a very contextually specific translation of human rights, with overwhelming references to a socialist worldview and left-leaning politics.

A defining characteristic of this generation of human rights defenders was their status as victims of human rights abuses themselves. Contrary to the members of most activist circles that came into being in the late 1990s, defenders who coalesced around organizations like İHD and TİHV did not assume a position of detached, impartial human rights expertise. Although many people in İHD and TİHV mobilized their professional identities as lawyers and doctors while performing particular forms of advocacy such as litigation or reporting, their involvement in human rights work primarily followed their political engagement. The victim status of early human rights defenders that was tied to their political identity led to their designation as "suspect citizens" by the state. Rights defenders were openly denounced by some key institutions such as the National Security Council and the Army, with the allegation that they used human rights as a cover for treacherous activity against the "indivisibility of the nation and the state." Particularly between 1984 and 1999, when the low-intensity warfare between the Turkish state and the outlawed Kurdistan Workers' Party (*Partiya Karkeren Kurdistan*—PKK) was at its peak, portrayals of human rights defenders as PKK sympathizers had led to events such as the infamous police rally in Istanbul in 1992, where the officers publicly chanted "To hell with human rights!" (*Kahrolsun insan hakları!*) (Bozarslan 2001).

As a result of this overwhelming stigmatization and despite the early defenders' ambition to define themselves as part of a "mass social movement" (*toplumsal kitle hareketi*), human rights advocacy did not gain popular support in mainstream Turkish society. It remained mostly marginalized, championed to a large extent by some professional segments, intellectual dissidents, and direct victims of human rights abuses who due to their political, ethnic, or religious identities were already marked as "the other" (Cizre 2001). Like what Teresa Caldeira (1992) describes in Brazil, human rights have come to be associated with "rights for terrorists," and human rights defenders have come to be seen as "enemies of the state" within the public realm in Turkey.[2]

This marginalization and lack of popular support in the domestic realm was one reason that compelled human rights organizations to form alliances with transnational advocacy networks in order to enhance their impact in the national polity. A well-known case is the partnering of İHD's Diyarbakır Branch with the international lawyers at Essex University Law School and with the London-based Kurdish Human Rights Project to systematically submit complaints to the European Court of Human Rights about violations perpetrated in the Kurdish regions (Kurban, Erözden and Gülalp 2008). Although this proved to be an effective means of publicizing state-led violations and holding the state accountable in front of international jurisdiction, it nevertheless contributed to the official repertoire to frame and persecute human rights advocacy as a foreign-born/sponsored activity and an imperialist plot. İHD's Diyarbakır Branch was shut down by executive order in 1997. Many local İHD offices were attacked by ultra-nationalist, paramilitary groups, either backed or overlooked by the state. In 1998, İHD's then president Akın Birdal was critically wounded in an attack on the İHD Ankara branch. The shooters were never found. After the shooting, Birdal was brought to trial for "separatist propaganda" and was made to serve fifteen months in prison (Cizre 2001).

Although transnational support and connections have always been crucial for Turkish human rights defenders to continue their work, the same defenders also maintained a deep criticism of global capitalism and the international political order it was connected to. This was reflected in their selection of transnational allies and their refusal to partner with foreign governments as well as certain non-governmental entities such as the Soros Foundation. Human rights defenders within İHD and TİHV have been quite vocal about their criticism of international donors and Western bodies that sought to disseminate the ideas of free market liberalism through patronage. Despite the strong anti-imperialist standpoint of the early defenders, human rights politics could not escape from being associated with imperialism in the eyes of the mainstream Turkish public.

Although the politics of human rights was marginalized and criminalized, this did not preclude the institutionalization of human rights within the state. Early instances of this institutionalization included the appointment of a Minister of State Responsible for Human Rights in 1991 and the formation of the Human Rights Research Committee within the Parliament in 1992.[3] Institutionalization of human rights at the governmental level accelerated following the 1999 Helsinki summit, which granted candidate status to Turkey. In 2001, the Human Rights Presidency was established under the Prime Ministry, which included the Human Rights High Committee and the Human Rights Advisory Board. In 2003, provincial and sub-provincial human rights boards were formed. Finally in 2012, the Human Rights Presidency was replaced by the National Human Rights Institution of Turkey. A very small number of those institutions have actually contributed to human rights advocacy in the country—such as the critical human rights violation reports produced by the Parliamentary Commission in 1997 and 2000 and the Minority Report produced by the Human Rights Advisory Board in 2004. With these exceptions, state-run human rights institutions were widely criticized due to their lack of independence, authority, and transparency (Alemdar 2011, Altıparmak 2007, Oğuşgil 2015).

At the non-governmental level, the increasing circulation of human rights discourse found its reflection in the rights-based organizations that mushroomed in the late 1990s. Following the enhancement of associational freedom in the country through legal reforms, a great number of organizations appeared in the civil society that applied human rights repertoire to a wide range of issues including women's rights, child labor, human trafficking, illiteracy, hunger, and access to safe water. While this might be regarded as the popularization of human rights as opposed to its prior marginalization in the society, some critics argue that this proliferation turns the concept of human rights into empty rhetoric and undermines its effectiveness (Cizre 2001).

Against this historical background, current EU-related human rights reforms are best understood as the retranslation of the already-translated human rights rhetoric in Turkey, in a way to accommodate the changing context of the human rights agenda both in the world and in the country. This new agenda, informed by the expansion of global capitalism and Turkey's EU candidacy, requires a liberal reclamation of human rights by way of redefining it as less threatening and more in line with the ideals of good governance. Human rights trainings for government workers are ideal sites to trace this retranslation, where the revolutionary-leftist vernacular of Turkish human rights discourse is both contested and managed by way of employing multiple strategies of articulation and silencing. These retranslation strategies denote the continuing negotiations and struggles about how to frame human rights in Turkey.

TRANSLATION AT WORK:
THE VISIBILITY OF THE FOREIGNER IN THE ROOM

On a bright summer day in Ankara, in her home garden, Nilay, a professor of translation studies and a longtime experienced translator, described to me what she considered to be an ideal translation situation. Her serene voice and perfect intonation complemented her elegant posture and warm, yet composed, disposition:

> The main form of translation for conference settings is simultaneous translation. And the most important thing in those settings is to become a mere voice and to be completely forgotten about after a while. The tone of your voice, the form of your delivery and your coherence . . . Even though the audience continues to hear your voice through the headphones, the only thing they see should be

what is in front of them. And if you manage to completely synchronize with the speaker, and are flowing along with your excitement, coherence, and concurrent stream, the audience forgets about you. If they are aware of the translator, if the translator goes on rambling, has difficulty in understanding [the speaker], or if you [as the translator] are saying something completely unrelated and telling a sad story while the speaker is laughing and saying something [else], then translation anxiety erupts among the audience because they can't speak the language. For instance, someone might say, "I can't follow what's going on because I don't know the language. People sitting next to me can follow it but I'm not proficient enough." . . . Therefore, a good translator has to be someone who can blend in entirely after a while, completely becoming invisible, undetectable . . . [the translator] should be imperceptible, should refrain from disturbing the audience with the smell of his or her perfume, behavior, attire . . . while the training is under way.

Despite this shared convention about the "invisibility" of an ideal translation situation, the actual translation practices I encountered during human rights seminars were anything but invisible. Translation was a highly detectable material aspect of training, involving translation booths, headphones, and sometimes sequential speaking that could hardly go unnoticed. The dominant image that comes to mind when one thinks of conference translation is *simultane çeviri* (simultaneous translation). This form of translation often features translators in soundproof booths located somewhere remote in the conference venue who translate the speeches of those on stage for audiences who follow their translation through headphones (Image 3). Although larger meetings connected to human rights training programs included conference translations of this sort, most of the translation events I encountered in the field were rather different.

The more-common form of translation employed by smaller human rights training programs featured translators engaged in "*ardıl çeviri*" (consecutive translation), who translated the presenters' speeches one or two sentences at a time as they stood right next to them on stage. Contrary to high-tech simultaneous translation situations, these practices made translators highly visible figures during the training process (Image 4). Additionally, translators were employed to conduct private simultaneous translation for non-Turkish-speaking observers who wanted to watch the training sessions that were held in Turkish (Image 5). In those specific instances, even though the foreign observers and translators were usually located somewhere in the corner of the room, the ongoing simultaneous translation in the form of a constant whisper remained highly perceptible by training audiences.

The actual translation situations I encountered in the field were therefore close to Walter Benjamin's ([1968] 1999) depiction of an ideal translation: Transparent, serving as a constant reminder of the original and of its foreignness, inciting discomfort and annoyance that is caused by an encounter with the foreign. However, in contrast to Benjamin's depiction, training participants considered the transparency of translation to be an indication of its poor quality. For instance, they criticized the training materials, which were translated from English to Turkish, claiming that they "smelled like translation" (*çeviri kokuyor*). The smell of translation indicated that the text was choppy and that it was not flowing as it would, had it originally been written in Turkish. Just like the smell of the translator's perfume, which according to Nilay should be avoided in an ideal translation situation, the smell of translation distracted and caused discomfort among the training participants. It suggested that what is given away by the smell—the foreign origin of the text or the message—was in fact something that had to be disguised. Rather than going invisible, translation worked as a conspicuous site to expose the foreign origin of the human rights training.

Furthermore, translation also served as a medium through which participants commented on the presence of foreigners in the seminar. These comments were usually in line with the historical register of the foreigner in Turkish nationalist imaginary as the colonial intruder waiting to partition the country (Bora 2003, 2004). Take the following excerpt depicting the dialogue between two police officers during juvenile justice training:

Participant 1: Are they translating everything?
Participant 2: They are learning all of our secrets. If I were [the translator] I would not translate everything. They [the foreigners] know all of our features much better than we do.

The division between what should and should not be known by the dubious foreigners also delineated the border between what could and could not be said in their presence. Whenever that border was crossed, direct or indirect interventions to the translation process raised the tension in the training environment. The participants often interrupted the translators, asking them not to translate certain parts of controversial discussions that took place during the training. In other instances, for dialogues that were considered inappropriate for the foreigners to hear, the participants or the trainers quickly employed self-censorship. They interrupted and warned each other to say no more, reminding each other that there was an "outsider" listening to their conversation. Translation in those instances was seen as an undesirable incident enabling the "outsiders" to gain access to "our" secrets.

Consider the following encounter between the trainer, participants, and moderator of the training on the prevention of torture for judges and prosecutors. The trainees, consisting of judges and prosecutors, were already unhappy about discussing the problem of torture in Turkey in front of a representative of the Danish Human Rights Institute, which was the international NGO providing technical support for the project. The situation was made even more uncomfortable because the trainer of the session was a professor of law who taught at the Police Academy—an institution the participants perceived to be inferior to their own:

> *Trainer*: Cases of torture and mistreatment would diminish considerably if the prosecutors personally conducted the interrogation.
> *Participant 1*: If you teach this issue like that at the [Police] Academy, the police will get the wrong impression about what they should expect [from us, the prosecutors].
> *Moderator*: Our topic is the Istanbul Protocol [The Manual on Effective Investigation and Documentation of Torture and Other Cruel and Inhuman, Degrading Treatment or Punishment]. The doctors, the police, the judges and the prosecutors are all going to work together, collaboratively . . .
> *Trainer*: I don't represent the police here! I am making a statement about the responsibility of the prosecutors in preventing torture. I've made at least five statements about police responsibility prior to this!

(Some participants get up and leave.)

> *Participant 2*: Prosecutors may have been instrumental in cases of mistreatment by the police . . . There's no need to get touchy about that . . . These things did happen in Turkey. But the manner of speech is so important here!
> *Participant 3*: He [the trainer] is an academic; he is our professor (*hocamızdır*) . . . But his manner of speech does not suit him at all . . . I don't think that any prosecutor would say to the police "Do what needs to be done in detention, I'm not looking." I mean, one in a thousand [cases] maybe.
> *Moderator*: Ladies and gentlemen! May I remind you that all these statements are being translated!

Trainer: I am not here to represent the [Police] Academy! Working for the [Police] Academy means I'm starting out with a disadvantage already! I am striving to transform the police and to pull them within the boundaries of the law! In case you were wondering, I still can't bring myself to like the police after all these years! The police still scare me.

Moderator: Professor!

This episode displayed a familiar tension between different state institutions (the judiciary and law enforcement), caused by a disagreement over their division of labor (whose responsibility it is to conduct interrogations). The moderator thought that it was highly inappropriate for the foreign observer from the Danish Institute of Human Rights, sitting silently in the back and listening to the conversation, to be exposed to this tension. When coupled with outrageous remarks by one of the participants about how some prosecutors might in fact have been complicit in police brutality, the moderator decided that the border dividing the speakable and the unspeakable had been crossed, and he quickly shut down the discussion.[4]

The translators who took part in these training programs had the best insight into how the training audiences perceived the foreigners in the room. Cem, a translator I came to know after working together in many programs, described the government workers' perception of the figure of the foreigner as someone against whom the country had to be guarded by evoking the expression: "*Türk'ün Türk'den başka dostu yoktur*" (A Turk has no friends other than a Turk), which was common among the nationalist circles as well as the official administrative ones in Turkey. The roots of this expression, Cem went on to explain, stemmed from the identification of foreigners with the Crusaders and the "*gavur*" (infidels) who "since the Ottoman times have been holding a grudge against us." Seen as such, foreigners were always "suspect figures" who either had "malicious intent" regarding Turkey or were "seeking to serve their own interests."

The main attribute of the foreigner defined as such was hypocrisy. A recurrent theme to define the foreigner, hypocrisy laid bare the discrepancy between the messages conveyed within the trainings and the human rights policies implemented in the countries from which these programs originated. The post-9/11 era and the US-led "War on Terror" contributed heavily to this traditional repertoire of the hypocritical, suspect foreigner. Almost exclusively associated with "the Western powers," the foreigner came to embody the perpetrator of gross human rights violations, all the while posing as an apostle of human rights and democracy. A dialogue between two judges that I encountered on the shuttle bus to the Justice Academy illustrates how the participants of the Advanced Human Rights Seminar organized by the Ministry of Justice and the British Embassy made sense of the seminar in terms of hypocrisy:

> *Judge 1*: What do you mean advanced? What does advanced human rights mean?
>
> *Judge 2*: It means overdose. They now came up with the advanced version. (Laughs.) Now, they are saying things like "Can there be exceptions to human rights?" In the past they used to talk about human rights, now they are talking about national security. That's what I hear. You know about the bombings in the subway in England, right? After the explosion of the bombs, and after they themselves got hurt, now they started asking whether there might be any exceptions . . . For example, one of the questions they ask is, so there is a bomb planted somewhere in a building with a thousand people inside. Can we torture the person who knows where the bomb is? And we said: "Why are you asking us? If you are asking whether it is legitimate within the legal framework, the answer is no. It is a violation of human rights. But if you're asking in practical terms, you pay the price and you do it, if you're powerful enough."
>
> *Judge 1*: So how come it doesn't count as a violation when they do it?
>
> *Judge 2*: They used to call it a violation, now that's changed . . . [They say] What if we call it not torture but maltreatment . . . What if we do it only once . . . Well there are human rights, but what about the right of the English people to live in security?

TRANSLATORS' AMBIGUITY AND THE STATUS OF THE FOREIGN

Along with the government workers' perception of translation as an ambiguous situation, translators who served during the training programs were also marked as ambivalent figures. They were seen both as "collaborators" and "traitors" due to their proximity to the foreigner, and as "privileged insiders" who had unmediated access to the foreign. Translators were accused of revealing national secrets to foreign audiences. But at the same time, they were seen as powerful figures who could make the foreigner decipherable for the national.[5] In a setting where the national and the foreigner were clearly demarcated, translators transgressed these boundaries and occupied an in-between space. The ambivalent position of translators constituted an anomaly to the particular system of classification and "the national order of things" (Malkki 1992), which informed the perceptions of training audiences.

As Mary Douglas (1966) famously argues about "the matter out of place," anomaly in the form of ambiguity poses the utmost danger to the system of classification it transgresses.[6] For order to be maintained, anomaly must be confronted and dealt with. In a similar vein, translators transgressed the boundaries separating the inside from the outside by making confidential information available to the outsider. Therefore, they had to be dealt with so as to maintain the order that the trainees operated within. Intervening in translation and condemning the translators with treason were among the various ways the trainees sought to grapple with the ambivalent position of the translators. However, there were also many cases in which the translators were appreciated and treated fondly. Nilay, for instance, believed that translation formed a special bond between Turkish trainees and the translator, who mediated between the foreigners and the trainees. Translation did cause discomfort among the trainees, and led them to censor both themselves and the others. This, however, coexisted with a contradictory tendency to confess and to reveal secrets to the translator during the breaks. Nilay described the coexistence of what she called "*çevirmen kaygısı*" (translator anxiety) among the participants, with their urge to tell the translator the truth:

> When the participants find the translators alone, they talk to them for hours. But then afterwards, they say: "Please don't translate these [things] . . ." Like, "We're telling you these [things] but don't say them to the foreigner . . ." But you just told me all these things! What do you want me to do with them? They say: "You should know [the truth] but don't repeat it [to the foreigners]."

Disclosing insider information to someone closely associated with the foreigner may at first glance appear as a contradiction. However, this seemingly illogical act makes sense when thought of as a way to deal with the translators' anomaly. The participants, perceiving the danger posed by the ambivalent position of the translator (an insider who also has allegiances to the outside), attempt to pull the translator back from the margins to the inside. By treating her as a true insider who has the right to know the truth, the participants seek to restore the classificatory scheme that orders their world.

The threat associated with the ambivalence of the translators makes better sense when thought together with the relationships of power and dominance that are embedded in transnational translation processes. In dealing with translation, it is essential to note that one deals with a situation predominantly taking place on unequal ground. Asymmetrical relations between the West and non-West designate the status of different languages and their speakers in unequal ways as they come into contact with each other. The difference between two languages that are rendered in each other's terms does not have the same value for both languages. Languages are positioned hierarchically, which means translation is ridden with politics and asymmetrical relations of power (Apter 2001, Asad 1986, Spivak 1993).

Similarly, the hegemonic position of English in relation to Turkish influenced the tone of translations in human rights training programs, as well as the audiences' reactionary attitude towards them. What is more, the unequal positioning of English and Turkish rendered the translators' linguistic ability a marker of their class distinction.[7] Due to the particular symbolic status of foreign language acquisition in Turkey, the translators were perceived as elite, cosmopolitan figures, whereas most of the training audiences shared a small-town, lower-middle-class background.[8] This class difference between the translators and the audiences contributed to the anxiety mentioned previously by Nilay, caused by the inability of the trainees to fully control the communicative situations that they found themselves in.

The commonplace Turkish expression for the lack of ability to speak a foreign language (*dil bilmemek*) translates as "not knowing language." Rather than "not knowing *a foreign* language," it refers to "not knowing *any kind of* language." This means not having a means of communication and self-expression, which has the effect of silencing and ostracizing the nonspeaker. This feeling of ostracism built up further during human rights training programs, in which the trainees sometimes felt attacked by the representatives of foreign institutions, and were compelled to explain and defend themselves. The need to communicate and to express one's self for purposes of self-defense intensified the training audiences' frustration with "not knowing language." This frustration was caused on the one hand by a nationalist reaction to the dominance of the English language, and on the other by the felt necessity to speak in that language to successfully resist the conditions of dominance. Oktay, a psychologist working for the Directorate of Prisons and Detention Centers, expressed this dilemma in the following manner:

> I have this nationalist vein in me . . . And I reacted against the hegemony of English [language] education in elite schools . . . That's why I refused to work

on my English. I still think that the dominant language in Turkey should be Turkish. But now, when I'm in situations like this, I can't speak . . . It puts me at a disadvantage for sure.

The educational settings of human rights training programs therefore necessitated translation to enable communication, interaction, and understanding. These same settings also presented opportunities for some participants to distinguish themselves from the others by demonstrating their linguistic abilities. Although the ability to speak English and the symbolic social status that came with it was ultimately an object of desire, the performance of that ability by some participants during the training was seldom met with approval. For instance, during the training program for judges and prosecutors on the prevention of torture, a woman judge preferred to pose her question to the Danish trainer in English, despite the fact that translation was available on site. The rest of the trainees listened to her question in deep silence, and some participants turned to each other with raised eyebrows and grins. Cem, who was translating the training into English for the trainer, had to translate the judge's question into Turkish for the general audience before the trainer started to answer it. The judge participant, by addressing the Danish trainer in English, did not just perform her ability to communicate directly to the foreigner in the room—an ability that the other trainees lacked. She also (willingly or unwillingly) distinguished herself from the rest of the audience.[9] Another judge participant, whom I interviewed after the training, spoke of what happened during the seminar disapprovingly, claiming that the woman judge was just "showing off" by displaying her ability to speak English.[10] "Her question," he remarked, "wasn't even interesting."

Recalling similar events that happened during the training programs she translated, Selin thought that the trainees' attempts to speak English interrupted the whole process, causing the training to lose its focus by turning it into a medium for the trainees to demonstrate their linguistic abilities:

Even though there is translation available, they still want to ask their question in English, they want to demonstrate their English . . . But then what happens is that the training deviates from its purpose. The purpose of the training is to educate the audience. It is not for you to show off. When you ask the question in English it actually makes it more complicated. Because most of the time they really can't speak English. The foreigner doesn't understand it either . . . There is translation available. If they asked [the question] in Turkish, the translation would be very clear. But because their English is in fact not good, the [foreign] speaker doesn't really understand it either. It creates an unnecessary ambiguity. . . . All this happens so that they can demonstrate their English and talk to the foreigners directly.

The perceived high status that was attached to the ability to speak English led government workers to use this ability, or to react to people who demonstrated this ability strategically, in order to manage hierarchical situations in the classroom. For instance, both Selin and Cem reported that trainees frequently employed "competing with the translator" as a way to restate their authority in circumstances in which they felt threatened. In my interview with Cem, he reported that the judges and prosecutors were especially prone to becoming involved in this "*statü yarışı*" (status competition) in order to confirm their superior position within the bureaucratic hierarchy:

Cem: The fact that they get into a *statü yarışı* (status competition) and try to prove something to the translator is completely puzzling to me.

Elif: What kind of a status competition are you talking about?

Cem: They have an attitude like, "OK, so you are the translator and you are important but we studied law for so many years, and look at where we are now."

Elif: Why is it that they get into a status competition with the translators? Because I've seen it happening, too. . . .

Cem: They get into a status competition with me because they haven't yet grasped the concept that every job has to be performed by its expert. They immediately start questioning their educational history. "In our days, English language classes were taught by agricultural engineers, physical education teachers. We weren't given [proper language education]." They start having anxieties, like "We wish we were able to express ourselves here," etc. If you ask me, everybody should do their own job. I mean, a judge or a lawyer doesn't necessarily have to know how to express themselves in English. Even if they do, they don't necessarily have to speak it. I mean there are people who do this professionally. But because these people [the trainees] want to be everything in the world, it's a big problem . . . It's a complex, like "OK, so you can speak this language without an accent and you are very close to the foreign expert. But it's not like we are unimportant people." I believe it has to do with an inferiority complex.

Government workers' relationship to both English and the translators was also closely tied to the privilege of economic, social, and symbolic distinction that was often attributed to the foreigner. For instance, Hasibe, the social worker from the juvenile justice training program, shared with me her feelings about Anika, the Dutch project coordinator, one evening during dinner:

> In my personal life, I struggle with the aspects of feudal culture continuously. But I get so annoyed when someone comes from the outside to teach me about the individual, the family, and the child. It's as if my culture is all bad and theirs is all perfect. Is that it? If they know it all, why is it that [in their countries] thirteen-year-old girls get pregnant and families break up? When that's the situation, I feel like I'm being played here for Anika's personal satisfaction. Of course, Anika is a symbol . . . Why am I being subjected to the impositions of some people who come from England or France or wherever? . . . Of course Anika is optimistic about the future. Anika speaks five languages, she has already solved her own problems, and she's here to teach me how to solve mine.

As Hasibe's comment demonstrates, the trainees combined the ascribed status of the foreigner as a powerful intruder with the perceived privilege of the translators to define human rights trainings as "impositions from outside." This juxtaposition led the trainees to equate a situation of language inequality with transnational legal systems of human rights monitoring and institutional standardization, and enabled them to depict the latter as "unfair." As a result, human rights training programs generated a field of encounters shaped by an amalgamation of hierarchies that inform transnational politics, socio-economic distinctions, gender relations, and professional identities. Not surprisingly, then, within this field of encounters, translation and the ability to speak English seldom configured as an area of expertise. Instead, linguistic capability emerged as the means through which people strategically managed both hierarchies among themselves and the relations of power between them and the foreign/international parties.

SENSITIVE TRANSLATIONS FOR SENSITIVE PEOPLE

In addition to elucidating the configuration of foreignness within the human rights training programs, translation also provided the means to manage these foreign configurations. This designated the translators' work in the trainings as not just the transmission but also the mediation of the things said. As Selin aptly put it, translators did not just translate from English to Turkish. They also translated what was said into the state language:

> State employees in Turkey have a specific language they speak . . . It's very interesting, and you can ask all the translators about it. We encounter such difficulty when translating it. There are no clear statements . . . They think that the more complicatedly they speak, the more valuable it will be . . . We can now decipher it somehow . . . We got used to it in time and with experience.

The state language described by Selin indicated the appropriate form of communication within the official governmental domain in Turkey. Similar to Miyako Inoue's (2003) description of the "Japanese women's language," state language both delineated a set of linguistic beliefs about a delimited zone of language with specific norms and forms, and functioned as an emblem of national-institutional particularity. State language embodied official standpoints and sensibilities, bureaucratic hierarchies, and distinctions that made up the domain of speech within which interactions with the Turkish state were carried out.

Foreign experts who served in human rights training programs for government workers did not always come informed about these proper forms of communication. Even if they did, the forms of address and sentence construction in English did not always convey the linguistic markers of politeness and respect in Turkish. A very simple example is the distinction between the formal and informal forms of address in Turkish (*sen/siz*), which the singularity of the word "you" in English fails to capture. Verbal, tonal, and dispositional differences that defined the proper and improper forms of speech in the Turkish official realm could easily go unmarked in the conditions of discourse that informed the foreign experts' ways of speaking. In those instances, the duty to ensure that these unmarked differences appeared properly in the foreigner's discourse fell upon the translators. This made editing an integral and significant part of the translation work.

Although translators often expressed their obligation to translate everything that had been said during training as part of their professional responsibility, they nevertheless did (sometimes radically) edit what they translated. When translating back and forth between Turkish government workers and foreign experts, translators employed several methods to adjust the tone, meaning, and mode of utterances to fit them into the appropriate communicative genre for the Turkish bureaucracy.[11] They rephrased foreign utterances by adding certain forms of address that the originals did not contain. Or they replaced certain words with others in order to prevent audience reaction. For instance, Hakan, a translator with ten years of experience working for both private businesses and the state, explained how he adjusted the tone of address during translation to acknowledge bureaucratic hierarchies:

> When translating for a director general, a group of judges and prosecutors, or a similar group of decision makers, especially if the person [whose speech I'm translating] is a foreign NGO member—which means that because of their way of working and the language that they use they are not used to addressing someone superior to them—I add an introductory expression such as "*efendim şimdi de . . .*" (now, sirs and madams, let's . . .) to adjust the tone . . . I start with "*efendim*" (sir/madam). I pay great attention to my tone because there is more than one way of saying the same thing.

Similarly, Selin recounted her first experience of translating for human rights trainings to describe how she learned the necessity of replacing certain words in order to appease the specific sensibilities of training audiences:

> The first thing that I was told [by the project team] was, "The foreign trainer may say things like 'I am going to teach you,' etc. Don't ever use the word '*öğretmek*' (to teach) while translating." There was a huge uproar [in the audience], like "Who is this person coming from outside and teaching us things?" I had to be very careful about choosing words . . . So they told me that I had to express things very softly and humbly. Because of course the foreign [trainer] doesn't know about it . . . and if I'm not aware of this sensitivity I would just translate exactly what s/he said . . . I said things like "This is what we are going to discuss; this is what we are going to talk about . . . We are going to exchange information on these matters."

The adjustment of the tone of speech for an audience that was stratified along bureaucratic hierarchies also required alterations in other aspects of foreign expressions, such as verbal modes or active/passive sentence constructions. When I was helping with copyediting for the translation of the material for one of the training projects, the strongest feedback we received from the test audience was about the wording of the instructions in the book. Instructions written in an imperative mode such as "*Daha fazla bilgi için 12. sayfaya bakın*" (Turn to page 12 for more information on this) were received very negatively, as an improper and disrespectful way of addressing the readers. For the following week, I had to rewrite all of the similar sentences in a propositional/passive mode such as "*Daha fazla bilgi için 12. sayfaya bakılabilir*" (It is possible to turn to page 12 for more information on this).

Similarly, the trainees reacted to active and direct forms of sentence construction employed in the original texts, which appeared at the beginning of each chapter to inform the trainees about the learning expectations. The wording of the learning expectations also had to be changed, as shown in the charts here.

Before Editing

Bu bölümün sonunda sizden:	By the end of this section you are expected to:
eğitime katılmayla ilgili rahat hissetmeniz,	feel comfortable about participating in the classroom,
tüm iş arkadaşlarınızın isimlerini bilmeniz,	know all of your colleagues by their names,
diğer iş arkadaşlarınızın katkı ve tecrübelerine saygı göstermeniz beklenmektedir.	respect your colleagues' experiences and contributions.

After Editing

Bu bölümde:	What is aimed in this section is that:
eğitime katılma konusunda rahat hissedilmesi,	the classroom participation becomes comfortable,
tüm katılımcıların isimlerinin bilinmesi,	all the participants are known by their names,
tüm katılımcıların katkı ve tecrübelerine saygı gösterilmesi hedeflenmektedir.	all of the participants' experiences and contributions are respected.

The imperative mode, the active form of sentence construction, and the direct form of address that was in the original text came across as offensive to the trainees. Rewriting them in the passive form had the effect of blurring the subject of the sentences and removing the trainees from a position of receiving orders. Another way to accommodate this sensibility was through the mobilization of gender identities. This method was actively used by some international NGOs that preferred to work with soft-spoken, young women translators. Translators who fell under this specific profile were thought to sound less intrusive and more agreeable, and they were especially sought after for meetings with high-level government workers in order to decrease possible tension.[12]

In addition to adjusting the tone of speech, translators sometimes skipped or erased certain words to tame a discourse that training audiences might consider subversive. For instance, Ebru, a young translator, explained to me how she had to skip the word "*Sayın*" (Mr. or Honorable) when translating the phrase "Mr. Öcalan," during a training for high-level government workers:

> Once there was a group meeting . . . for high-level government workers on human rights. They talked about Öcalan, the IRA, and lots of stuff. The foreign guest kept saying "Mr. Öcalan," and I, as a naïve and inexperienced person, kept translating it as "Sayın Öcalan," "Sayın Öcalan." The participants sitting right next to me all turned bright red. And . . . there was no intention at all . . . really . . . to honor him or something. It's just because that's how it is said in English, they said "Mr. Öcalan." . . . At the end of that session, [a group of participants] approached me, and they grilled me: "How could you say that, as a Turkish girl?" I felt so terrible. After that, I translated [Mr. Öcalan] as "Öcalan" [without "Mr."].

Likewise, Selin testified that she had to get around using the word "*diktatörlük*" ("dictatorship") when translating the expression "Atatürk dictatorship" during a training for army officials:

> Especially the police, the military . . . There are some topics they are very sensitive about . . . For instance, I once conducted a translation about Atatürk. There was this foreign man. He came from a university. He conducted this study, a very good study, on Atatürk. He read all the unpublished letters of Atatürk, translated them, tried to learn them. And he wrote a book about those . . . So he used the word "dictatorship" in one part of his speech. Now if you say "*Atatürk diktatördü*" (Atatürk was a dictator) in the presence of people who admire Atatürk, where there are military officers, you would encounter huge reactions. Nevertheless, I could not find any other words to use instead of the word "dictator" there . . . The sentence itself was not negative at all. Just the word "dictatorship" . . . So I had to use the words "*askeri diktatörlüğü*" ("military dictatorship") . . . What else could I do? There were no synonyms I could use . . . I couldn't have done any interpretation. I didn't want to erase it, either . . . Afterwards, a question came immediately from the audience: "You used the word "*diktatörlük*" ("dictatorship"). Atatürk was not a dictator . . ." The man [the foreign expert] explained what he meant by the word dictator . . . in a military sense. So he really didn't mean it in a bad way. But [the way he used it] was totally unfamiliar in Turkish

. . . I couldn't say things like, "Atatürk was a military dictator." The translator has to be sensitive in those instances . . . The meeting continued after my shift, and I told the translator taking over after me: "Look, ask the foreigner beforehand if he's planning to use the word "dictator" again. This is a sensitive subject. He is making this speech to admirers of Atatürk. Make sure that you ask what he means by it, what other synonyms you can use." That's what I advised. Sensitivities like this . . . You find similar sensitivities in every situation.

The two men—Mustafa Kemal Atatürk and Abdullah Öcalan—who are the subjects of these sensitive translations symbolize the key building blocks of the republican nationalist paradigm in Turkey. Mustafa Kemal Atatürk is considered the founder of modern Turkey and his cultlike figure disallows a thorough analysis of the authoritarian nature of the early republican regime (Image 6). Abdullah Öcalan is the leader of PKK—the main opponent of the Turkish state in low-intensity warfare that has been going on for the last thirty years.[13] Under arrest since 1999, Öcalan is often marked as the penultimate enemy of the state and the nation (Image 7). So much so that addressing him as "*Sayın*" has previously been punished on the grounds that it constitutes "praising the criminal and crime." He is commonly addressed in the mainstream media by just his surname, "Öcalan," or by an abbreviated version of his name, "Apo." In more nationalistic media outlets, he is also referred to as "the separatist head," "the terrorist leader," and "baby murderer."

With such high stakes, both of these accounts indicate sensitive translation events that translators were expected to manage properly. In Ebru's case, we see a form of respect—the word "*sayın*"—overflowing from the foreign discourse into its Turkish translation. This overflow, which the translator was not yet skilled enough to edit, caused an immense discomfort among members of the audience. What is interesting about this case is that the audience blamed the translator for the improperness of the foreign trainer's utterance. They criticized the translator for not applying the official filtering to the foreign trainer's discourse before reproducing it in Turkish. During the coffee break, Ebru was surrounded by the government workers, who grilled her and blamed her for not being a proper Turkish girl for translating "Mr. Öcalan" as "*Sayın Öcalan*." This event clearly indicates that what is expected from the translator is more than just a linguistic transplant. The translator is also expected to function as a checkpoint to prevent unspeakable dogmas from sneaking into the official governmental domain.

In the event narrated by Selin, we see a better management of the subversive discourse. The translator informed the foreigner about the sign value of the word he used, and she mediated between the two parties to come to terms with the meaning of the normally unspeakable word by establishing its difference from what usually makes it unacceptable. Although the speaker used the word "dictatorship," which could be translated into Turkish in a straightforward manner as "*diktatörlük*," Selin preferred to put a qualifier in front of the word and translated it as "*askeri diktatörlük*" ("military dictatorship") to give it an aura of technicality. By doing so, she could claim that the way the foreign speaker used the term endowed it with a specific technical meaning that was different from the ordinary use of the word "*diktatör.*"

Although by managing it successfully Selin rendered the subversive discourse speakable, her translation produced an effect similar to Ebru's. Instead of allowing the phrases "*Sayın Öcalan*" and "*Atatürk diktatörlüğü*" to permeate the official discourse, both Selin and Ebru employed what Lawrence Venuti (1995) calls the "domesticating method" in their translations, and reshaped foreign utterances by deleting or twisting them to make sure that they fit into the official language. Following Frederick Schleiermacher, Venuti argues that the translator can decide to appropriate either the "domesticating method" or "the foreignizing method" while translating. The domesticating method is employed when translation is meant to appropriate foreign cultures for domestic agendas. Conversely, the foreignizing method is employed with the intention of disrupting the target language and the cultural codes it is engrained in. According to Venuti, the method of translation ultimately reflects a "political decision." Translation, which is capable of affirming or transgressing discursive values and institutional limits in the target language, is "a cultural political practice" shaped by power relations between the target and the source languages, the exchange value of the foreign word, and the specificities of the audience of translation. Shaped by political decisions, both Selin's and Ebru's translations ended up not transgressing, but enforcing, the established conventions of the language into which the foreign utterances were translated. Translation did not push the limits of the official state discourse by letting it assume unaccustomed forms (Asad 1986). As a consequence, translation failed to reshape the state language.

One of the ways to effectively domesticate subversive discourses was to claim their "untranslatability" (cf. Rafael 2005, 105). For instance, Selin claimed that the way in which the foreign expert used the word "dictator" could not be translated accurately because it did not have an equivalent that conveyed the same meaning in Turkish. Similarly, in Amnesty International's human rights trainings, the project coordinator in multiple instances had to argue that there was no proper translation of the word "amnesty" available in Turkish. The Turkish word *af*, which literally means forgiveness or pardon (as well as amnesty), often provoked reaction among the trainees. This reaction was once expressed by a high school teacher in a question he posed to the project coordinator at the beginning of the training: "Exactly whose amnesty are you advocating for?" Against the historical background, which led to the stigmatization of human rights as "rights for terrorists" in Turkey, people who considered themselves the embodiments of the state found the word amnesty unnerving.

Despite claims of untranslatability, the discourse of human rights was in fact widely translated into Turkish during the 1980s. This translation, without a doubt, was informed by a very specific political register. Borrowing heavily from the revolutionary-leftist vernacular, this translation enabled the opposition at a very specific moment, when every other political outlet was rendered unavailable by the authoritarian military regime. *"Katil devlet hesap verecek!"* ("The murderer state will pay for it!"—one of the most common slogans at human rights rallies) may not have been the most accurate translation of the liberal universal human rights rhetoric. Nevertheless, in the context of its production, it proved to have considerable political efficacy.

Against this backdrop, claiming the untranslatability of the marked idioms of suspect human rights language (like amnesty) in human rights training programs actually worked as a strategy to manage the established threatening status of the language of human rights by way of claiming its irrelevance or inaccuracy. This irrelevance, more than anything else, has to do with the changing context of the human rights agenda in Turkey. In the current context of EU accession and economic structural transformations, claims of untranslatability emerge as an essential part of the current liberal reclamation of human rights in the country.[14]

POLITICS OF TRANSLATION AND THE LIBERAL RECLAMATION OF HUMAN RIGHTS RHETORIC

The episodes I laid out in this chapter make it clear that the ability to facilitate and mediate between training parties requires mastery over the cultural concepts and perceptions, social conventions, and political connotations dominating human rights trainings for government workers. Translators working in these environments were required to conduct not just "linguistic" but also "semiotic" translation, which made "evaluation" an essential aspect of their work. Translation, seen as such, is not so much about matching sentences in two different languages in an automated fashion. It is instead a skillful decision-making process about how to reproduce the effect of different utterances embedded in different cultural conditions by making them relevant to the context into which they are being translated.

Translation decisions, which the translators were expected to master as part of their duty, reflect what Talal Asad calls "a skill learned in life" (1986, 155). All of the translators I interviewed in the field described this learning process as an informal, intuitive one that happened through experience. In Hakan's words, "You observe, make mistakes, and learn from your mistakes." This experiential, intuitive learning process that shapes translation decisions is also heavily informed by the politics of translation. This politics, in turn, is determined by the power relations between the target and source languages, and the exchange value of the foreign utterances in the specific translation situations featured in human rights training programs.

What is essential to note here is that the politics of translation that are displayed in human rights training programs run counter to the established conventions in the literature about how transnational power relations condition translation processes. According to Apter (2001), Asad (1986), Brennan (2001), Spivak (1993, 2000), Venuti (1995, 2003), and many others, the situation of power that determines the orientation of translation is heavily informed by the domination of Western languages over Third World ones. Asad contends that the likelihood of the translator's language to subject itself to the transforming power of translation is contingent upon institutionally defined power relations between the languages (1986, 157). However, my fieldwork in human rights training programs shows that despite the institutional and structural inequality that positions English and Turkish aysmmetrically, the official state language that dominates these trainings almost never bent.

Despite the overwhelming value of English in the global language market, within the specific discursive field of human rights training programs, the power of English as an abstract language did not suffice to push Turkish official discourse to its limits. On the contrary, the force of concrete utterances located within the specific communicative situation of human rights trainings overrode the discrepancy between the market values of Turkish and English, and introduced Turkish as the language towards which translations had to be oriented. The force of concrete utterances in human rights training programs was measured against the official state language that served as the norm, regulating the linguistic practices within those trainings. The state language, shared by law enforcement agents, the military, the judiciary, and other state actors, served as "the standard measure of the value of linguistic products" (Bourdieu 1991, 56) that were produced during human rights training programs for government workers in Turkey. In a context in which managing the audience was the primary concern of the training, it was mostly the domesticating method that translators were compelled to employ while translating the speech of foreign experts for government workers. By doing so, translators (and the project teams directing them) modified foreign utterances, sometimes even took actions to ensure that they appeared familiar, acceptable, and legitimate to the training audiences.

Another important takeaway of this chapter is that translation, just like performance, never comes ex nihilo, and that it is citational and reiterative (Butler 1997). This argument is captured by the history of the human rights movement in Turkey, which exposes the current human rights training programs as retranslation processes. The translation events I recounted in this chapter demonstrate that the denial of and distancing from previous human rights translations are an essential part of the current transnational standardization process in Turkey. Against the backdrop of the historical and political context in which human rights were cast as "rights for terrorists," human rights training programs claim the familiarity of the foreign or the domesticity of the universal with an aim to manage the (pre-)established suspect status of human rights rhetoric in Turkey. In order to manage this suspect status, human rights training programs turn to asserting the irrelevance or inaccuracy of previous translations, or they claim the "untranslatability" of the marked idioms of suspect human rights language—like "amnesty." Among other things, these retranslations run the risk of conveying the message that a rights-informed approach to governance is really not that different from what has already been taking place. We can trace the outcome of this message and its effects in the police reaction towards the crowds during recent incidents such as the Gezi Protests, Kobane riots, and the Ankara bombing.

The Turkish government workers' encounters with the transnational and the mediation of the transnational through the politics of translation underlines the processual aspect of these encounters. Translation in human rights training programs corresponds to a field of sociocultural, political management that spatializes, contextualizes, and situates the utterances together with their sources and targets to manage hierarchical structures. As described in Sally Engle Merry's (1979) analysis of dispute management, management of the foreign through translation does not lead to the resolution or settlement of long-standing grievances or prejudices that are associated with human rights or with Europe in the Turkish nationalist imaginary. Rather, this field of management allows government workers to both resist and come to grips with transnational human rights regimes.

As well as providing Turkish government workers with the means to communicate their reactions to these regimes, translation also provides them with the means to figure ways of accommodating these regimes. In the next chapter, I focus on one such method of accommodation—the emergence of the figure of the foreigner as a technology that can be appropriated by government workers to create effects within their own institution. By citing and referencing the foreign in order to strategically borrow its authority, government workers find ways of fitting themselves into the changing governmental structures brought about by Turkey's accession to the EU.

5 DRAMAS OF STATEHOOD AND BUREAUCRATIC AMBIGUITY

As the leader of a dynamic country whose experience in transforming itself is being watched closely by a wide audience, I myself also feel the responsibility to lead by example.
—**Abdullah Gül, Eleventh President of the Republic of Turkey**[1]

IF TRANSNATIONAL STANDARDIZATION PROCESSES—such as those foreseen by Turkey's EU accession—are understood as a field of encounters and negotiations that enable various national and transnational actors to interact and come to terms with each other, then human rights training programs for government workers can be viewed as part of what Mary Louise Pratt (1991) calls "contact zones." According to Pratt, contact zones indicate highly productive social spaces where the opposing parties of deeply asymmetrical power relations meet, clash, and grapple with each other. In addition to forging absolute heterogeneity of meaning through practices of transculturation, bilingualism, collaboration, and miscomprehension, contact zones also include intensive efforts of self-representation on the part of subordinated, marginal groups in response to the assertion of power exercised by dominant parties. Although one could rightfully argue that the power dynamics involved in the relationship between Turkey and the EU are nothing like the violence of colonialism and slavery cited by Pratt, zones of contact between Turkish government workers and representatives of "the imagined Western gaze" (Ahıska 2003) nevertheless feature similar attempts of self-representation by both parties in order to manage and respond to a perceived situation of subordination and dominance that often colors the EU harmonization process.

Whereas in the previous chapter I focused on translation practices to underline the centrality of negotiations and adjustments for human rights training programs, in this chapter I attend to the performances that were enabled by those translations. Typically organized and implemented by a consortium of institutional partners that included state institutions, domestic NGOs, international experts, and EU offices, these training programs constituted sites of encounter where ordinary government workers experienced and interacted with the otherwise abstract "European standards of good governance" in their more tangible forms and as embodied by foreign or domestic human rights experts or representatives of civil society and international institutions. Furthermore, these training programs featured venues where government workers from different offices interacted with one other in a highly monitored and charged social setting.

I argue that it is through these multiple encounters that Turkish government workers come to "know their place"[2] within the larger national governmental mechanism and amidst a highly volatile transnational standardization process. This "knowing" is an active process that includes affirmation, contestation, negotiation, avoidance, and aversion, by which government workers manage what I call the risky business of governance—the slippery terrain of bureaucratic arrangements that shift according to changing constellations of power and influence.

Human rights training programs featured both formal and informal venues of performance, ranging from inauguration events and certificate ceremonies (Image 8) to ice breakers, role-plays, and group presentations employed in the classroom (Image 9). As Erving Goffman (1956) noted, performance in the form of self-presentation happens the moment that people find themselves in the presence of others. Bearing out his observation, both high-level representatives of the state who appeared in ceremonial events and government workers who partook in human rights training programs found themselves in situations requiring them to present themselves in a certain way, in front of an audience that observed them closely. Performances of government workers in front of both national and international audiences in those venues provide us with a useful vantage point to understand the field of governance that they dramatize.

Before moving any further, though, let me clarify some important points about my use of performance as an analytic to study the interactions between government workers and those whom they consider outsiders in human rights trainings. Like process-based studies of society, studies that take performance as their mode of analysis seek to underline the primacy of deviations and deflections from normative frameworks, in an effort to better delineate the improvisational texture of the everyday life (Turner 1986). In doing so, those studies show the ways in which flexibility, flaws, hesitations, and lapses, rather than ideal formal structures, constitute the actual condition of lived realities in a variety of places. One of the most important outcomes of this mode of study is the emergence of ordinary people as a dynamic unit of analysis—as rule breakers, negotiators, strategists, and tricksters, actively taking part to shape their living conditions with varying degrees of success (De Certeau 1984, Scott 1985). Practice- and performance-based studies thus help to make visible the struggles of the poor and the oppressed, and demonstrate how these groups creatively respond to the workings of power by employing various tactics and strategies (Conquergood 1992).

It certainly is a worthy endeavor to focus on marginalized groups with the aim of portraying them as more than passive receivers of policies and order that are often generated elsewhere. However, taking into account national and transnational conditions of power still remains as a necessary component of studying such performances of resistance, which themselves are formulated dialogically within these conditions. In this regard, my focus on the performances of government workers in human rights training programs stands closer to disclosing "the performative nature of power" (Ebron 2002, 5) than attending to forms of resistance that happen at the margins of society. Despite transnational power differentials at play in human rights training programs, Turkish government workers by no means represent a disenfranchised group of people. Even though the hierarchy between Turkey and Europe is deeply engrained within the training settings (by way of positioning the two parties respectively as the learner and the learned), Turkish government workers who are endowed with the privilege to "subject others to authority" (Feldman 2008, 97) cannot really be considered oppressed. On the contrary, by employing various performative strategies to speak back to foreign experts or to mark a situation of cultural intimacy, government workers enact their membership in a powerful hierarchical institution. Performances of Turkish government workers during transnational interactions do not correspond to the response of the powerless to the powerful. They rather indicate competing enactments of power and status, which manifest themselves during hegemonic contestations between national and transnational pillars of governance.

PROTOCOL AND CYNICISM AT HARMONIZATION CEREMONIES

The formal venues of performance in human rights training programs included ceremonial events that were attended by high-level representatives of the state, the NGOs, and the donor agencies (usually the EU). They displayed highly ordered social settings organized according to the bureaucratic protocol that reflected national and transnational hierarchies. Both the performers and audiences at these events knew very well how to read these signs of hierarchy, encoded in the order of appearance, seating assignment, and forms of address.

During these events, representatives of state institutions performed both their role and status by assuming certain forms of address that endowed their self-presentation with an official quality and dramatized their performance by highlighting it with additional markers of hierarchy, such as insisting on speaking before or after the representative of the NGO or the EU, or by demanding to be introduced in a certain way by the training's organizer. In line with Erving Goffman (1956) and Victor Turner (1986), I take dramatization to delineate a specific mode of performance in which the performers not only do things but also show their audiences what they are doing. Dramas as such highlight performances and make apparent the terms and rules of enactment (i.e., the system itself), which might otherwise remain obscure.[3]

The order of appearance in fact proved to be a rather significant part of the ceremonies, closely followed by audiences mostly composed of government workers. Once, for instance, during the closing ceremony of a project for the prevention of domestic violence, the Minister of Women and Family Affairs addressed the audience following the opening remarks of the EU representative. A low-level bureaucrat from the provinces I was sitting next to who had come to Ankara to attend this meeting turned to me and expressed his disapproval by saying, "Wouldn't it be more appropriate if it was our honorable minister who opened the convention?" (*Toplantıyı sayın bakanımız açsaydı daha şık olmaz mıydı?*) This statement not only made clear that the person expressing it was invested in the performance of statehood on the stage during the ceremony. This outspoken disapproval also became the way its speaker performed his membership in state bureaucracy.

Along the same lines, during a press conference to inaugurate a project corun by the Ministry of Interior and the General Directorate for the Status of Women, one of the young employees of the Directorate who was sitting next to me rushed to stand up when she saw that her supervisors had risen to applaud the director's entrance. Getting up in a hurry myself, I asked her whether it was bureaucratic etiquette to rise when a high-level state representative entered the room in these kinds of meetings. She whispered to me: "I guess so. This is my first time and I'm still learning." The sudden rise of a group within the audience to mark the entry of a powerful figure had quite an influence on the rest of the crowd—such as myself—forcing them to stand up as well. While this dramatic act enhanced the performance of statehood by the director by showing respect to the authority she embodied, it also allowed government workers within the audience to dramatize their performance of belonging to the Directorate. By rising upon the entry of the director, government workers employed by the Directorate not only performed their respect to this authority figure but they also showed the rest of the audience how they performed their respect. This is how the young employees of the Directorate, who were attending their first public ceremony, could pick up the rules of this performance to enact them in an appropriate manner next time around.

The presence of a certain kind of audience was an essential component of the situation, which made these ceremonies ripe for multilevel performances. The attendance of the representatives of transnational/foreign institutions such as the EU and several other NGOs that were closely associated with a sense of being under close scrutiny, emphasized the performative quality of such events. Under the eyes of their foreign others, government workers both on and off the stage dramatically enacted their social role and status. However, the foreigners in the room were not the only designated audience for the government workers' performances. By using the imagined gaze of the foreigner as a tool to further accentuate their performances, government workers also performed for their peers, mobilizing nationalist discourses and images that had wide circulation within governmental circles. They particularly employed the availability of translation to that end.

For instance, Hakan, one of the translators I quoted in my last chapter, pointed out that the audiences in training events used translation "to mark their place within the group by interacting with the foreigner in a specific way." In line with Hakan's statement, I also witnessed the audiences often turning Q&A sessions into opportunities for performance by asking challenging questions and raising controversial issues, which via translation could be directed at the foreigners. Hakan claimed that in those instances, government workers in the audience "perform Turkey, perform their institution. They also perform themselves in front of other participants, keeping in mind [the audience's] expectations from someone in their position, their rank . . . They almost make themselves stand out, particularly if they are young."

A good example of these kinds of performances occurred during a large meeting featuring a Canadian speaker presenting a talk titled: "Male Involvement in Ending Violence Against Women." The speaker supported his talk with examples drawn from both developed and developing countries to demonstrate the prevalence of gender inequality and violence against women around the world. Following his presentation, a vibrant discussion took place, featuring representatives of the state and civil society expressing competing views on the status of gender equality, male dominance, and discrimination against women in Turkey. It was not long before the floor was divided between those who found this talk "too feminist" and those who saw it as an opportunity to argue for the necessity of a more gender-sensitive framework for governmental policy. One of the male government workers who took the floor to express his views said: "I don't want to distinguish between the kinds of violence directed against women, men, children, or animals. I also think that it is necessary to talk about the forms of violence that are inherent to the policies of powerful states. No matter what I do, my children will grow up watching Hollywood films full of violence."

A loud round of applause followed this remark. Similar statements followed, articulating the nationalist sensitivity in regard to the hypocritical disposition of powerful Western countries, and expressing the audience's discomfort with the often didactic form of its encounters with the representatives of Western powers. Members of the audience brought up controversial issues such as human rights violations in occupied Iraq or Palestine, the unfavorable conditions of Muslim immigrants in Europe, and past atrocities in Bosnia, in which Western countries were themselves complicit. In a mixed audience composed of government workers and members of civil society, those who made or openly supported these comments marked themselves unquestionably as representatives of the state by performing the official discourse in front of the foreign presenter, members of civil society, and their colleagues. The government worker who made the original comment did not just talk back to a foreign figure whom he perceived to stand for the transnational authority by which he felt oppressed. He also reasserted a position of power that was engrained in the patrimonial framework of bureaucratic structures by tying it to a nationalist performance of standing up to the West in front of an audience that mostly shared his sensibilities.

Compared to their junior colleagues, senior government workers had an even wider range of performative tools that were available to them. For instance, Hakan reported that he often experienced situations in which older, more senior government workers spoke directly to him, asking him to communicate their question to the foreign speaker he was translating for by saying: "*Sor bakalım o zaman beyefendiye/hanımefendiye evladım . . .*" (Well, in that case my child, ask the gentleman/lady . . .). Utilizing the translator in this manner helped senior government workers create two effects: First of all, by re-fusing to talk to the foreign speakers directly, they undermined the position of the speaker as an appropriate interlocutor with whom they could discuss sensi-tive national matters. Secondly, by addressing young translators instead of the speakers, who might be closer to them in age, senior government workers were able to assert their generational authority. In an effort to mediate between gov-ernment workers and foreign speakers by way of managing both parties' utter-ances, Hakan confessed that he rarely communicated this indirect attitude to the foreigners for whom he translated. Even though the reaction that was built into the government workers' indirect form of address was often lost in trans-lation (and therefore went unnoticed by the foreign speaker to whom this at-titude was directed), Turkish-speaking members of the audience were able to follow this subtle performance of dismissal fairly easily.

Dramatizations of statehood in formal ceremonies included both "sincere performances" featuring government workers who "believed in the impression fostered by their own performance," as well as "cynical performances" in which the government workers' belief in their own acts displayed a more complicated nature (Goffman 1956, 10). Government workers who acted out cynical perfor-mances gave mixed messages to different audiences, not hesitating to contra-dict themselves by saying different things on and off the stage. This was the case with Yakup, the Ministry of Justice representative overseeing the juvenile jus-tice training program, whom I already introduced in chapter two.

It was well known from his offstage remarks that Yakup was critical of the training program and that he thought of EU projects in general as a field of op-portunistic gain. I had conversations with him during lunch or coffee breaks when he openly described projects as "dirty work" (*pis işler*) and referred to NGOs who take part in them as "project hunters" (*proje avcıları*). Nevertheless, when he went up to the podium to speak on behalf of his institution, he praised the noble cause of training that promoted the transformation of Turkey's gov-ernmental apparatus according to transnational standards. The wording of his praise, however, was always slightly off and it added a cynical tone to Yakup's per-formance. Here is a passage from Yakup's speech at the final certificate ceremony:

> You know, there are always those kinds of projects in Turkey that finally end up on dusty shelves of the archives. We were wondering whether this would be one of those projects . . . It turned out to be different . . . In the end, we did a very nice job, we achieved beautiful results . . . Our certificates have arrived. These

certificates are different than the ones you're used to . . . For instance, I have numerous certificates at home from the US and other places . . . They all say: Yakup Kaya has participated in this training that took place on this date. They say that I've physically been present at those trainings. They don't say whether I've learned anything. But here, you've really learned something. Both the UNICEF representative and the Undersecretary of the Ministry have signed these certificates manually. They're not print signatures.

The cynicism of Yakup's speech was traceable in his sarcastic references to the recent project inflation in Turkey, to higher bureaucratic authorities who were usually oblivious to the training programs, and to certificates that usually meant little, if anything. Despite the fact that it gave Yakup's performance an insincere appearance, this cynicism did not necessarily render his dramatization of statehood unsuccessful. As many scholars of the state argue, cynicism inherent in the performances of governmental authority or compliance with it does not necessarily render that authority illegitimate or weak.[4] On the contrary, cynicism emerges as a necessary attitude to maintain and enhance contemporary state power and the forms of structural violence and malign neglect by which states rule.

Yakup's cynical enactment of the state in fact added to the authority of his performance by marking him as an insider to the exclusive governmental circles he represented on stage. As Lea (2008) and Steinmüller (2010) both argue, cynical attitude signals both one's access to an intimate order of knowledge that is only available to a closed community and one's self-confidence to cast ironic and deprecating asides regarding that same community. Although on the one hand it indicates a disbelief in the social convention underpinning the community, cynicism on the other hand marks its users as capable social actors who have special access to the making of the social convention they disbelieve. As much as communicating his criticism towards the training programs, Yakup's employment of cynicism in fact established his bureaucratic status as a capable representative of the ministry.

His cynical engagement with human rights training programs also helped Yakup put a healthy distance between himself and harmonization initiatives, widely regarded as politically contingent projects rather than established state policies. Operating in an incoherent field that is made even more volatile as a result of harmonization, Yakup's cynicism helped him engage with human rights and harmonization from a distance, giving him space to reverse his attitude if or when the tide turns. Although cynicism at first glance might suggest a withdrawal from involvement,[5] Yakup's cynical performance did not indicate his disengagement either with the state or with the EU. On the contrary, it was by way of ironic remarks, sarcastic comments, and a cynical attitude that many representatives of the state actively engaged with the EU and all that is brought about—and destroyed—by the accession process in Turkey.

IMPROVISATION AND PARODY IN THE CLASSROOM

Although they took on a particularly spectacular form at the harmonization ceremonies, dramatization and performance were also central to the pedagogical design of human rights training programs. Icebreakers, energizers, case studies, role-plays, and coolers were often utilized to make training sessions participatory and interactive. In addition to preparing the participants for the training, these techniques were also used with the hope of sensitizing government workers with regard to human rights abuses.

In role-playing exercises with grave scenarios such as rape or child abuse, dramatization created a grim environment. In some rare cases, these exercises enabled sincere moments of confession or revelation during which some government workers who may have personally experienced such situations came out and shared their experiences. Once, for instance, during the training for health care workers on the effective documentation of torture, one of the participants—a young, softspoken physician—came out to talk about her own experience of going through examination after being sexually assaulted. Her brave public testimony helped strengthen the training's message that health care workers should take a victim-oriented approach while preparing medical reports. Another example happened during the juvenile justice training, when one of the judge participants talked about his experience of growing up in an orphanage to a small group that included a social worker, a trainer, an organizer, and a translator after dinner over beers. Although this act of sincerity helped bring the people in the group closer, its effect stayed at a more personal level, establishing an understanding between the particular actors who witnessed that act. Unlike the former example, this private personal revelation did not contribute to strengthening the message of the training in the classroom.

Aside from those rare enactments of sincerity, when participants were asked to dramatize their work environment they often did it with exaggeration and mockery, marking performances as parody. Two such parodies that occurred during the juvenile justice training are particularly illuminating:

As part of the weeklong training camp, the trainers encouraged the participants to put together a skit for the evening attractions. The performance, inspired by the popular game show *Saklambaç* (Hide-and-Seek—the Turkish version of the US TV show *The Dating Game*), included three episodes of matchmaking, featuring one police officer looking for his dream prosecutor, and one attorney and one court social worker, each looking for their dream judges. The police officer, the attorney, and the court social worker all prepared questions that mimicked the flirtatious tone of the exchanges that occurred between prospective romantic partners on the original TV show. They posed their questions to three suitors in order to choose their ideal bureaucratic supervisor. The questions all drew heavily on the stereotypes of each professional group, with its working relations and habits. For instance, the police officer asked questions to assess how much of his "off the books" practices each prosecutor would overlook. The attorney asked questions to find out how sympathetic each judge would be towards his defense. The social worker questioned the judges to see which one would give her enough time to prepare the social investigation report and take her report seriously.

This innocent-looking little game in fact crossed many lines, both regarding the norms of relationship between hierarchically positioned government workers and the limits of disclosure about the inner workings of the system in the presence of outsiders. The police officer, who went first, initially generated some laughs, but as things started to heat up, he wrapped up his questions and ended his performance by respectfully kissing the hand of the prosecutor he chose.[6] The young attorney who went for the second round was less successful at managing the situation. He wanted to take advantage of the occasion to critique the judicial system, but he pushed the limits of the parody too far. By the end of his performance the air had turned sour, leaving the court social worker who was next in line panicked about how she was going to handle the rest of the game.

At the end of the skit, everyone involved—including the trainers—agreed that it went terribly. The trainers had to spend the rest of the evening doing damage control, making sure that this unsuccessful parody would not adversely affect the next day's training.

It is instructive to compare this little game of hide-and-seek with another—this time successful—improvisation that was put on display a couple of days later. This second performance was organized as a role-playing exercise in the classroom, in which different government workers assumed each others' positions in a mock trial of three boys facing allegations of extortion and armed robbery (Image 10). As opposed to the previous game, the roles were distributed very carefully to make sure that bureaucratic hierarchy was not upset. The child suspects were played by an attorney and two social workers. A young woman probation officer was given the part of the prosecutor and a woman prosecutor assumed the role of the court social worker. The rest of the parts—the judge, the attorney, the court recorder, and the bailiff—were all played by judges.

The performance opened with the judge ordering the bailiff around in the courtroom and reminding him to go to the bank during the lunch break to take care of some personal business for the judge. Upon judge's orders, the children, looking disheveled and confused, entered along with their attorney. The social worker was summoned and asked whether she had a chance to meet with the defendants. Needless to say, she hadn't. The children were sent out to have a brief consultation with the social worker. The trial resumed after the defendants returned to their places. The judge asked the children their identification information, which they answered in total incoherence. He then asked the prosecutor to read her indictment. The attorney representing the children denied the allegations, adding that her clients were questioned illegally by police officers instead of the prosecutor: They were beaten at the police center and were forced to sign false statements. As the judge went on to question the children, the court recorder announced that she could not record the proceedings because the power just went out.

The performance, frequently interrupted with rounds of applause and laughter, was a total hit. All the actors masterfully performed the dysfunctional, hierarchical operation of the court in a humorous way, with impeccable timing and insight that carried their improvisation to success.[7] As an absolute comedy of errors, the performance displayed the intimate, embarrassing episodes that government workers experienced every day and the shortcuts that they took to manage those situations without upsetting the bureaucratic hierarchy. What primarily made the mock trial successful was the strategic selection of the actors who played each other's parts. With the exception of the young woman probation officer who played the part of the prosecutor, all of the actors were assigned to depict positions that were lower than their rank. That way, when they performed their role with humor, it was not taken as disrespectful and offensive. Neither the judge who played an overly eager bailiff nor the judge who played a combative attorney got the kind of reaction the young attorney in the hide-and-seek game had to face. Contrary to the attorney, the judges who depicted the faults of lower-rank court operatives were regarded as cooperative, perceptive, and funny. The only actor who had to play a part higher than her rank displayed such a self-effacing performance that she got off the hook quite easily. Being a young, attractive, soft-spoken woman and a psychologist by training, the probation officer won the sympathy of her superiors from the beginning. During her performance, when she stood up to read the prosecutor's indictment, she started laughing and begged for prompting. She completed her part with the help of the judges and prosecutors in the audience. As a result, her confession of her inability to mimic the court discourse reinforced the judicial hierarchy rather than unsettling it. As opposed to the hide-and-seek game that turned the tables around by ascribing power over their superiors to lower-rank government workers, the mock trial kept those hierarchies intact.

What was clearly enacted in the mock trial was a field of "social/cultural intimacy" (Herzfeld 1997) and the "flexibility" of doing things (Ahıska 2009, 2010) that defined the commonality upon which the government workers' collective experience/identity was based. As the comparison between the hide-and-seek game and the mock trial reveals, the flexibility of these improvisations, just like the flexibility of the governmental field, was in fact limited by the structure of bureaucratic hierarchies. The extent of flexibility that was available to government workers was proportional to their rank in both real-life situations and their creative reenactments.

Depicted as corruption and arbitrariness in the lexicon of good governance, this uneven flexibility materialized as judges treated the bailiffs like their personal assistants, judges and prosecutors reprimanded attorneys and court social workers, prosecutors let police officers question child suspects, and all the officials wrestled with long working hours, limited resources, and conflicting ethical, professional, and personal imperatives. Nevertheless, as the mock trial also made clear, the only way this embarrassing social intimacy could be performed in front of both foreign and domestic audiences was by way of parody—in a form in which they should not be taken seriously.[8] Thus, performed in a safe way, inefficiencies within the bureaucratic system were confirmed as structural problems that were nobody's fault. It then made sense that in order to manage these problems, government workers had to resort to flexibility. The parody of bureaucratic intimacy ultimately did exactly the opposite of what the designers of the role-playing exercises intended. Instead of sensitizing government workers and inciting them to confront and question their everyday actions, parodies helped safeguard the impression of statehood while confirming the inevitability of the government workers' practices.

THE FOREIGNERS PERFORM BACK

Along with the dramatization of statehood and the performance of national bureaucracy, the presentation of self in the presence of national and international others also enabled government workers to talk back to and confront those whom they considered to be the foreign audiences of national dramas that were taking place in the classroom. When performing before representatives of the imagined Western gaze, Turkish government workers used various methods to engage with those representatives, either directly or through the use of cynicism, and to call on the West for accountability.

As I already alluded to in the previous chapter, government workers appropriated mediated communication via translators to perform themselves and to make powerful statements to confront the foreigners. While in trainings that featured English as the language of communication the inability to speak English could cause exclusion from the realm of interaction, there were times when the participants effectively turned this exclusion around by either refusing to speak directly to foreigners, demanding that foreigners speak in Turkish, or sabotaging translation by mumbling, speaking too fast, using culturally specific idioms, or telling culturally specific jokes. The inability to speak English (as much as the ability to speak it) was employed extensively by trainees to seize the opportunity to talk back to the foreigners.

While translation and the various performances it enabled introduced some effective means of confronting and talking back to the foreigners, conversations with foreign parties at the same time produced some surprising outcomes, too. For one thing, these conversations made government workers realize the heterogeneity and complexity behind seemingly uniform transnational structures. This happened because the contact zones that opened up spaces for performance by government workers contained opportunities for the foreigners to perform back, also by using tools of dramatization and self-presentation. See, for instance, the following quote, taken from a training program on women's human rights, featuring an exchange through translation between Erhan, a prosecutor, and Maria, the chief trainer from Ecuador who worked for the UN Security Council:

> *Erhan*: Forgive me, but it's so rare that I get to interact with a representative of the UN, I can't help but ask a question that I've been bottling up inside for so long . . . Do you really think that the UN is an organization that works to maintain world peace? In Rwanda, for example, people were slaughtered with blades provided by France—a member of the UN Security Council. Where was the UN? In Cambodia, people were buried in the rice fields.

Where was the UN? In Bosnia, thousands of Bosnians and Croatians were massacred. Where was the UN? Most of the human rights violations in the world are perpetrated by members of the UN Security Council . . . Do you really think that the UN is living up to its promises under these conditions?

Maria: Absolutely not! I wouldn't have had the shame, blood in me if I wouldn't have [sic] agreed with you . . . And I am speaking here as a human rights expert. Someone who has worked for a long time on human rights . . . I totally agree with you that the UN is not acting as it should. The Security Council members are the most powerful countries of the world. Most of the weapons trafficking is done by the same countries . . . So, why do I work there? I keep working there because there are 5 countries holding power but 120 member countries. Sooner or later the right thing will be done. Where was the UN during Rwanda? You know where? They were sitting in New York trying to decide who should be in power, bureaucratic procedures. These are the realities of war . . . The UN is not there, but people such as myself are there, I assure you. Not many, but I assure you they are there.

This interaction, depicting a moment when the performance of national sensitivity by Erhan was reciprocated with an equally powerful performance of transnational human rights sensibility on the part of Maria, signified a moment of rupture when the foreign expert emerged as more than a representative of the Western gaze embedded in international human rights structures. Conversations like this, in which foreigners turned around and put on an unexpected performance, created a fissure in the widespread nationalist narrative about the figure of the foreign. The extent to which this fissure might change how government workers think about human rights, however, remained quite vague. Following the training in which this conversation took place, all of the participants I interviewed praised the trainer for her courage and honesty in coming out and articulating the controversies in the UN's human rights policies. However, it became all the more clear to them that human rights could not be detached from the systems of governance underlying their practice.

Even though such performances by foreign experts did not necessarily change how Turkish government workers saw human rights, they nevertheless affected how this group received those foreigners. These performances enabled by personal contact, which might even establish friendships at an individual level, complicated the idea of the foreigner as a suspicious figure waiting to destroy the country. Long-term training programs in which government workers spent time with the project team and foreign experts were more likely to generate interactions that might cause personal rapprochements. At those times, a foreigner's influence and position of power transformed this figure into an effective tool that Turkish government workers could employ strategically to navigate the mazes of national bureaucracy.

Although Maria's performance had a surprising effect on government workers participating in the training program on women's rights, her strategic self-representation was not a singular event by any means. In fact, many people I spoke with who were involved in human rights training programs reported a visible transformation over time in the profile of the foreigners who came to Turkey to serve as experts or trainers. For instance, Nilay, a translator from the previous chapter, stated that unlike their colleagues from ten to fifteen years ago, the foreign experts who were recently sent to Turkey were very knowledgeable and sensitive towards the norms of conduct within the national bureaucratic realm in Turkey. These foreigners who "knew their places/limits" (*hadlerini bilen*) within the complex cultural and institutional hierarchies maintained appropriate bodily dispositions, proper attire, and a correct attitude when interacting with Turkish government workers. Counteracting the stereotype of detached, condescending international experts in similar developmental settings (Coles 2002), these humble experts were received much more positively within the governmental circles populating human rights training programs.

This revision in the self-presentation of the foreigners seldom indicated a change on a personal basis. Rather, this revision was first and foremost an institutional strategy employed by organizations providing technical assistance for human rights training programs. This strategy was especially evident in the selection of the individual experts who would be representing these organizations in training seminars. During my fieldwork, I noticed that even though there were still experts coming from Western European countries such as the Netherlands and Denmark, foreign human rights experts were increasingly composed of the nationals of countries such as Albania, Georgia, and Ecuador. Although most of them lived and worked in the US or Western Europe, these experts still had the ability to situate themselves and address their audiences in ways that were not available to their Western European colleagues. For instance, Edan, the Albanian human rights law expert commissioned by the Swedish NGO providing technical assistance to the human rights training for judges and prosecutors, chose to begin his session with the following remark:

> At the hotel [where] I am staying, the young man at the desk asked me where I am from, and I said, "I am Albanian." He said, "Albanian? Really?" And he said, "Oh, then we are *kardaş, kardaş* (brothers, brothers)." It is true. There is a big Turkish influence in Albania, so many words we have in common. And I know that there is a big Albanian influence in Turkey, too. So I feel equal in front of you . . . We are equal, so interrupt me whenever you like.

Edan's national origin helped him position himself as equal to the trainees as per the number-one rule of the adult education technique. Furthermore, his national origin equipped him with additional tools to further perform his affinity with training participants by explicitly stating his country's shortcomings in the field of human rights. Before he started talking about human rights in Turkey, Edan stated the following:

> I come from Albania, which is an interesting case study, having problems similar to maybe your country . . . In Albania, after forty-five years of communist regime, in 1991 everything had to change. Nevertheless, most of the judges and prosecutors were trained [during the communist era] and they operate in the communist mentality . . . Let me give you an example from my country . . . I will give an example from my country because I know that it is a messed-up country.

Whereas training programs asked participants to perform and discuss the social/cultural intimacies that defined the governmental field in Turkey, these not-so-foreign experts found ways of reciprocating those performances by explicitly recounting the intimate embarrassments that underpinned their own national condition. Throughout the seminar, Edan did not refrain from articulating the problems of his "messed-up country" in front of his own others. In a similar vein, Maria gave examples of legal malpractice and patriarchal mentality in Ecuador's courtrooms before asking her audience about comparable practices in Turkey. When I asked her to explain why she chose to address her audience in this particular way and why she situated herself in the training as she did, Maria said that in the past she had been in the same position as the trainees, and therefore was capable of understanding where they were coming from:

> You know, I had the same reaction as a trainee myself. These people used to come and tell us—we used to call them "white blond stools [sic] with blue

eyes"—they [would] tell us how things should be, and it is reactionary . . . [The trainees] are all prosecutors and judges. They are persons in positions of power who are coming to this seminar . . . because they are compelled by the minister of justice to attend . . . And on top of that I say "And you must do as we have done!" Of course [they] are going to hate [it] . . . And even more, I will create a resistance against the knowledge, against the message that I want to get through . . . So, the pedagogical tool is the reverse. I am here to learn. You see? Number one, we are equals. We come from the same roots. My society is the same [as yours] . . . And of course if this [trainer] is a man, if this is a male coming from the first world—tall, blond, blue eyes, or tall or short but speaking in English, he is in a big, big problem and disadvantage [sic], number one, because he himself believes he is superior, while he is absolutely despised by the people he is trying to teach . . . [Instead] if you come and say: "I have been in the same position and now I want to learn about your opinion, give me your opinion so that I will understand," the barriers are erased. And then we can talk.

Although she was a UN employee who was commissioned by the Swedish human rights NGO providing technical assistance for the training, throughout the entire seminar Maria made sure that her self-presentation did not hinge upon what those two institutions stood for. She even made effective use of the Swedish representative of the NGO observing the seminar, joking that "the Scandinavian blond skinny lady in the room" was surely clueless about what the trainer and trainees were talking about. Underlining her difference from the parties usually associated with the transnational expertise in such training environments, Maria carefully revised the system of classification ordering the stratification of the training. The antinomy between Maria and the "blond skinny lady" helped her designate the trainees and herself as "us"—putting Maria and the trainees in the same boat against "the Scandinavians" and their kind.

These unorthodox ways in which the untypical "non-Western" foreign experts performed themselves in human rights training programs corresponded to a strategic re-presentation of the transnational, designed for a better reception of the human rights regimes for audiences such as the ones in Turkey. With the hope of persuading Turkish government workers to embrace the universal in this way, the "non-Western" representatives of transnational NGOs sought to disconnect the universal from "the West," with which it is usually associated. These nonintrusive, non-condescending experts and pedagogical approaches intentionally emphasized connectedness by performing the similarity between the foreign emissary and the national situation. The unintended consequence of this approach, however, was to give trainees the message that "the universal" was just another "other." Needless to say, the success and the effects of this endeavor to disconnect the universal from "the West" were situational, and they coexisted with a frequent opposite tendency to collapse and conflate all things foreign.

THE POWER OF THE FOREIGN

One of the most significant (and surprising) outcomes of the strategic revision of the representation of the transnational in harmonization projects was the materialization of the image of the foreigner as a Janus-faced figure with a dual effect: Both an external impostor that intervenes in things that are not his or her business and a powerful possible ally that is capable of pushing for change. The power of the foreign, which civil society had widely and effectively employed in the past to speak out against the Turkish state, hereafter became available within the governmental realm as a result of the encounters at harmonization projects.

This newfound "promise of the foreign" (Rafael 2005) was at times strategically appropriated by some government workers to push back against institutional structures that put them at a disadvantage. A good example of such an appropriation was the training program organized by Amnesty International (AI) in collaboration with the Presidency of Religious Affairs (*Diyanet*) to educate male and female religious officials on discrimination and violence against women. Although both AI and *Diyanet* saw the trainings as a way to reach the larger public, the women employees of *Diyanet* quickly turned these events into tools for their own empowerment. Once the program was approved by the administration, both women bureaucrats who were employed in the *Diyanet* headquarters and women religious officials who were working at the local levels took over the organization and planning of the trainings to create an opportunity to challenge the masculinist hegemony that conditioned their own working environments.[9]

Similarly, Nazan, a young woman prosecutor stationed in a mid-Anatolian city who was also the only woman participant in the training for judges and prosecutors on women's human rights, sought alliance with the women trainers and organizers in order to seek refuge from the sexism that prevailed in her own institution. As a result of her honest criticisms of her colleagues' patriarchal dispositions, Nazan was invited to participate in a post-training roundtable meeting with the representatives of women's groups that provided technical assistance to similar trainings. At the meeting, Nazan gave a presentation reporting how some judge participants openly admitted to manipulating the testimonies of domestic violence victims in order to assess reduced punishments for the perpetrators. Akin to the women employees of *Diyanet*, Nazan developed relationships with the non-governmental, foreign figures she encountered during the training for building support networks that were not available within her workplace.

Needless to say, this shift in the "political culture towards the foreign" (Spadola 2004) that redefined the foreigner as a resource rather than an obstacle was highly situational and inchoate. Nevertheless, it had substantial effects in various government offices, at times shaping the ways other "outsiders" of the governmental realm (such as domestic NGOs) were perceived. I witnessed such an occasion featuring an interaction between the representatives of an NGO working with the Ministry of Justice on several projects on prisons and detention centers and some employees of the ministry, when I joined the NGO for a visit to the Ministry's headquarters following an eventful replacement of the director general of prisons and detention houses. The replacement of the director general was widely attributed to internal power struggles within the ministry. The NGO representatives wanted to visit the new director general to introduce themselves, inform him about the projects they ran with the previous director general, and learn whether it would be possible to continue working in the prisons under the new administration. Following a formal meeting with the new director general, the NGO representatives and some ministry employees sat down together to assess the situation. Here is an excerpt from my field notes capturing the dialogue between Zeki, the NGO representative, and Fehmi, the ministry employee:

Zeki: I feel like we had a positive meeting. I was wondering how the [new director general's] attitude would be about working with the civil society. If he was against it, I would have sensed it.

Fehmi: I agree. I already explained the situation to him before you came. How we worked very well in the past. How working together with the civil society is now an established state policy.

Zeki: Of course! I mean there are two very specific laws around it.

Fehmi: Yes . . . I mean we definitely want to continue doing projects. But there might be some delays due to the new administration. I particularly want us to prioritize the juvenile detention centers . . . We also want to continue taking law school students to detention houses.

> *Zeki*: We want to continue our project with the prison psychologists. Do we
> need any permits for that? How should we obtain them?
>
> *Fehmi*: If you need anything, just contact me. Permits would take a long time.
> Procedures, reports . . . It's a lot of bureaucracy . . . You just come directly
> to me.
>
> *Zeki*: Great, so we'll just tell them that Mr. Fehmi from the Ministry is taking
> care of it.
>
> *Fehmi*: Sure . . . We want to keep doing projects, but we have some financial
> problems at the moment . . . Believe me, we can barely feed the prisoners.
> I mean the projects and education are important, of course. But we have to
> feed our people first.
>
> *Zeki*: We may be able to solve the financial situation for you. The Netherlands
> Embassy was very pleased with the project we proposed last time. We might
> be able to keep getting money from them.

This dialogue neatly captures how Fehmi, who occupied a specific position of power within the ministry, made an effective use of both the NGO's visit and the work of the NGO to assess the shift in the balance of power within his institution and to calculate how the new administration will affect his position. For these purposes, Fehmi and his colleagues mobilized the institutional outsider both to realize their agenda with regard to the changes they would like to see in the detention houses and to access external (financial, political, social) resources to gain leverage within the ministry.

As much as it was triggered by a deliberate reconfiguration of the transnational at the harmonization projects, this increasing strategic deployment of the foreigner within governmental circles was in fact made possible due to the uneven, patchy quality of the state, an observation by anthropologists working in various places.[10] As those studies have already shown, "the state" in Turkey and elsewhere does not correspond to a monolithic entity. As one of its most prominent theorizers put it, the state rather resembles a field of competing positions, dispositions, relations, performances, and practices that are occupied, embodied, and carried out in concrete hierarchical social situations to gain recognition and legitimacy for power and influence over the control of official resources (Bourdieu [1977] 1999). Envisioned as a site of struggles, this field is an entity defined by the shared "fundamental presuppositions," "investments," and "beliefs" among the parties involved "in the value of what is at stake in the struggles they are waging" (Thompson in Bourdieu 1991).

One could argue that this patchy quality of the state became even more pronounced in Turkey during the AKP rule. Throughout the four terms that it reigned, different components of national bureaucracy—including the army, the judiciary, and the police—became battlefields for the party to establish itself as the uncontested sovereign authority. Since it first came to power in 2002, AKP has incessantly made and broken alliances with different bureaucratic offices (and competing groups seeking to establish hegemony in them) that are divided over social, political, and economic agendas. The struggle between different groups that make up state institutions thus influenced how the figure of the foreigner would be deployed in order to create effects in the governmental realm.

THE RISKY BUSINESS OF GOVERNANCE

To conclude this chapter, I would like to elaborate on some important aspects of the performances I described so far, in order to point out the insights that they provide for an understanding of the governmental field in Turkey. Yakup's cynical enactment of statehood, the two improvisations at the juvenile justice training, and Fehmi's strategic use of the outsider to manage his institution's unstable conditions all underline the prominence of risk in those performative situations. When performing in and for their institutions, government workers had to deal with a field that was uneven, unpredictable, and volatile, despite its widespread normative depiction as a stable and monolithic entity.

As Fehmi had strategically used a non-governmental entity to test the grounds of his institution, the participants of juvenile justice training tested the limits of their place within the larger bureaucratic machinery through improvisation. Yakup's cynicism towards the EU and its byproducts can be seen as another way of managing the instability of the bureaucratic realm as it undergoes transformation. Yakup displayed a cynical attitude towards human rights trainings in part because he wanted to avoid close association with programs that might cause him trouble in the future.

In his study on risk, ritual, and performance, Leo Howe (2000) argues against the classification established by Lévi Straus, which posits ritual in opposition to games in which players can come off as either winners or losers. Contrary to Lévi Straus' assertion, Howe claims that ritual performances involve as much risk as plays or games because they convey much more than merely following the rules of the ritual. While in general I find it useful to think of performance as containing an essential element of risk, I nevertheless think that the evidence Howe provides to support his argument renders the rules themselves as uncontested, established determinants. Contrary to this depiction, a close look at the governmental realm in Turkey reveals that the rules that organize this realm can be as volatile and effervescent as their practices and performances. What makes performance risky is first and foremost the indeterminate character of the rules themselves.

Although bureaucratic reform appears inherent in the harmonization framework that regulates the governmental realm in Turkey, an overinvestment in reform might end up causing some government workers to one day disappear from their offices. During my over two-year tenure as a researcher and worker in human rights training programs, I witnessed several government workers who served as the contact people for various EU projects get mysteriously re-appointed to virtually inactive positions in their institutions. This led government workers both on and off the stage at human rights trainings to take reform policies and projects with a grain of salt. Government workers in trainings and elsewhere performed their duties and presented themselves with the knowledge that government policies, as well as government employment, rested on extremely slippery ground. Even though harmonization and reform appeared to be an established state policy, this appearance by no means guaranteed what was going to happen tomorrow from the perspective of the people who worked for the state.

Both Fehmi and Yakup's enactments of their positions and their self-presentations in their respective governmental circumstances were attempts to grapple with this extremely precarious entity called the state. While on the one hand their duty compelled them to perform various attributions of statehood such as grandiosity, reverence, strength, and perseverance, on the other hand their position in this ostensibly stable constellation forced them to be cynical and calculative in their engagement.

What gets confirmed in the government workers' cynical performances in human rights trainings is the level of ambiguity inherent to organizational practices and bureaucratic structures. Contrary to the perception of both bureaucracy and standardization as ambiguity reducing, secrecy, uncertainty, and incalculability are in fact central to their operation (Anand 2015, Best 2012, Feldman 2008, Mathews 2008). The same operational vagueness and opacity are also encountered in grant/aid economies, whereby perceived inequities in the distribution of material and social capital, fortune, and justice lead to gossip, rumors, and accusations of malevolence on the part of grant givers and receivers (James 2012). Faced with all this ambiguity that emanates from both government work and the harmonization industry, government workers in human rights trainings generally employed a risk-aversive attitude. They took great pains not to make a commitment in an official capacity. In the trainings I participated in, the powerful narratives of violation and suffering at times moved some participants. Even so, those who were moved made it clear that all they could promise was a heightened personal awareness and sensitivity. They stressed that they were not speaking on behalf of their institutions—that they did not have authorization to make institutional commitments.

Failing to constrain or contain ambiguity in the bureaucratic domain, human rights training programs did not end up producing institutional responsibility, accountability, or transparency. The pedagogical spaces of human rights trainings instead produced a certain community of knowers that coalesced around the performances of embarrassing intimacies. I conclude the book with an elaboration of those communities.

CONCLUSION
Of Fragments and Violations

IN HIS BOOK *The Nervous System*, Michael Taussig writes: "There is no anthropology of the ruling class that rules over us, just as there is no sociology of it either . . . Failing that revelation, we fall back to our fantasies about the center, fantasies that in some curious back handed and effortless manner constitute that center" (1992, 134). Moving from similar concerns, the primary goal of this book has been to undo the fantasies attributed to both the state and the EU accession in Turkey. The fetishism that surrounds both of those entities—the fetishism that derives from the fantasies that endow them an "auratic and quasisacred quality" (116)—continues to shape the experiences of the state at the margins and the center. More often than not, these experiences take on a violent form. Although the majority of this book has been dedicated to displaying the fragmented and contested condition of the Turkish state, this does not take away from the gravity of violations and acts of injustice that are carried out in its name. No matter how uneven and patchy it may be, this constellation still holds the capacity to inflict death and suffering on many people inside and outside its jurisdiction.

This capacity for violence materializes in the heavy assaults carried out periodically in the Kurdish regions that kill, maim, and banish people from their homes, in the government's increasing control over the media by means of intimidation and arrests, and in the widespread criminalization of different oppositional sectors within the society who dare to demand accountability, justice, and peace—all in the name of the continuation/perpetuity of the state (*devletin bekası*).[1] Europe's implication in this state of affairs becomes traceable in the competing references made to its various constituents in order to both contest and legitimize the aforementioned securitization practices. While the victims seek to appeal to various EU bodies, the European Court of Human Rights, and the European public to activate a human rights sensibility, those who plan, implement, and support the armed operations, round-the-clock curfews, impeachments, bans, and censorship rely on the national security paradigm that is endorsed by the very same parties, activated most recently in the border control agreement signed between Turkey and the EU.

All of those experiences of state violence bring to the fore one question that has to be engaged with in light of the evidence presented in this study: Despite the fragmented, contested, uneven condition of the governmental realm that manifests itself in the human rights training programs, a tremendous stability arises from the violence that is inflicted via various mechanisms of the state.[2] How to make sense of this? How can we account for the coexistence of the consolidated, blatant display of violence and the volatile, precarious nature of the bureaucratic field in Turkey? I wish to address this question, as I conclude, by further elaborating the outcome of bureaucratic intimacies that are exhibited throughout the encounters between Turkish government workers and their various partners in harmonization projects.

As I have demonstrated in the preceding chapters, one of the most important products of human rights training programs is an active performance of cultural intimacy that defines the world of government workers as they engage with the delineation of the bureaucratic field in line with professionalism and expertise. These bureaucratic intimacies are enacted as the government workers protest, contest, question, and complain about the new governmental standards that are promoted in these programs and as they confide, confess, and pour out their grievances about their off-the-books practices that are condemned in the meantime. In line with the translation of human rights into bureaucratic rationalization and the establishment of good governance in the country, those off-the-books practices government workers resort to while managing their daily work are cast as the primary reason leading to human rights violations. Aiming to both respond to what they consider to be foreign impositions and redeem their governmental legitimacy, government workers draw from a range of repertoires pertaining to bureaucratic distinction, self-sacrifice, paternalistic care, and nationalistic sensitivity that mark their position as insiders to both the national order and the bureaucratic field in Turkey.

As Michael Herzfeld (2015) underlines in his definition of cultural intimacy, this mark of belonging primarily rests on a set of collective secrets that are internally uniting and externally embarrassing, which provide a resource for in-group solidarity. He also notes that this cultural intimacy becomes particularly manifest in transnational encounters featuring unequal parties. The high-stake situation that arises from the obligation to put on a specific form of self-display—one that runs counter to the national reality—paradoxically results in an overflow of the performance of those collective secrets. Similar to Herzfeld's formulation, Taussig (1999) also maintains that public secrets, which form the very basis of society, social formations, and power, exhibit a highly performative character. The efficacy of public secrets relies on their spectral radiance in everyday life, with the members of society acting "as if" they do not know "that which is known by everyone." Public/collective secrets, thus, operate amidst "an uncanny dialect of concealment and revelation" (Surin 2001, 206), and their social value depends on "being palpable and performed" (Herzfeld 2015, 25) more than being hidden and invisible.

This incitement to tell that which has to remain secret takes on a specific form, which can also be traced in the human rights training programs in Turkey. As I demonstrated in my depiction of translation events and performative situations that saturate these training programs, government workers respond to the training by experimenting with the boundaries of the sayable and unsayable in the presence of their multiple others. While some government workers make contradictory remarks inside and outside of the classroom, others deepen the sincerity of their statements by filling in the elusions of what they publicly said during more intimate conversations at lunch or coffee breaks. Still some others police what their colleagues, translators, or trainers reveal during the training by interjecting remarks and demanding that the ongoing conversations be stopped. Regardless of their particular outlook, what lurks behind all of those performances is an intimate order of truth that is alluded to both in the telling and untelling of public secrets.

As Meltem Ahıska (2009, 2010) argues, this intimate order of truth in Turkey corresponds to "an ostensibly flexible field" of doing things that predominantly shapes both the society and the state. This flexibility materializes in the creative solutions people find to compensate for the lack of resources, the shortcuts that they take to avoid bureaucratic red tape, and the mobilization of personal connections to manage a governmental situation that is already executed arbitrarily. In the official realm, this flexibility sometimes takes a routine institutional form, exemplified in the "cleansing" operations that Ahıska refers to in her work, where directors in public institutions commonly wipe out the traces of previous administrations by burning documents, demolishing buildings, and reappointing the personnel. More violent enactments of this flexibility include forced disappearences under custody, extrajudicial killings, arbitrary arrests, and states of emergency that are used to dissolve the rule of law in what are considered to be "suspect" geographies.

As Ahıska also maintains, the presence of different registers of truth—an intimate order alongside an official one—brings forth mechanisms of boundary management, where external and internal truths are manifested in various and calculated ways via different statements and practices. Looking at human rights training programs where similar practices take place, we see that boundary management involves telling as much as hiding. As I demonstrated in my chapter on translation, although government workers often intervene in translation processes to keep the state language intact, this reactionary stance coexists with a seemingly paradoxical urge to tell some selected outsiders the truth. Similarly, although performances of statehood include episodes in which government workers demonstrate a rehearsed enactment of their institutions in official capacity, performative situations inside and outside the classroom also include cynicism, improvisation, and parody, in which embarrassing secrets of intimate orders are revealed, albeit in a form they cannot be critically engaged with.

One striking example of these revelations happened during the police training on the prevention of domestic violence. The trainer of the session, Chief Inspector Sertan, tried to appease the participants' protests that the new procedure concerning the handling of domestic abuse victims was infeasible. Speaking to the complaints about understaffed police centers that would complicate the implementation of the procedure, Chief Inspector Sertan jokingly asked me to cover my ears for a minute. Then he delivered a passionate lecture about how if they called the police officers napping in the patrol cars back on duty and refused to send officers to chase random personal business upon the prosecutors' or the governors' whimsical demands, police chiefs would surely have enough people to run the centers properly. During his lecture, the participants smiled and nodded with a combination of embarrassment and amusement, with the recognition of a common sociality that confirmed that their trainer was one of them. In another instance, while explaining the benefits of professionalization within the police, Sertan invoked some off-the-books practices police officers often employ to manage their workload. Listing a number of code words such as "aspirin," "novalgin," "baby aspirin," and "grippin" that refer to various extralegal remedies utilized in policing, he continued: "Think of the difference between interrogating and taking testimony. We started taking testimonies only recently. Before, we used to interrogate. When I say the difference between interrogation and taking testimony, I believe it must be only Elif Hanım who doesn't understand what I'm talking about . . ." Giggles from the audience erupted immediately.

In both instances, the revelation of inner truths concerning extralegal, violent practices of the police, which alluded to the intimate order that organizes the force, happened not only despite but also with a clear acknowledgement of my presence as an outsider. Although those revelations were arguably made with an underlying message of disapproval, and were utilized as evidence for the necessity of police reform, I encountered similar revelations at other times, some of which referred to even more violent practices. Once, for example, during the juvenile justice test training, a young woman police officer told me in a private conversation over lunch how she likes to beat up adolescent boys who are brought to the police center with allegations of extortion, and who protest their apprehension by cursing at her using sexual remarks. She gave details about how she asks two of her male colleagues to hold the boys by each arm and how she kicks their genitals because it makes them most ashamed. On yet another occasion a gendarme officer confessed during the coffee break that even though he strictly denied the use of violence against the Kurdish youth in the previous class, he often encountered confined Kurdish boys who are tied up in stress positions by lower-rank soldiers.

As shocking as these episodes might be, it is important to step back for a minute to think more about their effects on the boundaries of the intimate orders that they reveal. I argue that these unexpected and complex practices/ performances of telling/not telling in human rights training programs ultimately expand the community of insiders to the bureaucratic intimacy in Turkey. With the expansion of the governmental field in line with a good governance paradigm as foreseen by harmonization, this field now includes members of civil society, experts, translators, and in some instances even foreigners, who as a result of their close encounters with Turkish government workers come to possess the knowledge of the local mechanisms of power. This insider knowledge includes the secrets of the ostensibly flexible field of national bureaucracy and the means of its management. The knowledge of this intimate order of truth that in Herzfeld's words is a source of embarrassment also includes the involvement of government workers in human rights violations via acts of abandonment as well as acts of cruelty and care. An important outcome of this exposure to the performances of bureaucratic intimacy is the understanding it generates of those violations. Witnessing the narratives of contingency, precarity, material hardship, and neglect that surround the worlds of government workers, the experts, trainers, organizers, and translators of training programs develop a particular understanding of those worlds and their products.

Human rights training programs, thus, generate a community of knowers of bureaucratic secrets while attempting to forge a community of believers in human rights values. Strategies of the participatory adult education framework seek to establish an egalitarian, judgment-free, and sincere learning environment where the trainees can talk openly without fear, and transform as a result of those open discussions. Rather than a sincere belief in human rights values or a dutiful submission to national and transnational human rights regimes, those open discussions form an association that is loosely tied around a common understanding of what the state really corresponds to in Turkey.

This common understanding does not necessarily bring sympathy or tolerance for the violations perpetrated by government workers. The knowledge of the intimate bureaucratic order in fact generates a multitude of sentiments and dispositions. As I laid out in various chapters, while some members of civil society such as Nesrin (Chapter 3) come out with a more nationalistically oriented human rights sensibility as a result of their engagement with government workers, others such as Fehmi (Chapter 5) look for ways to strategically use their newly acquired insider knowledge to deepen their access into government offices with the hope of making a difference. While some expert trainers such as Dr. Simden (Chapter 2) are able to mobilize their insider status to draw from a particular professional ethics to cultivate political consciousness, promote a progressive pro-human rights message, and conclude the training on a more hopeful note, others such as Oya and Selma (Chapter 2) feel increasingly hopeless the more they learn about the impasses inherent in everyday governmental situations.

The multitude of dispositions among this group finds its reflection in the variety of feelings and attitudes among the government workers themselves. As I also laid out previously, human rights trainings generate an array of bearings among the trainees, too. Whereas upper-level bureaucrats such as Yakup (Chapter 5) display an openly cynical attitude, lower-level functionaries such as Hasibe, Gizem, and Fatma (Chapter 2) grapple with feelings of frustration due to the disparity between their actual working conditions and the aspired-to standards of governance. While the trainings' emphasis on professionalism empowers some government workers, such as Superintendent Fırat (Chapter 2), to engage in expert dialogues with more elite officials such as judges or prosecutors, others, such as Judge Neriman (Chapters 1 & 2), become resentful of accusations of "too much" (i.e., oppressive) care.

Although their shared knowledge of the intimate bureaucratic order unites these otherwise disparate actors by marking them as insiders in the bureaucratic field in Turkey, their level of belonging varies according to their profession, rank, status, gender, and age. These different levels of belonging also determine the level of access different insiders have to public secrets. It is important to stress that I do not claim to have equal knowledge of extralegal police activities with Chief Inspector Sertan or other police officers. Nevertheless, his open reference to a host of generally known but officially unacknowledged tools of policing in my presence makes obvious an implicit shared knowledge. This gesture has the double effect of both bestowing upon me some sort of insider status and taking away the shame in openly discussing the violent practices of the police. When combined with other intimate secrets—such as inefficient organization, undereducated, overburdened staff, and underserved facilities— these violent shortcuts suddenly become understandable, if not acceptable. It is this understanding that emanates from the community of knowers emerging from human rights training programs.

This community of knowers does not exactly correspond to a community of complicity that Hans Steinmüller (2010) describes in his study of state formation and the use of cynicism in China. To argue that the group of trainers, experts, organizers, and translators that are involved in human rights training programs all become complicit in the violations perpetrated by the state would be empirically inaccurate and unfair. The knowledge and understanding that this community shares instead breeds a certain form of shamelessness[3] that renders the previously embarrassing events openly sayable. The good governance paradigm puts the reform-oriented, developmental, pedagogical engagement of human rights training programs as an alternative to the naming and shaming strategy that human rights defenders have traditionally resorted to in Turkey. While taking away the shame in stating the intimate order of truth that underpins the governmental realm, the format and context of trainings (and the particular form those statements must take) prevent the training parties from really confronting the violence of that order. What is more, the revelation of extralegal, unacknowledged, violent practices of government workers that are mostly sanctioned at the official level ultimately fails to produce any legal-administrative (as well as moral-ethical) consequences. This, I argue, is the most significant outcome of the bureaucratic intimacies that are exhibited throughout human rights training programs in Turkey.

What happens when a public secret that belongs to the intimate order of truth crosses the boundary to become publicly registered, but that registration fails to bring any consequences? A possible answer can be found in the recent court case concerning the extrajudicial killings that happened in the Kurdish town of Cizre between the years 1993 and 1995, in which all the defendants were acquitted "due to a lack of sufficient, credible evidence."[4] In the final hearing, answering a question about his membership in the infamous clandestine counterguerilla organization JITEM (Gendarmerie Intelligence and Counter-Terrorism), one of the defendants declared: "I did my duty. I have not participated in anyone's death. I have not worked at JITEM. I do not know what JITEM is. I only know of Je t'aime. And that means I love you in French."[5]

JITEM, which has been the primary mechanism of extrajudicial securitization practices throughout the Kurdish regions since the 1980s, and whose existence before 2005 is still contested officially, is perhaps the most notorious public secret that constitutes the intimate order of truth in Turkey. While this is so, the level of shamelessness that surrounds the aforementioned testimony demonstrates the robustness of the mechanisms of impunity that are at play in the governmental realm. This indirect performance of state violence via sarcasm is a blatant display of its performers' confidence in those mechanisms. Taking away the shame in talking about human rights violations (such as those undertaken by JITEM) and failing to punish the perpetrators in the meantime leads to the further enforcement of impunity, as well as boosting the violators' confidence in it.

Regularization of the governmental realm via standardization of norms, institutions, procedures, personnel, and facilities seldom curbs governmental power. Instead, it surrounds that power with an aura of legitimacy. Reorganization of the bureaucratic field according to stipulations of professionalism and expertise ultimately transforms state violence into governmental force by rendering it more calculable, technical, and exacting.[6] Human rights training programs add a further twist to this transformation by expanding the boundaries of the bureaucratic field in Turkey, providing spaces for experimenting with what is sayable within that expanded field, and drawing out the shame in playfully performing public secrets. These unforeseen, perhaps unintended, consequences of bureaucratic reform in Turkey explain why the harmonization process does not necessarily lead to a less violent form of governance in the country.

It is true that harmonization intensifies the fragmented nature of the state and that it also adds to the slipperiness of the governmental realm, as well as to the repertoires of its management. The unexpected sites of alliance between governmental and non-governmental figures also testify to the fact that restoring the power and reach of the state through good governance does not entirely preclude the sites of resistance to it. Nevertheless, the increasing state violence that accompanies this contested makeup should serve as a reminder that aggressive state practices do not necessarily hinge on a consolidated organizational structure. My aim in this book has been to expose by way of ethnographic engagement that governmental mechanisms (including national and transnational human rights networks) are inhabited by multiple, diverse actors who occupy this field with varying stakes. Ultimately, my hope is that this exposition would contribute to the efforts demanding accountability and justice for the violations perpetrated by those mechanisms.

NOTES

INTRODUCTION

1. Steedman 1992, 76.

2. The riots were the culmination of a number of government policies that fueled the dissent of Gezi protesters. These included increased pressure on organized labor through privatization and subcontracting, drafting of legislation to limit women's reproductive rights, stricter regulation of the sale of alcohol, increasingly sectarian Sunni-oriented policies that led the government's war against the Asad regime in Syria, naming the new Bosphorus bridge after the Ottoman Sultan Yavuz Süleyman, who had ordered a massive Alevi slaughter, and government proposals to build new hydroelectric and nuclear plants. In Istanbul, the number of people who joined the protests reached 1.5 million people, corresponding to 16 percent of the city's population. (Yörük and Yüksel 2014).

3. Although Gezi Park continues to exist at the time of this writing, President Erdoğan's recent declarations indicate that the government's urban renewal plans for the neighborhood are still on the table: http://www.diken.com.tr/erdoganin-akli-hep -gezide-isteseler-de-istemeseler-de-taksime-kisla-yapilacak/.

4. See Alessandrini, Üstündağ, and Yildiz 2013.

5. http://www.theguardian.com/world/2014/may/29/gezi-park-year-after-protests -seeds-new-turkey.

6. According to the Turkish Medical Association report, police intervention had caused eight deaths and thousands of injuries, among them 106 instances of severe head trauma and eleven cases that included the loss of an eye. (http://www.ttb.org.tr/ index.php/Haberler/veri-3944.html). Many people suffered from beatings and sexual harassment during mass arrests. Answering a parliamentary question posed by a member of the main opposition party, the Ministry of Interior declared that, in twenty days, the police used 130,000 cartridges of tear gas and three thousand tons of water to disperse the protesters (http://www.aksam.com.tr/guncel/ne-kadar-biber—gazi-ve-su-kullanildi/ haber-215796).

7. The full name of the project was: "Implementation Capacity of Turkish Police to Prevent Disproportionate Use of Force" (CRIS Number: TR2009/0136.07): http://

www.egm.gov.tr/SiteAssets/Sayfalar/insanHaklarıFaaliyetRaporu/?H%20Faaliyet%20 Raporu%2002.08.2013.pdf.

8. The project consisted of two parts: first, analysis of existing conditions for the use of police force in Turkey, their comparison with German, Austrian, Dutch, and Spanish standards, and the development of police service regulations "for the topical fields of leadership, tactical communication, crowd control, and use of force"; second, training of trainers in a total of sixteen one-week courses on the developed service regulations. The second part of the project was inaugurated on May 6, 2013. The European Commission evaluated the mid-term performance of the project as "good to very good."

9. http://bim.lbg.ac.at/en/projects-twinning/turkey-implementation-capacity-turk ish-police-prevent-disproportionate-use-force-twinning.

10. In total, I undertook participant observation in thirty-five human rights train- ings and interviewed over one hundred interlocutors, among them, foreign and interna- tional human rights experts, foreign and national civil society workers, academics, and government workers who participated in the trainings.

11. Latour's definition of immutable mobiles shows slight variations between his earlier and later writings. While in his earlier work Latour defines immutable mobiles as rather rigid forms that are used in the universalistic stratification of locally variable phenomena (1987), he later revises this definition by attributing more contradictory qualities to those metrics that may seem immutable at first glance. He writes, for in- stance, that immutable mobiles themselves get transformed as they are transported into various places. He also pays more attention to the making, fine-tuning, dissemination, and upkeep of immutable mobiles that testify to their malleability (2005). Borrowing from Latour, many anthropologists use the concept "immutable mobiles" to study glo- balization and standardization processes in various places (Collier and Ong 2005, Dunn 2005, Kayaalp 2012). Despite the nuances involved in Latour's definition of the concept, however, many of those studies take immutable mobiles as fixed forms that can be ab- stracted, translated, compared, and combined to transform locally specific phenomena without being transformed themselves (also see Star and Griesemer 1989).

12. https://www.law.ox.ac.uk/research-subject-groups/centre-criminology/centre border-criminologies/blog/2016/03/turkey-safe-third.

13. https://www.amnesty.org/en/latest/news/2016/06/eus-reckless-refugee-returns -to-turkey-illegal/.

14. https://www.opendemocracy.net/kerem-oktem/zombie-politics-europe-turkey -and-disposable-human.

15. Talberg (2002) writes that the EU uses an effective combination of both enforce- ment and management strategies to ensure compliance of the member and candidate countries with the regulatory agreements. While enforcement strategies include moni- toring and economic and political sanctions, management strategies include capacity building, rule interpretation, and transparency. EU most notably began to employ ca-

pacity building in the 2004 to 2007 enlargement period. During what is regarded as "the largest enlargement so far," ten new countries including the Czech Republic, Estonia, Latvia, Lithuania, Hungary, and Poland joined the EU. These Eastern European and Central European countries were considered far removed from the EU standards. Capacity building strategies were thus deployed as the means to assist these countries to meet the required membership criteria. For a good ethnographic example of the techniques, human resources, and relationships that go into international capacity building efforts for achieving Europeanization, see Coles 2002 and 2008.

16. A useful comparison would be James Ferguson's (2006) account of development in Africa as market oriented and primarily carried out by international civil society. Contrary to this, Mosse (2005a) argues that the new aid framework reaccommodates the role of both the state and self-organizing society as complementary mechanisms for development in a "post-Washington consensus" world while maintaining the central role of market rationality in fostering international development. Similarly, Merilee Grindle (1997) traces the mid-1990s shift in the development agenda and finds that it results in the convergence of capacity building and good governance.

17. According to Grindle, capacity building for state institutions encompasses a variety of strategies that have to do with increasing the efficiency, effectiveness, and responsiveness of government performance (1997, 5).

18. Following Andrew Barry (2001), I take "political" to refer to the ways in which artifacts, activities, or practices become objects of contestation and dissensus. "Technical," by contrast, is regarded as something that exists outside of the contested space of politics.

19. See, for instance Appadurai 1990, 1996, Ferguson 2006, Hannerz 1996, Inda and Rosaldo 2002, Riles 2001, Tsing 2005.

20. In a 2006 BBC interview, former president of the European Commission José Manuel Barroso stated that he does not expect Turkey to become a full member of the EU at least until 2021 "Interview with European Commission President Jose Manuel Barroso on BBC Sunday AM." http://ec.europa.eu/commission_barroso/president/pdf/interview_20061015_en.pdf.

21. For the full text of Turkey's Negotiating Framework that lays out principles governing the negotiations between Turkey and the EU see: https://ec.europa.eu/neighbourhood-enlargement/sites/near/files/pdf/turkey/st20002_05_tr_framedoc_en.pdf.

22. For a complete list of the negotiation chapters see: https://ec.europa.eu/neighbourhood-enlargement/sites/near/files/20170301-overview_negotiations_turkey.pdf.

23. For more detailed information on how the screening and negotiation process works, see: https://ec.europa.eu/neighbourhood-enlargement/policy/steps-towards-joining_en.

24. The 1963 Ankara Agreement had established a customs union between Turkey and the European Economic Community.

25. See, for instance, Aktar 2012.

26. For a similar analysis of AKP's relationship with NATO in search of political legitimacy, see Tuğal 2007.

27. The Copenhagen Criteria, adopted at the June 1993 summit of the EU Council, lists the political requirements candidate countries should comply with for EU membership.

28. http://www.cnnturk.com/2005/dunya/09/03/ab.olmazsa.ankara.kriteri.der.ge ceriz/122622.0/index.html.

29. There are different interpretations of what the underlying reasons for the switch in the AKP's foreign and domestic policy might be. According to one interpretation, AKP's pragmatic approach towards EU membership has led the government to revert to a passive activism in its relationship with the EU, due to the high domestic cost of passing high-stake reforms such as the Kurdish initiative (Avcı 2011). Another interpretation correlates AKP's authoritarian turn with the 2013 corruption scandal that implicated top-level AKP officials as well as Erdoğan himself, which prompted the ongoing power grip by means of executive decisions and legal regulations that reversed the government's former reforms (http://www.radikal.com.tr/yazarlar/baskin-oran/yetmez -ama-evet-meselesi-maddeleri-ogreniyoruz-1206882/).

30. *Public Perceptions on Turkish Foreign Policy*, research issued annually by Kadir Has University, in May 2016 reported that EU's approval rate has improved to 62 percent: http://www.khas.edu.tr/news/1367. However, according to the *Social Political Tendencies* research report again issued by Kadir Has University in January 2017, the rate of EU support among the Turkish public fell to 45.7 percent in less than a year following the July 2016 failed coup attempt: http://www.khas.edu.tr/news/1498.

31. http://europa.eu/rapid/press-release_MEMO-12–359_en.htm.

32. For example, see a recent working paper released by the Finnish Institute of International Affairs: http://www.fiia.fi/en/publication/480/turkey_under_the_akp/.

33. See: http://avrupa.info.tr/fileadmin/Content/2016__April/2016.04_EP_Resolution _on_Turkey.pdf.

34. See: http://www.consilium.europa.eu/en/press/press-releases/2016/07/18–fac-tur key-conclusions/.

35. See: http://edition.cnn.com/2016/07/18/asia/turkey-attempted-coup/.

36. The roots of the EU lie in the treaty that established the European Coal and Steel Community in 1952, signed between the six founder states: Belgium, France, Germany, Italy, Luxemburg, and the Netherlands. In 1959, the European Community was set up to further extend the economic cooperation between the members. In 1967, the European Coal and Steel Community and the European Community were brought together with the European Atomic Energy Community under the rubric of the European Communities. In 1993, the Maastricht Treaty signed among the member states established the EU as not just an economic cooperation but as a political entity. Today the EU does not just represent an economic market with a single currency and customs union. It also designates a political entity with a common domestic and foreign policy.

37. Those fears came into view most recently in the Brexit campaign, in which leaving the EU was portrayed as synonymous with regaining the right to decide on national matters and reestablishing control over national resources in Britain.

38. See, for instance, the speech of Vaclav Havel, former president of the Czech Republic, addressing the European Parliament on the eve of his country's accession to the EU in 1994: "The European Union is based on a large set of values, with roots in antiquity and in Christianity, which over two thousand years evolved into what we recognize today as the foundations of modern democracy, the rule of law and civil society" (quoted in Hsu 2010a, 1). Also see Gupta 1997 for the definition of the European Community as a specific form of transnational imagined community that is unified by experiences of colonialism and late capitalism.

39. For a recent collection of essays that elaborate the challenges of ethnic diversity in Europe, also see Hsu 2010b.

40. For more on the Islamic State see: http://www.bbc.com/news/world-middle-east -29052144.

41. See: http://www.avrupa.info.tr/en/accession-negotiations-720.

42. See, for instance, an interview of the former Turkish Minister of EU Affairs, Egemen Bağış, by Stephen Sackur of HARD TALK on BBC World on January 3, 2012, where both Bağış and Sackur discuss Turkey's EU membership on the basis of "attitudes," "values," and "beliefs": http://www.theglobetimes.com/2012/03/05/hold-on-tight-europe -turkeys-coming/.

43. See Silverstein 2014 on the particular role of statistics as a tool of commensurability and intervention in Turkey by the EU.

44. For Turkey's 2016 progress report, see https://ec.europa.eu/neighbourhood-en-largement/sites/near/files/pdf/key_documents/2016/20161109_report_turkey.pdf. For Turkey's 2015 annual progress report see https://ec.europa.eu/neighbourhood-enlargement/ sites/near/files/pdf/key_documents/2015/20151110_report_turkey.pdf. In both documents, the details of financial assistance Turkey receives from the EU appear under Chapter 33: Financial and Budgetary Provisions.

45. For a diverse array of studies that approach Turkey's EU accession from this perspective, see the rest of the essays in the special issue of the *European Journal of Turkish Studies* on EU-Turkey: Sociological Approaches. See particularly Alemdar 2009, Fırat 2009, and Yankaya 2009.

46. See, for instance, Asad 2000, Brown 2004, Mamdani 2008, Rancière 2004, and Weizman 2011.

47. For CIA involvement in the coup, see Birand 1987, Çelikkol 2005, Paul 1981. For analyses of the coup from a political economy perspective, and especially the effects of IMF policies and January 1980 austerity measures (that were said to require "political stability") for the process leading to the coup, see Ahmad 1981, Marguiles and Yıldızoğlu 1984, Pamuk 1981, Yalpat 1984.

48. For first-hand testimonies of the establishment of the İHD and the history of the human rights movement in Turkey, see İHD 2006, İHD/TİHV 1999, Kanar 1999.

49. See, for instance, the testimony of the Chilean human rights defender Joe Eldridge, who says: "Human rights entered my vocabulary on September 11, 1973, when it was suddenly denied to one-third of the Chilean population" (Keck and Sikkink 1998, 91). Similarly, renowned Turkish political science professor Baskın Oran had told me in an interview: "When the Human Rights Center was first established in Ankara University in 1978, we had no idea what the use of human rights might be. None of us paid attention [to the Center]. Afterwards, the military regime taught all of us what human rights meant."

50. For a collection of insightful essays on the strategic adoption of the global discourse of human rights (which entails a lower risk of violent repression) by networks of former political activists from various factions throughout the Middle East and North Africa, see Beinin and Vairel 2011, especially Göker 2011, Hersant 2011, Stork 2011, Vairel 2011.

51. Also see Ferguson 2002 and Malkki 1994, 1998 for an elaboration of the conditions of membership in the world society of nation states in general.

52. In a similar vein, in 1928, during the early years of the republic and before its acceptance into the League of Nations, the Turkish government had signed the Geneva Declaration on the Rights of the Child as a sign of its participation in the international area of sovereign states (Libal 2001).

53. For a more detailed analysis of the inheritance of the project and tactics of the political left by the Islamist social movements in the Middle East in general, see Zubaida 2001.

54. The relations between MAZLUMDER and other notable human rights organizations in Turkey have periodically been stalled following the adverse statements that MAZLUMDER released regarding LGBT rights in 2010. These statements led the organization to be removed from the Human Rights Joint Platform, which includes organizations such as the İHD, the Helsinki Citizens' Assembly and Amnesty International Turkey.

55. See Dağı 2004 for the adoption of the ideas of human rights and democracy by what he calls "post-Islamist intellectuals" in Turkey. Also see Zubaida 1994 for a comparative analysis of the appropriation and transformation of human rights thought by the Muslim thinkers in Egypt and the Arab world.

56. These reforms were the changes that came into effect in the Turkish Civil Code (2001) and the passing of the new Law of Associations (2004). In addition to the EU accession process, a long-lasting cease-fire between the outlawed Kurdistan Workers' Party (*Partiya Karkeren Kurdistan*—PKK) and the army, following the capturing and arrest of PKK's leader Abdullah Öcalan in 1999, also contributed to the loosening of government controls over political expression and social organization.

57. The introduction to one of STGM's manuals reads: "Despite all the impossibilities and challenges, it is important to remind the newly established civil society insti-

tutions that aim to improve the society's quality of life that they should keep trying: Don't complain, don't complain about the issues that are not in your power, about the obstacles stemming from external factors. Change the issues that are in your power . . . Do not complain about problems either. In fact, a civil society institution, by nature, exists for solving problems. Let's not forget, if everything functioned the way it should have, there would be no need for civil society institutions." In a similar vein, the motto of one of the most well-known volunteer organizations in Turkey is: "*Eleştirmek için değil, değiştirmek için gönüllüyüz*" (We volunteer not to criticize but to change).

58. See, for instance, the Third Sector Foundation of Turkey (*Türkiye Üçüncü Sektör Vakfı*), heavily supported by the Turkish private sector.

59. Although it shares some fundamental elements with the EU (such as the European flag), and it cooperates with the EU on issues regarding human rights, legal standardization, rule of law, and democratic development, CE is an international organization that is entirely separate from the EU structure. Apart from the European Court of Human Rights, which is the executive body of the European Convention of Human Rights, CE does not have any decision-making power. With a membership base that is almost twice the size of the EU, CE covers a much more comprehensive area. Turkey has been a member of CE since 1949.

60. People in İHD refused to call themselves "*aktivist*" (activist), using the word "*hak savunucusu*" (rights defender) instead. They also refused to use the acronym STK (*sivil toplum kuruluşu*—civil society institute), instead preferring the acronym STÖ (*sivil toplum örgütü*—civil society organization) because of the former's proximity to the official discourse and the discourse of transnational developmentalism.

61. See, for instance, Appadurai 1990, 1996, Collier and Ong 2005, Tsing 2005.

62. See, for instance, Fassin and Rechtman 2009, Feldman and Ticktin 2010, Keck and Sikkink 1998, Malkki 1995, 1996, Merry 2006, 2011, Ticktin 2005, 2006.

63. Anna Tsing (2005) describes "travelling packages" as models of activism (or development) that are translated in specific ways to intervene in local scenes.

64. See, for instance, Ho 2009b, Riles 2010, Zaloom 2006.

65. Deeb and Marcus 2011, Holmes and Marcus 2005.

66. See, for instance, Abu-Lughod 1993, Caldeira 2000, Narayan 1993, Osanloo 2009, Özyürek 2006, Thiranagama 2011, Weston 1991, and Zinn 1979.

SETTING THE STAGE

1. Here and throughout the book, I use pseudonyms for all the informants I worked with.

CHAPTER 1

1. Cited in Feldman 2008, 97.

2. For example, see Baytaş 2002, Bener 1982, Pamukoğlu 2003, Pazarcıklı 2004. Also

see Karaosmanoğlu 1934 for a satirical portrayal of the relationship of state elites with the common people in fiction form.

3. Following Bourdieu's (1987) usage, I employ the term "field" to refer to an area of structured, socially patterned activity or practice pertaining to the characteristics of a specific professional world. It is a site of struggle and competition for control, which leads to a hierarchical system within the field (see Terdiman 1987). For more definitions of Bourdieu's field theory and its place in his theory of practice, see: Thompson, J.B. "Editor's Introduction" in Bourdieu (1991), especially pp.15–17; Johnson, R. "Editor's Introduction" in Bourdieu (1993), especially pp.6–9.

4. Furthermore, in everyday life the state is employed as a metaphor of power to create, maintain, and manage social hierarchies within the wider society (Alexander 2002, Sirman 1990).

5. For EU's definition of good governance, see Commission of the European Communities 2001.

6. Key works in this literature include Aretxaga 2003, Coronil 1997, Das and Poole 2004, Ferguson and Gupta 2002, Gupta 1995, Hansen and Stepputat 2001, Taussig 1997, Trouillot 2001.

7. Bourdieu's definition of distinction alludes to a class marker that takes into consideration cultural competence, aesthetic disposition, educational capital, bodily comportment, and tastes as a means to distinguish oneself from the working classes. By seeking to understand the imaginaries of distinction, I intend to grasp the network of a system of symbols and signifiers that define the terms of distinction at a given time in a given society.

8. The "mainstream Turkish political culture" and its nonliberal "state tradition" is often defined as the "prevalence of state interests over fundamental human rights, the model of passive deferential citizen, lack of tolerance for cultural, religious and ethnic diversity (and) the exalted role of the military and bureaucratic elite as guardian of the Western and secular character of the Turkish state" (Grigoriadis 2004, 8). This problematic definition, which assumes an overarching, uniform realm of governance, leaves little room to account for fractures and inconsistencies that may arise from governmental practices.

9. Metin Heper defines the bureaucratic *adab* as the knowledge of the proper way of doing things within the bureaucratic machinery, inherited by the Republican bureaucratic elite from their Ottoman predecessors. After the nineteenth century, the well-educated bureaucrats also came to be regarded as possessing knowledge of the West (Heper 2000).

10. Here, what I describe as "governmental legitimacy" is distinct from "political legitimacy" (see Heper 2000) because it accounts for the political/governmental divide that is central to the constitution of bureaucratic authority in Turkey. I take "political legitimacy" to refer to an important contestation between the state and the nonstate actors

in Turkey about the right to be politically engaged. The right to politics, which is a major organizing theme of the post-1980 political field in Turkey, should not be conflated with "governmental legitimacy," and it remains beyond the scope of this chapter.

11. Despite the bureaucratic elite's distinction from the political elite at the symbolic level, both Chambers (1964) and Frey (1965) show that there is a high level of permeability between these two groups in practice. Not only do bureaucrats share similar educational and occupational backgrounds with most politicians but they also tend to enter into active politics frequently, although the law requires them to resign from official duty prior to standing election.

12. Mustafa Kemal Atatürk, who is considered the founder of modern Turkey, has the title *baş öğretmen* (head teacher) among his other titles—general commander, head of the state, and father Turk.

13. Also see Altinay 2004 for an elaboration of the school along with the army as the nation's front in Turkey.

14. For example, in her detailed study of the courtroom practices in an Istanbul district, Koğacıoğlu shows how the judges and the prosecutors saw putting people in their proper place as a central component of their job and a natural outcome of their position (Koğacıoğlu 2009). Also see Alexander 2000 for an analysis of the state-owned Erzurum Sugar Factory as a built environment that molds proper citizen behavior.

15. For a compelling analysis of the configuration of the female body in the founding myth of the Turkish Republic through Sabiha Gökçen, Mustafa Kemal Atatürk's adopted daughter, see Altinay 2004.

16. The challenge of the educated periphery for the Kemalist-secularist governmental elite and the challenge of Islamist mobilization for the Kemalist-secularist political elite share similar characteristics. Akin to the new bureaucratic cadre replacing the traditional one, the Muslim popular movements effectively replace the Kemalist-secularist elite with an Islamist cultural/political/economic elite. Even though they are based on the mobilization of class-based political demands, Islamist populist movements do not end up challenging eliteness per se (Tuğal 2009, White 2002b).

17. National Programme for Adoption of the *Acquis Communautaire* details Turkey's road map to EU accession. Following the adoption of accession partnership by the EU Council of Ministers in December 2000, Turkey presented its National Programme in March 2001.

18. See, for instance, Council on Foreign Relations 2003.

CHAPTER 2

1. From Sugden 2004, 259.

2. Two instances that particularly materialized those circles during my fieldwork were the Public Ethics Symposium held by the Public Administration Institute for Turkey and the Middle East in Ankara on May 2009 and the briefing meeting of the Jus-

tice Watch Project run by the Human Rights Law Research Center of Bilgi University in Istanbul on April 2008. In both meetings, the participants, composed of academics, researchers, and the representatives of various government offices, fiercely debated whether public administration should be understood in terms of service provision or supervision that implies a hierarchical relationship between citizens and the government workers.

3. As David Graeber points out, the proliferation of corporate bureaucratic culture to state bureaucracies actually points towards an interesting and now-forgotten history of the rise of the modern corporation as a distinctly American form. Contrary to contemporary formulations of good governance, which advocates running governments more like businesses, the rise of the modern corporation in the late nineteenth century was based on the application of modern bureaucratic techniques to the private sector. At the time, these techniques were seen as indispensable for reorganizing the realm of production to operate on a large scale. Bureaucratic techniques were regarded as more efficient than the networks of personal and informal connections that until then had dominated the world of small family firms (2015, 11).

4. It is important to note that EU harmonization is not the first instance where bureaucratic reform became an agenda in Turkey. See, for instance, Chambers (1964) for an overview of the 1953 UN Technical Assistance Program, which was sent to the country by the Public Administration Division of the UN's Technical Assistance Administration upon the request of Ankara University's Faculty of Political Science. The program aimed to assess the strengths and weaknesses of Turkish administration and make appropriate recommendations for its reorganization on the basis of efficiency, meritocracy, and service provision.

5. Reflections of this calculative framework are visible in the reorganization of various areas of government service in the country. One of the most recent government initiatives includes the establishment of performance-based evaluation criteria in the health care sector. With the aim of promoting efficiency in state-run hospitals, the number of patients treated by health care professionals is taken into account when they are considered for promotion. The majority of health care professionals I worked with in the field criticized this practice, claiming that the quantification of health care services was essentially detrimental to maintaining their quality.

6. Some of these reform initiatives included changes in the Criminal Code and the Criminal Procedure Code in 2004, amendments to the constitution in 2004 and 2010; ratification of international instruments such as International Covenant on Economic, Social and Cultural Rights in 2003 and International Covenant on Civil and Political Rights in 2003; as well as the declaration of "Zero Tolerance for Torture" policy in 2003 by the AKP government.

7. The practice of obtaining medically relevant complaints by asking the patient specific questions.

8. The film was coproduced by the General Directorate of Women's Status and the Turkish National Police as part of the government's "zero tolerance towards domestic violence" policy.

9. Article 280 of the 2004 Turkish Penal Code No: 5237 details the health care professionals' obligation to report the signs of crimes they come across while performing their duties. According to the article, failure to do so is punishable by a prison sentence of up to a year.

10. For the relationship between governance and affect, see Aretxaga 2003, Navaro-Yashin 2006, 2007, Stoler 2004.

11. For a similar analysis of the clash of different forms of occupational expertise and how they shape the organizational environment in the World Bank, see Sarfaty 2012.

12. For a detailed analysis of gynecological examination in the Turkish context, especially in the form of state-enforced virginity examinations as a technology of governance, a practice of modern state-making and the disciplining of female national subjects, see Parla 2001.

13. The Institute of Forensic Medicine is a state institution that operates under the Ministry of Justice. It is the designated institution for undertaking medical investigation for the prosecution and judiciary. The Institute has been subject to widespread criticism regarding the controversial reports it produces. The connection between the Ministry of Justice and the Institute is also widely criticized, with the argument that the Institute should be an independent organization. Among others, the Turkish Medical Association (Türk Tabipleri Birliği—TTB) is one of the fiercest critics of the Institute.

14. The importance of the legitimacy of psychological evidence to prove torture and sexual assault stems from the argument that the signs of violence on the victims' psyche remain for a much longer period than the more physical signs. In most torture cases, victims can be detained for a prolonged period of time to deny them access to juridical means before their physical scars heal. Additionally, the development of technology enables torture to be carried out in more sophisticated ways to leave the least possible physical marks.

15. *Istanbul Protocol: Manual on the Effective Investigation and Documentation of Torture and Other Cruel, Inhuman or Degrading Treatment or Punishment* was adopted by the UN Commission on Human Rights and the UN General Assembly in 2000. For the complete text of the Protocol, see: http://www.ohchr.org/Documents/Publications/training8Rev1en.pdf.

16. Also see Ticktin 2006 on the devastating effects of ethically-driven neutral practices of humanitarianism in the absence of guiding political principles.

17. Raymond Williams's etymology for the words "expert" and "professional" suggests that the word "professional" came to refer to a wide range of vocations and occupations and was thought of in contrast to the word "amateur" by the late twentieth-century industrial society (1983, 129). Since the word "amateur," deriving from the words *amatore*

and *amator* (lover), designates someone who does something out of love, its antonym, the word "professional," suggests a line of work that is devoid of emotions.

18. Thanks to Sylvia Yanagisako for helping me formulate this argument.

CHAPTER 3

1. The legal framework for the EIMET program was the 1990 amendment of the provision of the Foreign Assistance Act of 1961 overseeing International Military Education and Training. This amendment authorized spending US security assistance dollars to train both military personnel and the civilian officials who work with foreign defense establishments. The amendment also earmarked $1 million of appropriated funds to provide training in human rights, civilian control of the military in a democratic society, military justice systems, and defense resource management (Hinkley 1997, 297).

2. Tess Lea argues that the rigidly democratic format of such workshops in fact constitutes their main source of power. When coupled with the particular ways interactions are structured to take place—"intensely participatory" and "oppressively inclusive"—these workshops become potent "because of the democratic and inclusive ways that they police and silence" (2008, 86). "The polite force of the gathering" thus creates "an unbearable pressure for agreement" (101).

3. Along with her academic identity, Professor Kuçuradi is a public figure in Turkey with a strong background in human rights work, who served on the 1998 National Committee for the Decade of Human Rights Education following the UN program with the same name. In addition to being a prolific scholar in the field of philosophy of ethics and philosophy of human rights, she has also served as a trainer or advisor in many human rights education programs.

4. Law No. 657 on Civil Servants, which regulates the working conditions of government employees, prohibits them from taking an active part in politics.

5. For a critical study of the human rights education for the oppressed, see Englund 2006.

6. I thank Nazan Üstündağ for bringing this point to my attention.

CHAPTER 4

1. See, for instance, Asad 1986, Ballestero 2014, Brenneis 2004, Callon 1986, Chakrabarty 2007, Englund 2006, Kayaalp 2012, Merry 2006, Povinelli 2002, Sarfaty 2012, Scott et al. 1997, Spivak 1993, Star and Griesemer 1989, Tsing 1997, 2005.

2. Even though Brazil and Turkey share similarities in the stigmatization of human rights advocacy as defending the rights of social outcasts, the definition of the outcast in Turkey is nevertheless very different from Brazil. While Caldeira argues that in the post–Cold War era Brazil has seen a change in the figure with which popular conceptions of evil are associated—from the communist guerilla to poor, common prisoners—in Turkey, the figure of the political transgressor still designates the ultimate outcast. Due

to Turkey's specific socio-political history of national homogenization and ethnic tensions, which was also molded during the country's Cold War experience, conventions about "political crime," a.k.a "terrorism," bear strong connections to fears of disintegration and annexation of the country. As opposed to the Brazilian case, "the poor, common prisoner," a.k.a. "the victim of fate" (*kader kurbanı*), is deemed much more worthy of compassion, thus of human rights, than the "evil terrorist" or "the enemy of the state" in Turkey.

3. Paradoxically, this period corresponded to the Demirel and Çiller governments, lasting between 1991 and 1995, considered to be the worst period of human rights violations, particularly in the Kurdish regions (Bozarslan 2001).

4. Elizabeth Povinelli defines "the unspeakable" as essentially different from "the inexpressible," "indeterminate," and "incommensurate": "the unspeakable refers to instances in which something can be described with a perfectly reasonable degree of accuracy, but can nevertheless not be described because of explicit social prohibitions, whether these prohibitions are legal, religious or personal in nature, or whether they are local or nonlocal in origin" (2002, 239). The line between the speakable and the "unspeakable" is an aspect of the "social nature of the interaction . . . and thus is determined by the terms of how and what is sayable in this context and how it relates to questions of social and subjective worth, and livability" (2001, 325).

5. For a similar elaboration of the ambivalence of translators and translation in Jerusalem's criminal trial courts, see Braverman 2007. Braverman reports that akin to their perception in the human rights seminars in Turkey, translators in the criminal trial courts in Jerusalem are seen at once as connectors and differentiators whose loyalty oscillates according to the situation at hand.

6. An excellent example of the heightened danger associated with the insider enemy is the amended paragraph of the infamous Article 301 of the Turkish Penal Code, which prohibits insulting the Turkish people, the Republic of Turkey, and governmental institutions and bodies (formerly known as "insulting Turkishness"). The law declares those discursive acts punishable with between six months and two years in prison. Before its amendment in 2008, the article included a paragraph that stated that committing this crime in a foreign country would increase the time of the sentence by one third. The 2008 amendment to Article 301 was mainly carried out due to the widely criticized charges brought against internationally renowned figures such as the novelist Elif Şafak and Nobel Prize-winning author Orhan Pamuk, as well as the tragic assassination of the Armenian journalist Hırant Dink in Istanbul following his conviction on the basis of the same article. In addition to removing the paragraph related to committing the crime abroad, the amendment changed the wording of the article—for example, replacing "Turkishness" with "Turkish people"—and made the prosecution of the law conditional upon the permission of the Ministry of Justice. Although the last paragraph of Article 301 was removed with this amendment due to external pressure, it still exemplifies how

the most drastic form of treason within the Turkish official imaginary is closely associated with disclosing what are considered "nationally sensitive" issues to foreigners. The paragraph not only delineates the borders of what can be said publicly but it also associates the scope of danger that comes with transgressing that border beyond the borders of the nation-state. When spoken in a foreign country, the unspeakable becomes even more abhorrent because it takes a national matter (controversies about Turkey's national polity, which even in their right place constitute transgression) out of its proper place.

7. A useful comparison to this is Lisa Hajjar's (2005) study of the Israeli military courts in occupied Palestine, where linguistic ability of the translators is mapped upon their ethnic and national identity.

8. Four of the six translators I worked with during my fieldwork had graduated from private high schools, and the other two went to Anatolian High Schools, which are selected public schools for honors students with a special emphasis on foreign language education.

9. The audience in this case was 90 percent male. The male domination of the audience was not uncommon, particularly at training seminars for judges and prosecutors. Although the gender composition of the training audiences does not necessarily reflect the gender composition of the judiciary, the gendered division of labor in the home (the unequal allocation of responsibilities related to child care, housekeeping, etc.) nevertheless caused women government workers to volunteer less frequently to participate in professional training seminars due to the travel requirement. In such male-dominated audiences, women participants resorted to status symbols like speaking in English more often as a way to overcome their minority status.

10. This perception should make the ethnographic vignette at the beginning of the section "Pedagogies of Accession" (describing the adult participative training workshop) more understandable. The awkwardness I felt after having stepped in to help translate the ongoing English interaction for the two non-English-speaking project team members arose from the fact that my behavior, especially as a newcomer, was perceived as highly pompous and arrogant.

11. Similarly, Andrea Ballestero (2014) shows that translation is not just a mechanical but also a poetic process whereby linguistic/symbolic/semiotic conversion indicates a shift between the genres of communication.

12. For an analysis of feminization as an age-old strategy to deal with the threatening status of the West in the late Ottoman and early Republican novels, see Gürbilek 2009. In line with what Gürbilek describes, gendered perception of translation as a feminine profession as well as the dominance of women translators in the field provided an effective tool to manage the threat coming from the "suspect" foreigner. This strategy proved to be viable particularly due to the specific history of the profession in Turkey, reported to me by Nilay, who was conducting a study on this topic when we met. Before it became available as a field of study in universities, the task of simultaneous translation

was undertaken by well-educated young women who served as executive secretaries, and who went to private schools thanks to their upper-class background. These young women, who would not stand a chance for employment in the diplomatic cadres of places like the Ministry of Foreign Affairs due to their gender, were nevertheless highly sought after for such secretarial positions.

13. The PKK and the Turkish state entered into a period of cease-fire following Öcalan's capture in 1999. Both sides resumed armed activities to some degree between 2004 and 2012. The conflict was interrupted once more between 2013 and 2015 with peace negotiations resuming between the guerillas and the government. The negotiations came to a halt in 2015 with the conflict spiraling between the two parties both due to domestic politics as well as the situation in the international arena that situated the PKK and the Turkish government as adversaries in the ongoing war in Syria.

14. Processes of translation perhaps provide one of the best mechanisms through which liberal reclamation of human rights can take place. For an excellent example of this, see Harri Englund's chapter "Poor Translations for Poor People," in which he describes how in the official documents the word "rights" was deliberately translated as "freedoms" in Malawi (2006, 47–70).

CHAPTER 5

1. From Abdullah Gül's address at Stanford Graduate School of Business (Stanford University, May 23, 2012).

2. As Dicle Koğacıoğlu explains in her work on courtroom practices in a working class district in Istanbul, the knowledge of one's proper place is contingent upon one's "awareness of the interplay between the social situation, power relations, the time and the place" defining the specific moments in which one has to act. The appropriate placement of the self requires a practical sensibility of the time, place, and ways of behaving in situations delicately situated within hierarchical social structures (2009, 15). Building upon White 1994 and Merry 1979, Koğacıoğlu argues that the knowledge of one's place helps the contending parties in the courtroom hierarchy to strategize and maximize their interests.

3. Unlike Goffman, who takes the dramatization of status as an everyday aspect of the presentation of the self, Turner believes that social dramas erupt in moments of crises that interrupt the daily flow of social action. This, according to Turner, turns dramas into "transformative performances."

4. See, for instance, Gupta 2005, Ismail 2006, Navaro-Yashin 2002, Sayer 1994, Wedeen 1999.

5. See, for instance, Hannah Arendt's definition of cynicism as "a vehement impulse to withdraw from worldly involvement" (1958, 310).

6. Kissing the hand of a person and putting it on the forehead is considered a sign of respect in Turkey. This widespread practice commonly denotes the recognition of

generational hierarchy, with young people expected to kiss the hands of their elders to greet them. It is also used in other platforms (such as conservative political ones) as a way to communicate the recognition of other forms of hierarchy, in which generational respect acquires a metaphorical form to mark humility and submission to the authority figure whose hand is kissed.

7. As Liisa Malkki insightfully articulates, a successful improvisation depends on a well-absorbed structural repertoire and a lifetime of preparation, learning, and practice that eventually enable practitioners to grasp "the things that go without saying" (2007b, 186). In a similar way, government workers in the juvenile justice training program could effortlessly improvise each others' roles because they had mastered the structure of this ostensibly flexible field, which was captured in a scene with which they were extremely familiar.

8. Parody in the juvenile justice training, as well as in other human rights training programs, assumed a function similar to what Erving Goffman attributes to practical jokes and social games: purposefully engineered situations in which embarrassments would be taken "unseriously" that ultimately work as defensive and protective techniques to safeguard the impression fostered by the performers before their audiences (1956, 7).

9. See Babül 2015 for a more detailed elaboration of the *Diyanet* trainings.

10. Recent publications in this literature include Fassin 2015, Feldman 2008, Gupta 2012, Hull 2012, Lea 2008, Navaro-Yashin 2012.

CONCLUSION

1. For the latest report published in March 10, 2017 by the UN Human Rights Office that details the massive human rights violations perpetrated in the Kurdish regions since June 2015, see: http://www.ohchr.org/Documents/Countries/TR/OHCHR_South-East_TurkeyReport_10March2017.pdf.

2. I thank Belgin Tekçe for helping me articulate this point.

3. I thank Nükhet Sirman for helping me articulate this point.

4. My thanks, again, go to Nükhet Sirman for bringing this case to my attention.

5. http://www.milliyet.com.tr/jitem-in-ne-oldugunu-bilmem-je-gundem-2143584/.

6. See Babül, forthcoming.

BIBLIOGRAPHY

Abu-Lughod, Lila. 1993. *Writing Women's Worlds: Bedouin Stories.* Berkeley: University of California Press.

Acar, Feride, and Ayşe Ayata. 2002. "Discipline, Success and Stability: The Reproduction of Gender and Class in Turkish Secondary Education." In *Fragments of Culture: The Everyday of Modern Turkey,* edited by Deniz Kandiyoti and Ayşe Saktanber, 90–111. New Brunswick, New Jersey: Rutgers University Press.

Açıkmeşe, Sinem Akgül. 2010. "Cycles of Europeanization in Turkey: The Domestic Impact of EU Political Conditionality." *UNISCI Discussion Papers* 23 (May 2010): 129–48.

———. 2014. "Avrupa Birliği'nde Genişleme." In *Avrupa Birliği: Tarihçe, Teoriler, Kurumlar ve Politikalar,* second edition, edited by Belgin Akçay and İlke Göçmen, 642–60. Ankara: Seçkin Yayıncılık.

Ahıska, Meltem. 2003. "Occidentalism: The Historical Fantasy of the Modern." *The South Atlantic Quarterly* 102 (2/3): 351–79.

———. 2009. "Arşiv Korkusu ve Karakaplı Nizami Bey: Türkiye'de Tarih, Hafıza ve İktidar." In *Türkiye'de İktidarı Yeniden Düşünmek,* edited by Murat Güney, 59–93. İstanbul: Varlık Yayınları.

———. 2010. *Occidentalism in Turkey: Questions of Modernity and National Identity in Turkish Radio Broadcasting.* New York: Tauris.

Ahmad, Feroz. 1981. "Military Intervention and the Crisis in Turkey." *Merip Reports* 93: 5–24.

———. 1993. *The Making of Modern Turkey.* London: Routledge.

Aktar, Cengiz. 2012. "The Positive Agenda and Beyond: A New Beginning for the EU-Turkey Relations?" *Insight Turkey* 14 (3): 35–43.

Alemdar, Zeynep. 2009. "Turkish Trade Unions and the European Boomerang." *European Journal of Turkish Studies* 9: 2–28.

———. 2011. "Sarmal Modeli Yarı Sarmak: Türkiye'de İnsan Hakları Kurumları-Devlet-AB İlişkisi." *Uluslararası İlişkiler* 7 (28): 111–28.

Alessandrini, Anthony, Nazan Üstündağ, and Emrah Yildiz, eds. 2013. "Resistance Everywhere": The Gezi Protests and Dissident Visions of Turkey. Special issue of *JadMag* Pedagogy Publications 1.4, Fall 2013. Washington,DC: Tadween Publishing.

Alexander, Catherine. 2000. "The Factory: Fabricating the State " *Journal of Material Culture* 5 (2): 177–95.

———. 2002. *Personal States: Making Connections Between People and Bureaucracy in Turkey*. Oxford, NY: Oxford University Press.

Allen, Lori A. 2013. *The Rise and Fall of Human Rights: Cynicism and Politics in Occupied Palestine*. Stanford: Stanford University Press.

Altınay, Ayşe Gül. 2004. The Myth of the Military Nation: Palgrave Macmillan.

Altıparmak, Kerem. 2007. "Türkiye'de İnsan Haklarında Kurumsallaş(ama)ma." In *Bürokrasi ve İnsan Hakları*, edited by Türkiye Barolar Birliği, 54–111. Ankara: TBB Yayınları.

Anand, Nikhil. 2015. "Leaky States: Water Audits, Ignorance, and the Politics of Infrastructure." *Public Culture* 27 (2): 305–30.

Anders, Gerhard. 2007. "Follow the Trial: Some Notes on the Ethnography of International Criminal Justice." *Anthropology Today* 23 (3): 23–26.

Appadurai, Arjun. 1990. "Disjuncture and Difference in the Global Cultural Economy." *Public Culture* 2 (2): 1–23.

———. 1996. *Modernity At Large: Cultural Dimensions of Modernity*. Minneapolis: University of Minnesota Press.

Apter, Emily. 2001. "On Translation in a Global Market." *Public Culture* 13 (1): 1–12.

Arat, Yeşim. 1991. "Social Change and the 1983 Governing Elite in Turkey." In *Structural Change in Turkish Society*, edited by Mübeccel Kıray, 162–78. Bloomington: Indiana University Press.

Arat, Zehra F. Kabasakal. 2007. "Collisions and Crossroads: Introducing Human Rights in Turkey." In *Human Rights in Turkey*, edited by Zehra F. Kabasakal Arat,1–16. Philadelphia: University of Pennsylvania Press.

———. 2008. "Human Rights Ideology and Dimensions of Power: A Radical Approach to the State, Property, and Discrimination." *Human Rights Quarterly* 30: 906–32.

Arat, Zehra F. Kabasakal, and Thomas W. Smith. 2014. "The EU and Human Rights in Turkey: Political Freedom Without Social Welfare." In *European Institutions, Democratization, and Human Rights Protection in the European Periphery*, edited by Henry Carey, 31–66. Lanham, MD: Rowman and Littlefield.

Arendt, Hannah. 1958. *The Human Condition*. Chicago: University of Chicago Press.

Aretxaga, Begoña. 2003. "Maddening States." *Annual Review of Anthropology* 32: 393–410.

Asad, Talal. 1986. "The Concept of Cultural Translation in British Social Anthropology." In *Writing Culture: The Poetics and Politics of Ethnography*, edited by James Clifford and George E. Marcus, 141–64. Berkeley: University of California Press.

———. 2000. "What Do Human Rights Do? An Anthropological Enquiry." *Theory and Event* 4 (4). https://muse.jhu.edu/article/32601.

Avcı, Gamze. 2011. "The Justice and Development Party and the EU: Political Pragmatism in a Changing Environment." *South European Society and Politics* 16 (3): 409–21.

Babül, Elif. 2012. "Training Bureaucrats, Practicing for Europe: Negotiating Bureaucratic Authority and Governmental Legitimacy in Turkey." *Political and Legal Anthropology Review* 35 (1): 30–52.

———. 2015. "The Paradox of Protection: Human Rights, the Masculinist State, and the Moral Economy of Gratitude in Turkey." *American Ethnologist* 42 (1): 116–30.

———. Forthcoming. "Morality: Understanding Police Training on Human Rights (Turkey)." In *Writing the World of Policing: The Difference Ethnography Makes*, edited by Didier Fassin. Chicago: Chicago University Press.

Balibar, Etienne. 1991. "Es Gibt Keinen Staat in Europa: Racism and the Politics in Europe Today." *New Left Review* 186: 5–20.

———. 2004. *We, the People of Europe? Reflections on Transnational Citizenship*. Translated by James Swenson. Princeton, NJ: Princeton University Press.

———. 2009. "Europe as Borderland." *Society and Space* 27 (2): 190–215.

Ballestero, Andrea. 2014. "What is in a Percentage? Calculation as the Poetic Translation of Human Rights." *Indiana Journal of Global Legal Studies* 21 (1): 27–53.

Barry, Andrew. 2001. *Political Machines: Governing a Technological Society*. New York: The Athlone Press.

Baytaş, Kemal. 2002. *Bir Bürokrat . . . Ve Devlet Baba*. İstanbul: Doğan Kitap.

Beinin, Joel, and Frédéric Vairel, eds. 2011. *Social Movements, Mobilization, and Contestation in the Middle East and North Africa*. Stanford, CA: Stanford University Press.

Bener, Erhan. 1982. *Bürokratlar*. İstanbul: Adam Yayınları.

Benjamin, Walter. [1968] 1999. "The Task of the Translator." In *Illuminations*, edited and with an introduction by Hannah Arendt, 70–82. New York: Harcourt, Brace & World. Reprint, London: Pimlico. Citations refer to the Pimlico edition.

Best, Jacqueline. 2012. "Bureaucratic Ambiguity." *Economy and Society* 41 (1): 84–106.

Bıçak, Vahit, and Edward Grieves, eds. 2007. *Turkish Penal Code*. Ankara: Seçkin Yayınevi.

Birand, Mehmed Ali. 1987. *The Generals' Coup in Turkey*. London: Brassey's Defence Publishers.

Bora, Tanıl. 2003. "Nationalist Discourses in Turkey." *South Atlantic Quarterly* 102 (2/3): 433–51.

———. 2004. "Nationalism in Turkish Textbooks." In *Human Rights Issues in Textbooks: The Turkish Case*, edited by Deniz Tarba Ceylan and Gürol Irzık, 49–75. Istanbul: The History Foundation of Turkey.

Bourdieu, Pierre. (1977) 1999. "Rethinking the State: Genesis and Structure of the Bureaucratic Field." In *State/Culture: State Formation After the Cultural Turn*, edited by George Steinmetz, 53–75. Ithaca, NY: Cornell University Press.

———. 1984. *Distinction*. Cambridge: Harvard University Press.

———. 1987. "The Force of Law: Toward a Sociology of the Juridical Field." *The Hastings Law Journal* 38: 805–53.

———. 1991. *Language and Symbolic Power*. Cambridge: Harvard University Press.

————. 1993. *The Field of Cultural Production*. New York: Columbia University Press.

Bourdieu, Pierre, and Jean-Claude Passeron. (1977) 1990. *Reproduction in Education and Society*. Second edition, with a foreword by Tom Bottomore and preface by Pierre Bourdieu. Thousand Oaks, CA: Sage Publications.

Bozarslan, Hamit. 2001. "Human Rights and the Kurdish Issue in Turkey." *Human Rights Review* (October–December 2001): 45–54.

Bozdoğan, Sibel, and Reşat Kasaba, eds. 1997. *Rethinking Modernity and National Identity in Turkey*. Seattle: University of Washington Press.

Braverman, Irus. 2007. "The Place of Translation in Jerusalem's Criminal Courts." *New Criminal Law Review: An International and Interdisciplinary Journal* 10 (2): 239–77.

Brennan, Thomas. 2001. "The Cuts of Language: The East/West of North/South." *Public Culture* 13 (1): 39–63.

Brenneis, Donald. 1994. "Discourse and Discipline at the National Research Council: A Bureaucratic Bildungsroman." *Cultural Anthropology* 9 (1): 23–36.

————. 2004. "A Partial View of Contemporary Anthropology." *American Anthropologist* 106 (3): 580–88.

Brown, Wendy. 2004. "'The Most We Can Hope For . . . ': Human Rights and the Politics of Fatalism." *The South Atlantic Quarterly* 103 (2/3): 451–63.

Bunzl, Matti. 2005. "Between Anti-Semitism and Islamophobia: Some Thoughts on the New Europe." *American Ethnologist* 32 (4): 499–508.

Burchell, Graham, 1996. "Liberal Government and the Techniques of the Self." In *Foucault and Political Reason: Liberalism, Neo-Liberaliam and Rationalities of Government*, edited by Andrew Barry, Thomas Osborne, and Nikolas Rose, 19–36. Chicago: University of Chicago Press.

Butler, Judith. 1997. *Excitable Speech: A Politics of the Performative*. London: Routledge.

Cabot, Heath. 2014. *On the Doorstep of Europe: Asylum and Citizenship in Greece*. Philadelphia: University of Pennsylvania Press.

Caldeira, Teresa P. R. 1992. "Crime and Individual Rights: Reframing the Question of Violence in Latin America." In *Constructing Democracy: Human Rights, Citizenship, and Society in Latin America*, edited by Elizabeth Jelin and Eric Hershberg, 197–211. Boulder, CO: Westview Press.

————. 2000. *City of Walls: Crime, Segregation and Citizenship in São Paulo*. Berkeley: University of California Press.

Calhoun, Craig. 2002. "The Class Consciousness of Frequent Travelers: Toward a Critique of Actually Existing Cosmopolitanism." *The South Atlantic Quarterly* 101 (4): 869–97.

Callon, Michel. 1986. "Some Elements of a Sociology of Translation: Domestication of the Scallops and the Fishermen of St Brieuc Bay." In *Power of Action and Belief: A New Sociology of Knowledge*, edited by John Law, 196–229. London: Routledge.

Can, Başak. 2015. "Human Rights, Humanitarianism, and State Violence: Medical Documentation of Torture in Turkey." *Medical Anthropology Quarterly*. Accepted author manuscript. doi:10.1111/maq.12259.

Canefe, Nergis, and Tanıl Bora. 2003. "Intellectual Roots of Anti-European Sentiments in Turkish Politics: The Case of Radical Turkish Nationalism." In *Turkey and the European Union*, edited by Ali Çarkoğlu and Barry Rubin, 127–48. Portland, OR: Frand Cass.

Carr, Summerson. 2009. "Anticipating and Inhabiting Institutional Identities." *American Ethnologist* 36 (2): 317–36.

———. 2010. "Enactments of Expertise." *Annual Review of Anthropology* 39: 17–32.

Casier, Marlies. 2009. "Contesting the 'Truth' of Turkey's Human Rights Situation: State-Association Interactions in and Outside the Southeast." *European Journal of Turkish Studies* 10: 2–20.

Castoriadis, Cornelius. 1987. *The Imaginary Institution of Society*. Translated by Kathleen Blamey. Cambridge: Polity.

Çelikkol, Ahmet. 2005. "12 Eylül Tarih Gündeminde." *Radikal İki* 466: 4.

Ceza Muhakemesi Kanunu No: 5271. http://www.mevzuat.gov.tr/MevzuatMetin/1.5.5271 .pdf. Accessed: March 13, 2017.

Chakrabarty, Dipesh. 2007. *Provincializing Europe*. Princeton, NJ: Princeton University Press.

Chambers, Richard L. 1964. "Turkey." In *Political Modernization in Japan and Turkey*, edited by Robert E. Ward and Dankwart A. Rustow, 301–27. Princeton, NJ: Princeton University Press.

Chatterjee, Partha. 1986. *Nationalist Thought and the Colonial World: A Derivative Discourse?* London: Zed Books.

Cizre, Ümit. 2001. "The Truth and Fiction About (Turkey's) Human Rights Politics." *Human Rights Review* (October–December 2001): 55–77.

Coles, Kimberley A. 2002. "Ambivalent Builders: Europeanization, the Production of Difference, and Internationals in Bosnia-Herzegovina." *Political and Legal Anthropology Review* 25 (1): 1–18.

———. 2008. "Election Day: The Construction of Democracy Through Technique." *Cultural Anthropology* 19 (4): 551–80.

Collier, Stephen J., and Aihwa Ong. 2005. "Global Assemblages and Anthropological Problems." In *Global Assemblages: Technology, Politics and Ethics as Anthropological Problems*, edited by Aihwa Ong and Stephen J. Collier, 3–21. Oxford: Blackwell.

Commission of the European Communities. 2001. *European Governance: A White Paper*. 428 final. Brussels: CEC.

Conquergood, D. 1992. "Ethnography, Rhetoric, and Performance." *Quarterly Journal of Speech* 78: 80–123.

Coronil, Fernando, ed. 1997. *The Magical State: Nature, Money and Modernity in Venezuela*. Chicago: Chicago University Press.

Council on Foreign Relations. 2003. *A New National Security Strategy in an Age of Terrorists, Tyrants and Weapons of Mass Destruction: Three Options Presented as Presidential Speeches.* New York: Council on Foreign Relations Press.

Cowie, Matthew. 1997. "Toward a Critical Pedagogy for Adult Education." In *Human Rights Education for the Twenty-First Century*, edited by George J. Andreopoulos and Richard Pierre Claude, 236–52. Philadelphia: University of Pennsylvania Press.

Cruikshank, Barbara. 1996. "Revolutions Within: Self Government and Self Esteem." In *Foucault and Political Reason: Liberalism, Neo-Liberalism and Rationalities of Government*, edited by Andrew Barry, Thomas Osborne, and Nikolas Rose, 231–52. Chicago: University of Chicago Press.

Dağı, İhsan. 2004. "Rethinking Human Rights, Democracy, and the West: Post-Islamist Intellectuals in Turkey." *Critique: Critical Middle Eastern Studies* 13 (2): 135–51.

Darder, Antonia, Marta Baltodano, and Rodolfo D. Torres. 2003. "Critical Pedagogy: An Introduction." In *The Critical Pedagogy Reader*, edited by Antonia Darder, Marta Baltodano, and Rodolfo D. Torres. London: Routledge-Falmer.

Das, Veena, and Deborah Poole, eds. 2004. *Anthropology in the Margins of the State.* Santa Fe, NM: School of American Research Press.

De Certau, Michel. 1984. *The Practice of Everyday Life.* Berkeley: University of California Press.

Deeb, Hadi Nicholas, and George E. Marcus. 2011. "In the Green Room: An Experiment in Ethnographic Method at the WTO." *Political and Legal Anthropology Review* 34 (1): 51–76.

Dembour, Marie-Bénédicte. 1996. "Human Rights Talk and Anthropological Ambivalence: The Particular Context of Universal Claims." In *Inside and Outside the Law: Anthropological Studies of Authority and Ambiguity*, edited by Olivia Harris, 19–41. London: Routledge.

Deringil, Selim. 2007. "The Turks and 'Europe': The Argument from History." *Middle Eastern Studies* 43 (5): 709–23.

Douglas, Mary. 1966. *Purity and Danger.* London: Routledge.

DuBois, Marc. 1997. "Human Rights Education for the Police." In *Human Rights Education for the Twenty-First Century*, edited by George J. Andreopoulos and Richard Pierre Claude, 310–33. Philadelphia: University of Pennsylvania Press.

Dunn, Elizabeth. 2005. "Standards and Person Making in East Central Europe." In *Global Assemblages: Technology, Politics, and Ethics as Anthropological Problems*, edited by Aihwa Ong and Stephen Collier, 173–93. Oxford: Blackwell.

Eade, Deborah. 1997. *Capacity-Building: An Approach to People Centered Development.* Oxford: Oxfam.

Ebron, Paulla. 2002. *Performing Africa.* Princeton, NJ: Princeton University Press.

Engelke, Matthew. 1999. "We Wondered What Human Rights He Was Talking About." *Critique of Anthropology* 19 (3): 289–314.

Englund, Harri. 2006. *Prisoners of Freedom: Human Rights and the African Poor*. Berkeley: University of California Press.

Evans-Pritchard, E. E. (1940) 1969. *The Nuer: A Description of the Modes of Livelihood and Political Institutions of a Nilotic People*. Reprint. New York: Oxford University Press.

Ewing, Katherine Pratt. 2008. *Stolen Honor: Stigmatizing Muslim Men in Berlin*. Stanford, CA: Stanford University Press.

Exum, Jelani Jefferson, and Feridun Yenisey, eds. 2009. *Turkish Criminal Procedure Code*. İstanbul: Beta Basım Yayım Dağıtım A.Ş.

Fassin, Didier. 2012. "Introduction: Towards a Critical Moral Anthropology." In *Moral Anthropology*, edited by Didier Fassin, 1–17. Malden, MA: Wiley-Blackwell.

———, ed. 2015. *At the Heart of the State: The Moral World of Institutions*. London: Pluto Press.

Fassin, Didier, and Richard Rechtman. 2009. *The Empire of Trauma: An Inquiry into the Condition of Victimhood*. Translated by Rachel Gomme. Princeton, NJ: Princeton University Press.

Feldman, Ilana. 2008. *Governing Gaza: Bureaucracy, Authority and the Work of Rule, 1917–1967*. Durham, NC: Duke University Press.

Feldman, Ilana, and Miriam Ticktin, eds. 2010. *In the Name of Humanity: The Government of Treat and Care*. Durham, NC: Duke University Press.

Ferguson, James. 1994. *The Anti-Politics Machine: "Development," Depoliticization and Bureaucratic Power in Lesotho*. Minneapolis: University of Minnesota Press.

———. 2002. "Of Mimicry and Membership: Africans and the 'New World Society.'" *Cultural Anthropology* 17 (4): 551–69.

———. 2006. *Global Shadows: Africa in the Neoliberal World Order*. Durham, NC: Duke University Press.

Ferguson, James, and Akhil Gupta. 2002. "Spatializing States: Toward an Ethnography of Neoliberal Governmentality." *American Ethnologist* 29 (4): 981–1002.

Finkel, Andrew, and Nükhet Sirman. 1990. "Introduction." In *Turkish State, Turkish Society*, edited by Andrew Finkel and Nükhet Sirman, 2–20. London: Routledge.

Fırat, Bilge. 2009. "Negotiating Europe/Avrupa: Prelude for an Anthropological Approach to Turkish Europeanization and the Cultures of EU Lobbying in Brussels." *European Journal of Turkish Studies* 9: 1–19.

Frey, Frederick. 1965. *The Turkish Political Elite*. Cambridge, MA: The MIT Press.

Gandin, Louis Armando, and Michael W. Apple. 2004. "New Schools, New Knowledge, New Teachers: Creating the Citizen School in Porto Alegre, Brazil." *Teacher Education Quarterly* 31 (1): 173–98.

Goffman, Erving. 1956. *The Presentation of Self in Everyday Life*. Edinburgh: University of Edinburgh Social Science Research Centre.

Göker, Zeynep Gülru. 2011. "Presence in Silence: Feminist and Democratic Implications of the Saturday Vigils in Turkey." In *Social Movements, Mobilization, and Contesta-*

tion in the Middle East and North Africa, edited by Joel Beinin and Frédéric Vairel, 107–24. Stanford, CA: Stanford University Press.

Goodale, Mark, and Sally Engle Merry, eds. 2007. *The Practice of Human Rights: Tracking Law Between the Global and the Local*. Cambridge: Cambridge University Press.

Goodwin, Charles. 1994. "Professional Vision." *American Anthropologist* 96 (3): 606–33.

Graeber, David. 2015. *The Utopia of Rules: On Technology, Stupidity, and the Secret Joys of Bureaucracy*. Brooklyn, NY: Melville House.

Grigoriadis, Ioannis N. 2004. "On Europeanization of Turkish Political Culture." Paper presented at the second Pan-European Conference on European Politics, Bologna, June 24–26 June 2004.

———. 2006. "Turkey's Accession to the European Union: Debating the Most Difficult Enlargement Ever." *SAIS Review* 26: 147–59.

Grindle, Merilee S. 1997. "The Good Government Imperative: Human Resources, Organizations, and Institutions." In *Getting Good Government: Capacity Building in the Public Sectors of Developing Countries*, edited by Merilee S. Grindle. Cambridge: Harvard University Press.

Gupta, Akhil. 1995. "Blurred Boundaries: The Discourse of Corruption, the Culture of Politics and the Imagined State." *American Ethnologist* 22: 375–402.

———. 1997. "The Song of the Nonaligned World: Transnational Identities and the Reinscription of Space in Late Capitalism." *In Culture, Power, Place: Explorations in Critical Anthropology*, edited by Akhil Gupta and James Ferguson, 179–202. Durham, NC: Duke University Press.

———. 2005. "Narratives of Corruption: Anthropological and Fictional Accounts of the Indian State." *Ethnography* 6 (1): 5–34.

———. 2012. *Red Tape: Bureaucracy, Structural Violence, and Poverty in India*. Durham, NC: Duke University Press.

Gupta, Akhil, and James Ferguson. 1997. "Discipline and Practice: 'The Field' as Site, Method and Location in Anthropolgy." In *Anthropological Locations: Boundaries and Grounds of a Field Science*, edited by Akhil Gupta and James Ferguson, 1–46. Berkeley, CA: University of California Press.

Gürbey, Gülistan. 1997. "Türkiye'de Bir Sivil Toplum Oluşumunun Önündeki Siyasi ve Hukuki Engeller." In *Ortadoğu'da Sivil Toplumun Sorunları*, edited by Ferhad İbrahim and Heidi Wedel, 117–35. İstanbul: İletişim Yayınları.

Gürbilek, Nurdan. 2009. "Avrupa'nın Cinsiyeti: Uysal Bakire, Yutucu Dişi, Fetihçi Oğul." In *Türkiye'de İktidarı Yeniden Düşünmek*, edited by Murat Güney, 94–109. İstanbul: Varlık Yayınları.

Hajjar, Lisa. 2005. *Courting Conflict: The Israeli Military Court System in the West Bank and Gaza*. Berkeley, CA: University of California Press.

Hale, William. 2003. "Human Rights, the European Union and the Turkish Accession

Process." In *Turkey and the European Union*, edited by Ali Çarkoğlu and Barry Rubin, 107–26. Portland, OR: Frank Cass.

Hannerz, Ulf. 1996. *Transnational Connections: Culture, People, Places*. London: Routledge.

———. 2007. "Cosmopolitanism." In *A Companion to the Anthropology of Politics*, edited by David Nugent and Joan Vincent, 69–85. Oxford: Blackwell.

Hansen, Thomas Blom, and Finn Steputtat, eds. 2001. *States of Imagination: Ethnographic Explorations of the Postcolonial State*. Durham, NC: Duke University Press.

Haskell, Thomas L. 1985a. "Capitalism and the Origins of the Humanitarian Sensibility, Part 1." *American Historical Review* 90 (2): 339–61.

———. 1985b. "Capitalism and the Origins of the Humanitarian Sensibility, Part 2." *American Historical Review* 90 (3): 547–66.

Heper, Metin. 1985. *The State Tradition in Turkey*. Walkington, UK: Eothen Press.

———. 2000. "The Ottoman Legacy and Turkish Politics." *Journal of International Affairs* 54 (1): 63–82.

Hersant, Jeanne. 2011. "Mobilizations for Western Thrace and Cyprus in Contemporary Turkey: From the Far Right to the Lexicon of Human Rights." In *Social Movements, Mobilization, and Contestation in the Middle East and North Africa*, edited by Joel Beinin and Frédéric Vairel, 125–42. Stanford, CA: Stanford University Press.

Herzfeld, Michael. 1987. *Anthropology Through the Looking Glass: Critical Ethnography in the Margins of Europe*. Cambridge: Cambridge University Press.

———. 1992. *The Social Production of Indifference*. Chicago: University of Chicago Press.

———. 1997. *Cultural Intimacy: Social Poetics in the Nation State*. London: Routledge.

———. 2015. "Anthropology and the Inchoate Intimacies of Power." *American Ethnologist* 42 (1): 18–32.

Hetherington, Kregg. 2011. *Guerilla Auditors: The Politics of Transparency in Neoliberal Paraguay*. Durham, NC: Duke University Press.

———. 2014. "Regular Soybeans: Translation and Framing in the Ontological Politics of a Coup." *Indiana Journal of Global Legal Studies* 21 (1): 55–78.

Hicks, Neil. 2001. "Legislative Reform in Turkey and European Human Rights Mechanisms." *Human Rights Review* (October–December 2001): 78–85.

Hindess, Barry. 1996. "Liberalism, Socialism and Democracy." In *Foucault and Political Reason: Liberalism, Neo-Liberalism and Rationalities of Government*, edited by Andrew Barry, Thomas Osborne, and Nikolas Rose, 65–80. Chicago: University of Chicago Press.

Hinkley, D. Michael. 1997. "Military Training for Human Rights and Democratization." In *Human Rights Education for the Twenty-First Century*, edited by George J. Andreopoulos and Richard Pierre Claude, 296–309. Philadelphia: University of Pennsylvania Press.

Ho, Karen. 2009a. "Disciplining Investment Bankers, Disciplining Economy: Wall

Street's Institutional Culture of Crisis and the Downsizing of 'Corporate America.'" *American Anthropologist* 111 (2): 177–89.

———. 2009b. *Liquidated: An Ethnography of Wall Street*. Durham, NC: Duke University Press.

Holmes, Douglas R., and George E. Marcus. 2005. "Cultures of Expertise and the Management of Globalization: Toward the Re-functioning of Ethnography." In *Global Assemblages*, edited by Aihwa Ong and Stephen J. Collier, 235–52. Oxford: Blackwell Publishing.

Hornberger, Julia. 2011. *Policing and Human Rights: The Meaning of Violence and Justice in the Everyday Policing of Johannesburg*. New York: Routledge.

Howe, Leo. 2000. "Risk, Ritual and Performance." *The Journal of the Royal Anthropological Institute* 6 (1): 63–79.

Hsu, Roland. 2010a. "The Ethnic Question: Premodern Identity for a Postmodern Europe?" In *Ethnic Europe: Mobility, Identity, and Conflict in a Globalized World*, edited by Roland Hsu, 1–17. Stanford, CA: Stanford University Press.

———, ed. 2010b. *Ethnic Europe: Mobility, Identity and Conflict in a Globalized World*. Stanford, CA: Stanford University Press.

Hull, Matthew. 2012. *Government of Paper: The Materiality of Bureaucracy in Urban Pakistan*. Berkeley: University of California Press.

Hunter, Ian. 1996. "Assembling the School." In *Foucault and Political Reason: Liberalism, Neo-Liberalism and Rationalities of Government*, edited by Andrew Barry, Thomas Osborne, and Nikolas Rose, 143–66. Chicago: University of Chicago Press.

Hwang, Hokyu, and Walter W. Powell. 2009. "The Rationalization of Charity: The Influences of Professionalism in the Non-Profit Sector." *Administrative Science Quarterly* 54: 268–98.

İHD, ed. 2006. '*20 Yıllık Kısa Kronoloji' Uzun İnce Bir Yoldayız: İHD 20 Yaşında*. Ankara: Basın Yayın Organizasyon İktisadi İşletme.

İHD/TİHV. 1999. "Türkiye İnsan Hakları Hareketi: Birikim ve Perspektifler." *Birikim* 118: 56–61.

Illich, Ivan, Irving Kenneth Zola, John McKnight, Jonathan Caplan, and Harley Shaiken, eds. (1977) 2000. *Disabling Professions*. Reprint, New York: Marion Boyars.

Inda, Jonathan Xavier, and Renato Rosaldo, eds. 2002. *The Anthropology of Globalization: A Reader*. Oxford: Blackwell.

Inoue, Miyako. 2006. *Vicarious Language: Gender and Linguistic Modernity in Japan*. Berkeley: University of California Press.

Ismail, Salwa. 2006. *Political Life in Cairo's New Quarters: Encountering the Everyday State*. Minneapolis: University of Minnesota Press.

James, Erica Caple. 2012. "Witchcraft, Bureaucrats, and The Social Life of (US) Aid in Haiti." *Cultural Anthropology* 27 (1): 50–75.

Jefferson, Andrew M., and Steffen Jensen (2009). "Introduction: Repopulating State Violence and Human Rights." In *State Violence and Human Rights: State Officials in the South*, edited by Andrew Jefferson and Steffen Jensen, 1–22. New York: Routledge-Cavendish.

Jenkins, Rob. 2001. "Mistaking 'Governance' for 'Politics': Foreign Aid, Democracy, and the Construction of Civil Society." In *Civil Society: History and Possibilities*, edited by Sudipta Kaviraj and Sunil Khilnani, 250–68. Cambridge: Cambridge University Press.

Kanar, Ercan. 1999. "İnsan Hakları: Bir Değerlendirme." *Birikim* 118: 41–51.

Kaplan, Roger F. S. 2001. "Turkey in the Middle East: The Islamic War with Itself." *Human Rights Review* (October–December 2001): 3–10.

Kaplan, Sam. 2006. *The Pedagogical State: Education and the Politics of National Culture in Post-1980 Turkey*. Stanford, CA: Stanford University Press.

Karaosmanoğlu, Ali. 2000. "The Evolution of the National Security Culture and the Military in Turkey." *Journal of International Affairs* 54: 199–216.

Karaosmanoğlu, Yakup Kadri. 1934. *Ankara*. İstanbul: İletişim Yayınları.

Kaufman, Edy. 1997. "Human Rights Education for Law Enforcement." In *Human Rights Education for the Twenty-First Century*, edited by George J. Andreopoulos and Richard Pierre Claude, 278–95. Philadelphia: University of Pennsylvania Press.

Kayaalp, Ebru. 2012. "Torn in Translation: An Ethnographic Study of Regulatory Decision-Making in Turkey." *Regulation & Governance* 6 (2): 225–41.

Keck, Margaret E., and Kathryn Sikkink. 1998. *Activists Beyond Borders*. Ithaca, NY: Cornell University Press.

Keyder, Çağlar. 1993. "The Dilemma of Cultural Identity on the Margin of Europe." *Review* 16 (1): 19–33.

———. 2003. "AB ile ABD Arasında Türkiye." In *Memalik-i Osmaniye'den Avrupa Birliği'ne, Çağlar Keyder*, 225–46. İstanbul: İletişim Yayınları.

Kiser, Edgar, and Justin Baer. 2005. "The Bureaucratization of States: Toward an Analytical Weberianism." In *Remaking Modernity: Politics, History and Sociology*, edited by Julia Adams, Elizabeth Clemens, and Ann Shola Orlof, 225–45. Durham, NC: Duke University Press.

Koğacıoğlu, Dicle. 2004. "The Tradition Effect: Framing Honor Crimes in Turkey." *Differences: A Journal of Feminist Cultural Studies* 15 (2): 118–51.

———. 2005. "Citizenship in Context: Rethinking Women's Relationships to the Law in Turkey." In *Citizenship and the Nation State in Greece and Turkey*, edited by Faruk Birtek and Thalia Dragonas, 144–60. London: Routledge.

———. 2009. "Bir İstanbul Adliyesi'nde Davranış Kalıpları, Anlamlandırma Biçimleri ve Eşitsizlik." In *Türkiye'de İktidarı Yeniden Düşünmek*, edited by Murat Güney, 110–57. İstanbul: Varlık Yayınları.

Kubicek, Paul. 2004. "Turkey's Place in the 'New Europe.'" *Perceptions: Journal of International Affairs* 9 (3): 55–8.

Kuçuradi, Ioanna. 2008. "The Philosophical Teaching of Human Rights: Teaching Human

Rights as Philosophy Courses." In *Value Education: Based on All the Religions of the World*, edited by Promilla Kapur, 671–81. Delhi: Kalpaz Publications.

Kurban, Dilek, Ozan Erözden, and Haldun Gülalp. 2008. "Supranational Rights Litigation, Implementation and the Domestic Impact of Strasbourg Court Jurisprudence: A Case Study of Turkey." In *JURISTRAS*. Athens: Hellenic Foundation for European and Foreign Policy (ELIAMEP).

Kyed, Helene Maria. 2009. "Traditional Authority and Localization of State Law: The Intricacies of Boundary Marking in Policing Rural Mozambique." In *State Violence and Human Rights: State Officials in the South*, edited by Andrew M. Jefferson and Steffen Jensen. New York: Routledge-Cavendish.

Lampland, Martha, and Susan Leigh Star. 2009. *Standards and Their Stories: How Quantifying, Classifying and Formalizing Practices Shape Everyday Life*. Ithaca, NY: Cornell University Press.

Latour, Bruno. 1987. *Science in Action: How to Follow Scientists and Engineers Through Society*. Cambridge, MA: Harvard University Press.

———. 2005. *Reassembling the Social: An Introduction to Actor-Network Theory*. Oxford: Oxford University Press.

Lea, Tess. 2008. *Bureaucrats and Bleeding Hearts: Indigenous Health in Northern Australia*. Sydney: University of South Wales Press.

Leistyna, Pepi, Magaly Lavandez, and Thomas Nelson. 2004. "Introduction—Critical Pedagogy: Revitalizing and Democratizing Teacher Education." *Teacher Education Quarterly* 31 (1): 3–15.

Lerner, Daniel. 1958. *The Passing of Traditional Society: Modernizing the Middle East*. Glencoe, IL: The Free Press.

Lévi-Strauss, Claude. 1973. *Tristes Tropiques*. New York: Penguin Books.

Lewis, David, and David Mosse. 2006. "Encountering Order and Disjuncture: Contemporary Anthropological Perspectives on the Organization of Development." *Oxford Development Studies* 34 (1): 1–13.

Li, Tania Murray. 2007. *The Will to Improve: Governmentality, Development and the Practice of Politics*. Durham, NC: Duke University Press.

Libal, Kathryn. 2001. "Children's Rights in Turkey." *Human Rights Review* (October–December): 35–44.

Lie, Jon Harald Sande. 2015. *Developmentality: An Ethnography of the World Bank–Uganda Partnership*. New York: Berghahn Books.

MacMillan, Catherine. 2010. "Privileged Partnership, Open Ended Accession Negotiations and the Securitisation of Turkey's EU Accession Process." *Journal of Contemporary European Studies* 18 (4): 447–62.

Malcomson, Scott L. 1995. "On European Union." *Transition* 68: 4–12.

Malkki, Liisa Helena. 1992. "National Geographic: The Rooting of Peoples and the Territorialization of National Identity among Scholars and Refugees." *Cultural Anthropology* 7 (1): 24–44.

———. 1994. "Citizens of Humanity: Internationalism and the Imagined Community of Nations." *Diaspora* 3 (1): 41–68.

———. 1995. *Purity and Exile: Violence, Memory and National Cosmology among Hutu Refugees in Tanzania.* Chicago: University of Chicago Press.

———. 1996. "Speechless Emissaries: Refugees, Humanitarianism, and Dehistoricization." *Cultural Anthropology* 11 (3): 377–404.

———. 1998. "Things to Come: Internationalism and Global Solidarities in the Late 1990s." *Public Culture* 10 (2): 431–42.

———. 2007a. "Professionalisme, Internationalisme, Universalisme." *Anthropologie et Sociétés* 31 (2): 45–63.

———. 2007b. "Tradition and Improvisation in Ethnographic Field Research." In *Improvising Theory: Process and Temporality in Ethnographic Fieldwork*, edited by Allaine Cerwonka and Liisa Helena Malkki, 162–88. Chicago: University of Chicago Press.

Mamdani, Mahmood. 2008. "The New Humanitarian Order." *The Nation*, September 29.

Mandel, Ruth. 2008. *Cosmopolitan Anxieties: Turkish Challenges to Citizenship and Belonging in Germany.* Durham, NC: Duke University Press.

Mardin, Şerif. 1973. "Center-Periphery Relations: A Key to Turkish Politics?" *Daedalus* 102 (1): 169–90.

———. 1990. *Türkiye'de Toplum ve Siyaset.* İstanbul: İletişim Yayınları.

Marguiles, Ronnie, and Ergin Yıldızoğlu. 1984. "Trade Unions and Turkey's Working Class." *Merip Reports* 121: 15–20, 31.

Mathews, Andrew. 2008. "State Making, Knowledge, and Ignorance: Translation and Concealment in Mexican Forestry Institutions." *American Anthropologist* 110 (4): 484–94.

Mayo, Peter. 2009. "Flying Below the Radar? Critical Approaches to Adult Education." In *The Routledge International Handbook of Critical Education*, edited by Michael Apple, Au Wayne and Louis Armando Gandin, 269–80. London: Routledge.

McDonnell, Lorraine M., and Richard F. Elmore. 1987. "Getting the Job Done: Alternative Policy Instruments." *Educational Evaluation and Policy Analysis* 9 (2): 133–52.

Meeker, Michael E. 2002. *A Nation of Empire: The Ottoman Legacy of Turkish Modernity.* Berkeley: University of California Press.

Mepham, John. 1987. "Turkey: Reading the Small Print." *Merip Reports* 149: 19–25.

Mercan, Ahmet. 1999. "İnsan 'Hak'larının Seyri." *Birikim* 118: 52–54.

Merry, Sally Engle. 1979. "Going to Court: Strategies of Dispute Management in an American Urban Neighborhood." *The Law and Society Review* 13 (4): 891–925.

———. 1992. "Anthropology, Law and Transnational Processes." *Annual Review of Anthropology* 21: 357–79.

———. 2006. *Human Rights & Gender Violence: Translating International Law into Local Justice*. Chicago: University of Chicago Press.

———. 2011. "Measuring the World: Indicators, Human Rights, and Global Governance." *Current Anthropology* 52 (3): 83–95.

Mitchell, Timothy. 2002. *Rule of Experts: Egypt, Technopolitics, Modernity*. Berkeley: University of California Press.

Montoya, Celeste. 2008. "The European Union, Capacity Building, and Transnational Networks: Combatting Violence Against Women through the Daphne Program." *International Organization* 62 (Spring 2008): 359–72.

Mosse, David. 2005a. *Cultivating Development: An Ethnography of Aid Policy and Practice*. London: Pluto Press.

———. 2005b. "Global Governance and the Ethnography of International Aid." In *The Aid Effect: Giving and Governing in International Development*, edited by David Mosse and David Lewis, 1–36. London: Pluto Press.

Müftüler-Bac, Meltem. 2005. "Turkey's Political Reforms and the Impact of the European Union." *South European Society and Politics* 10 (1): 16–30.

Nader, Laura. 1988. "Up the Anthropologist—Perspectives Gained From Studying Up." In *Anthropology for the Nineties*, edited by Johnetta B. Cole, 470–84. New York: The Free Press.

Narayan, Kirin. 1993. "How Native Is a 'Native' Anthropologist?" *American Anthropologist* 95 (3): 671–86.

Navaro-Yashin, Yael. 1998. "Uses and Abuses of 'State and Civil Society' in Contemporary Turkey." *New Perspectives on Turkey* 18: 1–22.

———. 2002. *Faces of the State: Secularism and Public Life in Turkey*. Princeton, NJ: Princeton University Press.

———. 2006. "Affect in the Civil Service: A Study of a Modern State-System." *Postcolonial Studies* 9 (3): 281–94.

———. 2007. "Make-Believe Papers, Legal Forms and the Counterfeit: Affective Interactions between Documents and the People in Britain and Cyprus." *Anthropological Theory* 7 (1): 79–98.

———. 2012. *The Make-Believe Space: Affective Geography in a Postwar Polity*. Durham, NC: Duke University Press.

Oğuşgil, V. Atilla. 2015. "Avrupa Birliği Yolunda Türkiye İnsan Hakları Kurumu'nun Birleşmiş Milletler Paris Prensipleri Işığında Değerlendirilmesi." *Bilig Yaz 2015 Sayı* 74: 175–98.

Öncü, Ayşe. 1991. "The Transformation of the Bases of Social Standing in Contemporary Turkish Society." In *Structural Change in Turkish Society*, edited by Mübeccel Kıray, 140–62. Bloomington: Indiana University Press.

Öniş, Ziya. 2008. "Turkey-EU Relations: Beyond the Current Stalemate." *Insight Turkey* 10 (4): 35–50.

———. 2013. "Sharing Power: Turkey's Democratization Challenge in the Age of AKP Hegemony." *Insight Turkey* 15 (2): 103–22.

Oran, Baskın. 2007. "The Minority Concept and Rights in Turkey: The Lausanne Peace Treaty and Current Issues." In *Human Rights in Turkey*, edited by Zehra Kabasakal Arat. Philadelphia: University of Pennsylvania Press.

Osanloo, Arzoo. 2006. "The Measure of Mercy: Islamic Justice, Sovereign Power and Human Rights in Iran." *Cultural Anthropology* 21 (4): 570–602.

———. 2009. *The Politics of Women's Rights in Iran*. Princeton, NJ: Princeton University Press.

Osborne, Thomas. 1994. "Bureaucracy as a Vocation: Governmentality and Administration in Nineteenth-Century Britain." *Journal of Historical Sociology* 7 (3): 289–313.

Özer, Nazan. 2006. Küreselleşme ve Bürokratik Seçkinler. Ankara: Lotus Yayınevi.

Özyürek, Esra 2005. "The Politics of Cultural Unification, Secularism, and the Place of Islam in the New Europe." *American Ethnologist* 32 (4): 509–512.

———. 2006. *Nostalgia for the Modern: State Secularism and Everyday Politics in Turkey*. Durham, NC: Duke University Press.

Pamuk, Şevket. 1981. "Political Economy of Industrialization in Turkey." *Merip Reports* 93: 26–30, 32.

Pamukoğlu, Osman. 2003. *Unutulanlar Dışında Yeni Bir Şey Yok: Hakkari ve Kuzey Irak Dağlarındaki Askerler*. İstanbul: Harmoni Yayıncılık.

Parla, Ayşe. 2001. "The Honor of the State: Virginity Examinations in Turkey." *Feminist Studies* 27 (1): 65–88.

Paul, Jim. 1981. "The Coup." *Merip Reports* 93: 3–4.

Pazarcıklı, Doğan. 2004. *Türklerin Tanrısı: Devlet*. İstanbul: Derin Yayınları.

Pieterse, Jan Nederveen. 2002. "Europe and Its Others." In *a Companion to Racial and Ethnic Studies*, edited by David Theo Goldberg and John Solomos. Oxford: Blackwell. doi: 10.1111/b.9780631206163.2002.00005.x

Povinelli, Elizabeth. 2001. "Radical Worlds: The Anthropology of Incommensurability and Inconceivability." *Annual Review of Anthropology* 30: 319–34.

———. 2002. *The Cunning of Recognition: Indigenous Alterities and the Making of Australian Multiculturalism*. Durham, NC: Duke University Press.

Pratt, Mary Louise. 1991. "Arts of the Contact Zone." *Profession* 91: 33–40.

Rafael, Vincente. 2005. *The Promise of the Foreign: Nationalism and the Technics of Translation in the Spanish Philippines*. Durham, NC: Duke University Press.

Rancière, Jacques. 2004. "Who is the Subject of the Rights of Man?" *The South Atlantic Quarterly* 103 (2/3): 297–310.

Redfield, Peter. 2005. "Doctors, Borders and Life in Crisis." *Cultural Anthropology* 20 (3): 328–61.

———. 2006. "A Less Modest Witness: Collective Advocacy and Motivated Truth in a Medical Humanitarian Movement." *American Ethnologist* 33 (1): 3–26.

Riles, Annelise. 2010. "Collateral Expertise: Legal Knowledge in the Global Financial Markets." *Current Anthropology* 51(6): 795–818.

Rose, Nikolas. 1996. "Governing 'Advanced' Liberal Democracies." In *Foucault and Political Reason: Liberalism, Neo-Liberalism and Rationalities of Government*, edited by Andrew Barry, Thomas Osborne, and Nikolas Rose, 37–64. Chicago: The University of Chicago Press.

Sampson, Steven. 1996. "The Social Life of Projects: Importing Civil Society to Albania." In *Civil Society: Challenging Western Models*, edited by Chris Hann and Elizabeth Dunn, 121–42. London: Routledge.

Sarfaty, Galit. 2012. *Values in Translation: Human Rights and the Culture of the World Bank*. Stanford, CA: Stanford University Press.

Sayer, Derek. 1994. "Everyday Forms of State Formation: Some Dissident Remarks on 'Hegemony.'" In *Everyday Forms of State Formation: Revolution and the Negotiation of Rule in Modern Mexico*, edited by Gilbert M. Joseph and Daniel Nugent, 367–77. Durham, NC: Duke University Press.

Schudson, Michael. 2006. "The Trouble With Experts—and Why Democracies Need Them." *Theory and Society* 35: 491–506.

Scott, J. C. 1985. *Weapons of the Weak: Everyday Forms of Peasant Resistance*. New Haven, CT: Yale University Press.

Scott, J. W., Kaplan, C., Keates, D., eds. 1997. *Transitions, Environments, Translations*. New York: Routledge.

Sharma, Aradhana, and Akhil Gupta, eds. 2006. *The Anthropology of the State: A Reader*. Oxford: Blackwell.

Shore, Chris. 2000. *Building Europe: The Cultural Politics of European Integration*. London: Routledge.

Silverstein, Brian. 2014. "Statistics, Reform, and Regimes of Expertise in Turkey." *Turkish Studies* 15 (4): 638–54.

Sirman, Nükhet. 1990. "State, Village and Gender in Western Turkey." In *Turkish State, Turkish Society*, edited by Andrew Finkel and Nükhet Sirman, 21–51. London: Routledge.

———. 1997. "Crossing Boundaries in the Study of Southern Europe." In *Tradition in Modernity: Southern Europe in Question*, Proceedings of the ISA Regional Conference for Southern Europe in Istanbul, June 20–21, 1997, edited by Çağlar Keyder, 45–54. Madrid: International Sociological Association. http://www.isa-sociology.org/uploads/files/Chapter%202%286%29.pdf

Slyomovics, Susan. 2005. *The Performance of Human rights in Morocco*. Philadelphia: University of Pennsylvania Press.

Spadola, Emilio. 2004. "Jinn, Islam and Media in Morocco." *Yearbook of the Sociology of Islam* 5: 13–24.

Spivak, Gayatri Chakravorty. 1993. "Politics of Translation." In *Outside in the Teaching Machine*. New York: Routledge.

———. 2000. "Translation as Culture." *Parallax* 6 (1): 13–24.

Stacy, Helen M. 2009. *Human Rights for the 21st Century: Sovereignty, Civil Society, Culture*. Stanford, CA: Stanford University Press.

Star, Susan Leigh, and James R. Griesemer. 1989. "Institutional Ecology, 'Translations' and Boundary Objects: Amateurs and Professionals in Berkeley's Museum of Vertebrate Zoology." *Social Studies of Science* 19 (3): 387–420.

Steedman, Carolyn Kay. 1992. *Landscape for a Good Woman: A Story of Two Lives*. New Brunswick, NJ: Rutgers University Press.

Steinmetz, George, ed. 1999. *State/Culture: State Formation After the Cultural Turn*. Ithaca, NY: Cornell University Press.

Steinmüller, Hans. 2010. "Communities of Complicity: Notes on State Formation and Local Sociality in Rural China." *American Ethnologist* 37 (3): 539–49.

Stoler, Ann Laura. 2004. "Affective States." In *Companion to the Anthropology of Politics*, edited by David Nugent and Joan Vincent, 4–20. Oxford: Oxford University Press.

Stork, Joe. 2011. "Three Decades of Human Rights Activism in the Middle East and North Africa: An Ambiguous Balance Sheet." In *Social Movements, Mobilization, and Contestation in the Middle East and North Africa*, edited by Joel Beinin and Frédéric Vairel, 83–106. Stanford, CA: Stanford University Press.

Strathern, Marilyn. 2000. "New Accountabilities: Anthropological Studies in Audit, Ethics and the Academy." In *Audit Cultures: Anthropological Studies in Accountability, Ethics and the Academy*, edited by Marilyn Strathern, 1–18. London: Routledge.

Sugden, Jonathan. 2004. "Leverage in Theory and Practice: Human Rights and Turkey's EU Candidacy." In *Turkey and the European Integration: Accession Prospects and Issues*, edited by Nergis Canefe and Mehmet Uğur, 241–64. London: Routledge.

Surin, Kenneth. 2001. "The Sovereign Individual and Michael Taussig's Politics of Defacement." *Nepantla: Views from South* 2 (1): 205–20.

Talberg, Jonas. 2002. "Paths to Compliance: Enforcement, Management, and the European Union." *International Organization* 56 (3): 609–43.

Tate, Winifred. 2007. *Counting the Dead: The Culture and Politics of Human Rights Activism in Colombia*. Berkeley: University of California Press.

Taussig, Michael. 1992. *The Nervous System*. London: Routledge.

———. 1997. *The Magic of the State*. London: Routledge.

———. 1999. *Defacement: Public Secrecy and the Labor of the Negative*. Stanford, CA: Stanford University Press.

Terdiman, Richard. 1987. "Translator's Introduction to the Force of Law: Toward a Sociology of the Juridical Field by Pierre Bourdieu." *The Hastings Law Journal* 38: 805–13.

Thiranagama, Sharika. 2011. *In My Mother's House: Civil War in Sri Lanka*. Philadelphia: University of Pennsylvania Press.

Ticktin, Miriam. 2005. "Policing and Humanitarianism in France: Immigration and the Turn to Law as State of Exception." *Interventions* 7 (3): 347–68.

———. 2006. "Where Ethics and Politics Meet: The Violence of Humanitarianism in France." *American Ethnologist* 33 (1): 33–49.

Trouillot, Michel-Rolph. 2001. "The Anthropology of the State in the Age of Globalization: Close Encounters of the Deceptive Kind." *Current Anthropology* 42 (1): 125–38.

Tsing, Anna Lowenhaupt. 1997. "Transitions as Translations." In *Transitions, Environments, Translations*. Edited by Cora Kaplan, Joan W. Scott, and Debra Keates. New York: Routledge.

———. 2005. *Friction: An Ethnography of Global Connection*. Princeton: Princeton University Press.

Tuğal, Cihan. 2007. "NATO's Islamists: Hegemony and Americanization in Turkey." *New Left Review* 44: 5–30.

———. 2009. *Passive Revolution: Absorbing the Islamic Challenge to Capitalism*. Stanford, CA: Stanford University Press.

Turam, Berna. 2007. *Between Islam and the State: The Politics of Engagement*. Stanford, CA: Stanford University Press.

Türem, Ziya Umut, and Andrea Ballestero. 2014. "Regulatory Translations: Expertise and Affect in Global Legal Field." *Indiana Journal of Global Legal Studies* 21 (1): 1–25.

Türk Ceza Kanunu No: 5237. http://www.mevzuat.gov.tr/MevzuatMetin/1.5.5237.pdf. Accessed: March 13, 2017.

Türker, Yıldırım. 2005. "Paşalar Cumhuriyeti." *Radikal İki* 466: 9.

Türkmen, Emir Ali. 2006. "Yirmi Yılın Artı ve Eksileri." In *'20 Yıllık Kısa Kronoloji' Uzun İnce Bir Yoldayız: İHD 20 Yaşında*, edited by İHD, 129–34. Ankara: Basın Yayın Organizasyon İktisadi İşletme.

Turner, Victor. 1986. "The Anthropology of Performance." In *The Anthropology of Performance*, edited by Victor Turner. New York: PAJ Publications.

Uğur, Mehmet, and Nergis Canefe. 2004. "Turkey and European Integration: Introduction." In *Turkey and European Integration: Accession Prospects and Issues*, edited by Mehmet Uğur and Nergis Canefe, 1–15. London: Routledge.

Vairel, Frédéric. 2011. "Protesting in Authoritarian Situations: Egypt and Morocco in Comparative Perspective." In *Social Movements, Mobilization, and Contestation in the Middle East and North Africa*, edited by Joel Beinin and Frédéric Vairel, 27–42. Stanford, CA: Stanford University Press.

Venuti, Lawrence. 1995. *The Translator's Invisibility: A History of Translation*. London: Routledge.

———. 2003. "Translating Derrida on Translation: Relevance and Disciplinary Resistance." *The Yale Journal of Criticism* 16 (2): 237–62.

Visier, Claire. 2009. "Turkey and the European Union: The Sociology of Engaged Actors and of Their Contribution to the Candidacy Issue." *European Journal of Turkish Studies* 9 [Online] http://ejts.revues.org/index3910.html

Watts, Nicole. 2001. "A Symposium On Human Rights in Turkey: Introduction." *Human Rights Review* (October–December 2001): 11–16.

Weber, Max. 1978. "Legal Authority with a Bureaucratic Administrative Staff." In *Max Weber: Economy and Society*, edited by Guenter Roth and Claus Wittich, 217–26. Berkeley: University of California Press.

Wedeen, Lisa. 1999. *Ambiguities of Domination: Politics, Rhetoric and Symbols in Contemporary Syria*. Chicago: University of Chicago Press.

Wedel, Heidi. 1997. "Türkiye Cumhuriyeti'nde Sivil Toplumun Nüveleri—Yeni Bir Seçkinler Örgütlenmesi mi?" In *Ortadoğu'da Sivil Toplumun Sorunları*, edited by Heidi Wedel and Ferhad İbrahim, 137–62. İstanbul: İletişim Yayınları.

Weizman, Eyal. 2011. *The Least of Possible Evils: Humanitarian Violence from Arendt to Gaza*. London: Verso.

Weston, Kath. 1991. *Families We Choose: Lesbians, Gays, Kinship*. New York: Columbia University Press.

———. 1997. "The Virtual Anthropologist." In *Anthropological Locations: Boundaries of a Field Science*, edited by Akhil Gupta and James Ferguson, 163–84. Berkeley: University of California Press.

White, J. B. 1994. *Money Makes Us Relatives: Women's Labor in Urban Turkey*. Austin: University of Texas Press.

———. 2001. "The Islamist Movement in Turkey and Human Rights." *Human Rights Review* (October–December 2001: 17–26.

———. 2002a. *Islamist Mobilization in Turkey: A Study in Vernacular Politics*. Seattle: University of Washington Press.

———. 2002b. "The Islamist Paradox." In *Fragments of Culture: The Everyday of Modern Turkey*, edited by Deniz Kandiyoti and Ayse Saktanber. New Brunswick, NJ: Rutgers University Press.

Williams, Raymond. 1983. *Keywords: A Vocabulary of Culture and Society*. New York: Oxford University Press.

Willis, Paul. 1977. *Learning to Labor: How Working Class Kids Get Working Class Jobs*. New York: Columbia University Press.

World Bank. 1992. *Governance and Development*. Washington, DC: The World Bank. http://documents.worldbank.org/curated/en/604951468739447676/Governance-and-development.

Yalpat, Altan. 1984. "Turkey's Economy under the Generals." *Merip Reports* 122: 16–24.

Yankaya, Dilek. 2009. "The Europeanization of MÜSİAD: Political Opportunism, Economic Europeanization, Islamic Euroscepticism." *European Journal of Turkish Studies* 9: 2–19.

Yeğenoğlu, Meyda. 2005. "Cosmopolitanism and Nationalism in a Globalized World." Ethnic and Racial Studies 28 (1): 103–131.

Yılmaz, Gözde. (2016). "From Europeanization to De-Europeanization: The Europeanization Process of Turkey in 1999–2014." *Journal of Contemporary European Studies* 24 (1): 86–100.

Yörük, Erdem, and Murat Yüksel. 2014. "Class and Politics in Turkey's Gezi Protests." *New Left Review* 89 (Sept–Oct 2014): 103–123.

Young, Iris Marion. 2003. "The Logic of Masculinist Protection: Reflections on the Current Security State." *Signs: Journal of Women in Culture and Society* 29 (1): 2–25.

Zaloom, Caitlin. 2006. *Out of the Pits: Traders and Technology from Chicago to London.* Chicago: University of Chicago Press.

Zinn, Bacca. 1979. "Field Research in Minority Communities: Ethical, Methodological and Political Observations by an Insider." *Social Problems* 27 (2): 209–19.

Zola, Irving Kenneth. (1977) 2000. "Healthism and Disabling Medicalization." In *Disabling Professions*, edited by Ivan Illich, Irving Kenneth Zola, Jonathan Caplan, John McKnight and Harley Shaiken, 41–67. Reprint New York: Marion Boyars.

Zubaida, Sami. 1994. "Human Rights and Cultural Difference." *New Perspectives on Turkey* 10: 1–12.

———. 2001. "Civil Society, Community and Democracy in the Middle East." In *Civil Society: History and Possibilities*, edited by Sudipta Kaviraj and Sunil Khilnani, 232–49. Cambridge: Cambridge University Press.

INDEX

Page numbers in *italics* indicate photo illustrations. The author's informants are listed under the pseudonyms used in the text.

Asef Bayat, *Revolution without Revolutionaries: Making Sense of the Arab Spring*
2017

Orit Bashkin, *Impossible Exodus: Iraqi Jews in Israel*
2017

Maha Nassar, *Brothers Apart: Palestinian Citizens of Israel and the Arab World*
2017

Nahid Siamdoust, *Soundtrack of the Revolution: The Politics of Music in Iran*
2017

Laure Guirguis, *Copts and the Security State: Violence, Coercion, and Sectarianism in Contemporary Egypt*
2016

Michael Farquhar, *Circuits of Faith: Migration, Education, and the Wahhabi Mission*
2016

Gilbert Achcar, *Morbid Symptoms: Relapse in the Arab Uprising*
2016

Jacob Mundy, *Imaginative Geographies of Algerian Violence: Conflict Science, Conflict Management, Antipolitics*
2015

Ilana Feldman, *Police Encounters: Security and Surveillance in Gaza under Egyptian Rule*
2015

Tamir Sorek, *Palestinian Commemoration in Israel: Calendars, Monuments, and Martyrs*
2015

Adi Kuntsman and Rebecca L. Stein, *Digital Militarism: Israel's Occupation in the Social Media Age*
2015

Laurie A. Brand, *Official Stories: Politics and National Narratives in Egypt and Algeria*
2014

Kabir Tambar, *The Reckonings of Pluralism: Citizenship and the Demands of History in Turkey*
2014

Diana Allan, *Refugees of the Revolution: Experiences of Palestinian Exile*
2013

Shira Robinson, *Citizen Strangers: Palestinians and the Birth of Israel's Liberal Settler State*
2013

Joel Beinin and Frédéric Vairel, editors, *Social Movements, Mobilization, and Contestation in the Middle East and North Africa*
2013 (Second Edition), 2011

Ariella Azoulay and Adi Ophir, *The One-State Condition: Occupation and Democracy in Israel/Palestine*
2012

Steven Heydemann and Reinoud Leenders, *editors, Middle East Authoritarianisms: Governance, Contestation, and Regime Resilience in Syria and Iran*
2012

Jonathan Marshall, *The Lebanese Connection: Corruption, Civil War, and the International Drug Traffic*
2012

Joshua Stacher, *Adaptable Autocrats: Regime Power in Egypt and Syria*
2012

Bassam Haddad, *Business Networks in Syria: The Political Economy of Authoritarian Resilience*
2011